'An excellent book covering all the key themes and well grounded in the literature surrounding the topic. The writing is clear, lively and accessible and the use of case studies is innovative and effective'.
    – **Martin Johnes**, *Senior Lecturer in History, Swansea University, UK*

What do we understand by the word 'sport'? How has the phenomenon of sport come about? How have historians attempted to explain its development?

This introductory text grapples with these questions, offering a thematic review of the historical development of sport. The book examines the subject on a global scale, exploring the relationship between sport history and topics such as modernization, globalization, identity, gender and the media. Informed by the latest research, the book provides students with a variety of ways into the topic through case studies, key issues, questions and suggested further reading sections. Ideal for those approaching the subject for the first time, *Sport in History* offers a wide-ranging perspective on the place of sport in modern society and provides methodological tools for thinking about sport from a historical perspective.

Jeffrey Hill is Emeritus Professor of Historical and Cultural Studies at De Montfort University UK, where he teaches on the FIFA International MA in the Management, Law and Humanities of Sport. He has published books and articles on both sport and popular politics, including *Sport, Leisure and Culture in Twentieth-Century Britain* (2002) and *Sport and the Literary Imagination* (2006).

D1446280

Sport in History
An Introduction

Jeffrey Hill

palgrave
macmillan

First published 2011 by
PALGRAVE MACMILLAN

Palgrave Macmillan in the UK is an imprint of Macmillan Publishers Limited, registered in England, company number 785998, of Houndmills, Basingstoke, Hampshire RG21 6XS.

Palgrave Macmillan in the US is a division of St Martin's Press LLC, 175 Fifth Avenue, New York, NY 10010.

Palgrave Macmillan is the global academic imprint of the above companies and has companies and representatives throughout the world.

Palgrave® and Macmillan® are registered trademarks in the United States, the United Kingdom, Europe and other countries.

ISBN: 978–1–4039–8790–7 hardback
ISBN: 978–1–4039–8791–4 paperback

This book is printed on paper suitable for recycling and made from fully managed and sustained forest sources. Logging, pulping and manufacturing processes are expected to conform to the environmental regulations of the country of origin.

A catalogue record for this book is available from the British Library.

A catalog record for this book is available from the Library of Congress.

10 9 8 7 6 5 4 3 2 1
20 19 18 17 16 15 14 13 12 11

Printed in China

For Mary, Katharine, Richard and Tim, and to all friends, old and new, for their help and encouragement

Contents

List of Illustrations

Acknowledgements

My thanks to all colleagues and friends in sport history whose help and inspiration is reflected in this book. I should also like to acknowledge the help of the many librarians, especially those at De Montfort University and the British Library, who have provided materials from which I have drawn. Thanks also to Terka Acton, whose idea this originally was, and to Kate Haines, Felicity Noble and Jenni Burnell at Palgrave for guiding me through the production process. Some parts of the book, especially Chapter 5, have benefited from ideas presented in a series of workshops on 'Sport, History, and Heritage: An Investigation into the Public Representation of Sport', made possible by financial assistance from the Arts and Humanities Research Council. I should like to acknowledge the support of the AHRC, and of all the colleagues from a variety of backgrounds who participated in the workshops.

Preface

There are now many books on the history of sport – so many indeed that it is becoming more and difficult to keep up with them. There are also several that provide an overview of sport, whether of individual sports, sport in particular countries, or the spread of sport throughout the entire world. Among the more noteworthy are: Allen Guttmann, *Sports: The First Five Millennia* (2004); Richard Holt, *Sport and the British* (1989); Tony Mason, *Association Football and English Society* (1980); Matthew Taylor, *The Association Game* (2008); Bill Murray, *World Football* (1996) and David Goldblatt *The Ball Is Round* (2006). Of a more theoretical and sociological nature are Alan Tomlinson's *The Sports Studies Reader* (2007) and Grant Jarvie's *Sport Culture and Society* (2006). Martin Polley's *Sports History: A Practical Guide* (2007) offers a lively (and unique) exploration of the methodologies of sport history.

The present book does not seek to compete with any of these excellent studies, though it is influenced by all of them. Its main aims are to provide a short historical perspective on sport for those embarking on a programme of sports studies. In this respect its aim is to show that 'sport', however we might define it, is something with quite a long history. It did not, as many media presentations of sport are inclined to suggest, emerge fully clothed at some point in the late-twentieth century. In doing this, the book does not assume that all readers will necessarily have a background in history, but expects that some readers will. In seeking to bridge this divide it will avoid over-detailed information on the development of sport – this can be found in the works mentioned above, as well as in a host of yet more specialized literature referred to in the further reading listed at the end of each chapter, as well as in the Select Bibliography. Nor will the present book attempt to immerse its reader in too many 'technical' matters of the discipline of history, and the many debates between historians that abound in the profession. Nonetheless, it will try to show how a historian works and thinks, and thereby to point up some of the differences, as well as the similarities, between historians and those who practise other disciplines. As a *historical* introduction to sport the book has to be, to some extent, about historians, since they are the people who make history. 'History' cannot be separated from 'historians'. Therefore the case studies that appear in each chapter are designed to draw attention to particular problems of interpretation or methodology and how they have been handled by particular historians; it is hoped that by focusing upon such matters readers might be encouraged to dig more deeply themselves into the writings of historians and to think critically about what they find there. By so doing they will gain an understanding of what history is, how it is constructed and how it is an infinitely contestable discipline. In the light of the variety of approaches we will find in the work of historians we might even come to the conclusion that it is more appropriate to use the term 'histories' than the general category 'history'.

The book, as its title says, is an *introduction*. Whatever value it might have will lie mainly in its cutting a path through what might seem to be the tangled thicket of the many books on sport; and also, perhaps, in having persuaded readers that a fully rounded understanding of sport needs a historical dimension. Understandably, sport studies often concentrate attention on *contemporary* issues and events, and seek to prepare students with the means of dealing with them. The result of this is that students are sometimes led to believe that what happened in the past is irrelevant; that it has no bearing on the present day. The fact that the great majority of our current sports emerged in former times, that their present make up still bears traces of that previous existence, and that the past offers us alternative notions of what sport might be, can easily escape our notice. Historians are alert to such perspectives. They are aware of the ways in which the past informs the present, and especially of why things change, and why in some cases they remain the same. They might even be better at explaining change than anybody else. This being so, a cardinal idea of this book is that change does not stop at the present. Historians fifty years hence will look back at some of our current sporting practices and perhaps consider them decidedly quaint. What we now consider terribly up-to-the-minute will soon seem *passé*. This leads me back to a fundamental point. It is often assumed that 'history' is a fixed entity composed of facts, events and people, and which bestows its meaning simply through the passing of time. 'History will reveal' (we say) whether some statesman or other has got it right, or made a big mistake. Not so. In itself 'history' reveals nothing, until historians have gone to work on the past and rendered it into a meaningful history. Who are the makers of history? None other than historians themselves.

CHAPTER 1

Sport Matters

In a seemingly paradoxical statement the chief sports correspondent of the *Times* newspaper, Simon Barnes, has speculated that 'perhaps sport matters because it doesn't matter.'[1] What he seems to have meant was that, compared with questions of world conflict, health, disease and the environment, the issues that so concern us in sport carry little weight. Thus, sport is something that can consume our attention as a distraction. Perhaps it serves as *a valuable* distraction from the worries of the world. It matters because it doesn't matter.[2] It is an interesting thought; an attempt to put things into proper perspective, by a writer who makes his living by communicating the issues of sport to us. Barnes's comment, though, prompts further questions for readers in the early twenty-first century. What, in the last analysis, *does* matter? In a world beset by financial disorder, pathetic attempts to tackle climate change and a cultural climate that spreads much banal shallowness, we should perhaps be rethinking many of the conventional wisdoms that the later twentieth century has bequeathed to us: about economic growth and how it is to be attained, about our political systems and how democracy is to be fulfilled, about global relations and the relationship between rich and poor within and between societies. And perhaps about sport, where it is going, and what it means to us.

There is another point: at the beginning of the new century sport is very big business globally. In this way it matters a great deal to a great many people. Their jobs are tied up in it, and much of their leisure activities are consumed by it. A rough estimate would make sport a $500bn worldwide industry. In the United Kingdom it accounts for approximately 2 per cent of all workers (approximately 576,000) and some 2 per cent of GDP.[3] Consider the staging of the Olympic Games in 2012. Securing this event involved much effort and expense by many people trained in economics and business, urban planning and transportation, architecture, and public relations, because it was assumed that being asked by the International Olympic

1

Committee (IOC) to stage the Games in their city would bestow value, not only to the city but also to the country in which the city was located. When the decision was announced by the president of the IOC in Singapore in July 2005, London emerged as the winner, albeit by a narrow margin it seems. It was an outcome greatly desired not only by those in sport in Great Britain, but also by an institution whose involvement in sport was of fairly recent origin: Her Majesty's Government. Some sixty years earlier London had staged the first Games after the end of the Second World War. Few other countries had expressed much interest, for obvious reasons, and Great Britain stepped in to claim some prestige for re-igniting the Olympic flame. The British government, and in particular its foreign secretary Ernest Bevin, was keen to give support, and lent both financial and moral backing to an event that by the standards of today seems low-key and rather cheapskate. (A recent book has described them as the 'austerity Games'.) This was an unusual move at a time when governments in Britain considered that the organization of sport was a matter for private individuals and associations (much as later governments were to regard the economy). When the bid was being prepared for the 2012 Games, all this had changed. Sport was now seen as something that improved the nation's physical and moral health, kept its youngsters off the street corners and which through 'mega' events like the Olympic Games might 're-generate' depressed areas of the urban landscape such as the East End of London. The opportunity of 2012 was not to be missed, and a mark of its perceived importance was that the prime minister of the day, Mr Blair, went to Singapore at a crucial moment in the IOC's deliberations to show the flag and press the flesh.

In a smaller way the growing sense that sport matters has been registered in the academic world by historians. Even as recently as the 1970s the idea that serious historians (especially those employed in academic jobs) should want to write about the history of sport seemed faintly ridiculous to many. It still is, though to a much lesser extent. Over the past 30 or so years there have been big changes. Sport history is now a buoyant branch of the discipline, with large organizations of scholars across the globe through whose auspices debate and discussion about the study of sport proceeds, and from which issues the publication of a steady stream of books now too numerous for any one individual to keep up with. It is important to retain a critical perspective on all this endeavour, and to ask whether much of what is produced is really worth reading. This might sound facetious, if not dismissive. It is not intended to be; it merely raises the question, which I believe is very important for anyone embarking on the study of sport at whatever level – why are we studying it, and how should we do it?

Let us try to offer an answer to this question. One of the complaints that critics of sport history have levelled against the subject is that its practitioners are simply 'fans with typewriters'.[4] In other words, they are people whose own love of sport has impelled them into writing about it. (Perhaps they are older historians who, instead of playing the game, now write about it).

But should history be constructed simply out of such personal reasons? We should, I think, answer 'no' to this question, while at the same time acknowledging that much history – 'respectable' history, that is, which has not been subjected to the strictures that sport history has sometimes endured – has also been fashioned with personal likes and dislikes in mind. How many historians of religion and the churches have been practising believers? Have military historians been ex-servicemen? And historians of government and the central administration – have they not formed close associations with those in the corridors of power? To what extent have all these people been *men*? Be that as it may, we need to establish an intellectually convincing justification for placing sport on the historian's agenda. My own manifesto would begin with the place sport occupies in society.

Social history

Some years ago, during an important phase in the development of British and, by extension, international historiography, a renowned historian, Eric Hobsbawm, sought to give direction to what was then a relatively new branch of the discipline. Social history, a part of the subject that had previously languished as a junior partner in what was known as 'economic and social history', suddenly came into its own in the 1960s. Social history deals with a wide range of topics related to how people live their lives; it includes, among other things, institutions (such as the National Health Service), social policy (the Poor Law), social relationships (class, gender, race), the family, consumption, lifestyle and population trends. As may be imagined from this potentially vast canvas, social history shades into various other subjects of history which have their own specialism: business, demography, economics, religion and intellectual matters to identify but a few. In recent years there has arisen a particular form of history that has close associations with social history. This is *cultural* history, a branch that is sometimes difficult to distinguish from social, but the principal characteristic of which is a concern with how things are *understood* by people through the ways in which they are represented to them.[5] It is therefore not so much about *what* happened as what people *thought* happened, and how they reacted to it. The 'revolution' (if that is an appropriate term) in social history had, as is usual with revolutions, a combination of causes. Some of it had to do with the impact of a seminal (i.e. influential) book – EP Thompson's *The Making of the English Working Class* (1963) – that quickly acquired a following among many younger scholars. Equally important, though, was the way in which British higher education was opening up at this time with the expansion of the 'new' universities.[6] This development brought a new generation of students into the universities with a greater proportion than previously who were from a working-class background and female. When such students themselves moved on into research and eventually got jobs in universities, they often introduced new perspectives in their teaching, with greater emphasis on subjects such as popular culture and politics, women, and leisure and recreation.

In an influential article in *Daedalus* (winter, 1971) – the journal of the American Academy of Arts and Sciences – Hobsbawm attempted to orchestrate these new developments in social history. The article was entitled 'From Social History to the History of Society'.[7] Its purpose was to explain the rise of social history, which at that point had undergone the same kind of explosive growth that sport history has experienced over the past 20 or so years. Social history, said Hobsbawm, was 'in fashion' but its 'copious development' had proceeded in an 'unsystematic' way. In an attempt to give the subject coherence Hobsbawm argued for an approach in which social history would embrace the totality of society, and at the same time offer what its companion disciplines of sociology and economics had been unable to formulate, namely a satisfactory explanation of social change. A short while after the publication of this article Hobsbawm directed some of the same concerns to his own specialist area of study, labour history. In this article, also in an American journal – the *Journal of Social History* (summer, 1974) – Hobsbawm said that all historians should have a model of society in their mind, and be able to theorize about how society works and how it changes. He talked of labour historians being able to relate their own particular bits of specialist study to what was going on in the bigger picture. He particularly noted how the development of labour history, which had been started for polemical purposes outside the academy, had meant that much of the history of labour had been written 'from within' the labour movement, was concerned with ideological issues important to labour activists and tended to equate the working classes with the organizations that operated in their name. He called for a more broadly based history alert to aspects of labour which had previously been suppressed or neglected – women, the casual labour force, workers who did not support 'progressive' causes, and so on. Above all, he reminded his readers that 'the history of labour is part of the history of society'.

For those inclined to take notice, these observations had a dual importance. They encouraged a reassessment of what the proper study of history should be, and they steered historians towards theory. The study of sport was one beneficiary of the reassessment. The first academic group of sport historians in Britain – the British Society of Sport History – was founded in 1982, taking its cue from a body established ten years earlier in the United States – the North American Society for Sport History – composed at that time mainly of men and women from physical education departments who wished to trace the origins of the sports they taught and coached. Though influenced by the Americans, the British initiative was prompted as much as anything by the appearance in 1979 of a book similar in stature in the world of sport to that of EP Thompson's in the broader field of working-class history: Tony Mason's *Association Football and English Society 1863–1915* (1980). Mason's was the first British book – and perhaps the first anywhere – to subject sport to rigorous academic method based upon a range of primary archival sources.

It examines from a thematic perspective the development of association football in England from the 1860s, when the game was extensive but found in a variety of forms, until the time of the First World War, when it had become a commercialized mass spectator sport organized into regulated competitions and subject to the overall supervision of the Football Association. The book has continued to spawn a succession of studies based on either individual sports or, as in the more recent past, broader thematic studies of sport's role as social practice.

Quite apart from its landmark status in opening up the study of sport, Mason's work was (and remains) typical of a dominant method in history writing that has been called *empiricism*. This means the practice of collecting information from a range of primary and secondary sources, analysing it and writing up the findings as history. For many, in schools and universities, this approach is the hallmark of 'doing history'; its validity is unquestioned. It has been and probably always will be the methodological orthodoxy. Yet some think this approach to be flawed; or to put it more accurately, the unquestioned faith in empiricism is thought to be flawed. Their scepticism is rooted in ideas about knowledge and truth that have come out of continental European philosophy, and which make of history a far more indeterminate and insubstantial process of knowledge formation and 'truth validation' than the orthodox method would have us believe. This is where theory comes in, and we should pause a while to consider it.

Theory

Hobsbawm's concern for theory was mostly a reflection of his own Marxist approach to history, and a belief that in the work of Marx and Engels there was an indication of why societies *change*. What, indeed, did Engels assert in his graveside oration at Marx's funeral in 1883? That Marx had uncovered the laws of movement in history just as Charles Darwin in his researches had laid bare the process of evolution in biology. Hobsbawm felt that, whether Marxists or no, historians should at the very least bring to their studies an appreciation of theoretical insights into this question of change. It has to be admitted though, that the take-up of theory among historians in general over the past 35 years has been very patchy. An illustration of this is provided if we consider the responses to the surge of what at the time was often referred to as 'structuralism': a set of ideas drawn mainly from continental European sources that first hit British historians in a big way during the late 1970s. The influences of philosophers such as Derrida and Foucault, sociologists such as Pierre Bourdieu, anthropologists such as Clifford Geertz, politico-cultural theorists such as Antonio Gramsci and literary theorists such as Stephen Greenblatt has varied enormously. In broad terms historians have been less interested in theory *per se* than have, for example, sociologists; for the historian the application of theory to the practice of writing history has been the key issue, and in this respect some theories have seemed more applicable than others. Thus some historians have been strongly persuaded by ideas coming from outside the discipline of history, while others (one might say the majority) have not. A harsh indictment of the latter might suggest that they have buried their heads in the sand, or at least retreated behind the ramparts of their citadel of ortho-doxy. To be fair, though, there are few historians who have not imbibed at least something of these theoretical positions, but only relatively few historians have carried them very far.

How far have they been carried in the study of sport? As someone who has been involved in this business for some while I have noticed, especially over the past 20 years, an increasing awareness at conferences and in publications of theoretically informed approaches. They have been particularly in evidence in work done on sport and identity (especially gender), a subject that became quite modish in the 1980s. There is still, however, a firm commitment to what I have called 'empiricism'. It is manifested in the tendency to see sport as a collection of fixed realities: the people who perform sport, those who administer it, and events and places where it all takes place. In this sense sport is a series of 'things' relating to physical activity of a competitive nature that takes place largely out of doors. It is an understanding of sport that has been fortified in the recent past by interesting developments in the representation of sport in museums and heritage sites.

The theoretically minded sport historian, however, has a different vision of the subject. The starting point is often an unease with the way sport is seen as something 'shaped' by other forces in society – politics, economics, demo-graphic patterns, ideas, social customs, religion, and so on. To be sure, no one would deny that these forces have their influences in sport, but in acknow-ledging this it is the reverse process – the ability of sport itself to exercise a determining influence over the way people think – that is often overlooked. Far from being marginal things, mere entertainments that do not 'matter', sporting activities are cultural agencies with *ideological* significance; that is to say, they have the power to give *meaning*.

Whose theories we adopt is, to a large extent, a matter of personal inclin-ation and interest. Personally I have found the work of the anthropologist **Clifford Geertz (1926–2006)** to be very illuminating for a historian inter-ested in how people's social and cultural rituals can reveal things about their society and its social relationships. Geertz's method of analysis is also intri-guing; he 'reads' customs and practices as a literary specialist might read texts, deconstructing them for what they say about matters that are not obvious from a cursory glance. His analysis, done in the course of fieldwork carried out in the 1950s, of the Indonesian cock fight, shows us that (in a famous phrase) the stories people tell themselves about themselves can be valuable source material for the historian. Yet more subtle, perhaps, is his reading of stories about sheep stealing in Morocco in the early twentieth century, using the technique of 'thick description'. Geertz disentangles the complex layers of meaning that reside in these stories, especially as between what they meant to contemporaries and what they might mean to observers coming to them some half a century later. Geertz, then, repays the cultural historian's close attention. One of the criticisms made of his work, however, is that he neglects the overarching power relationships of the societies he investigates (See Case Study Discussion 1).

Such a charge could not be made of another theorist whose influence among many historians and cultural analysts has been immense: the Italian philosopher and politician **Antonio Gramsci (1891–1937)**, who spent the last ten years of his life imprisoned by the fascist regime in Italy. Gramsci draws our attention to the political significance of everyday life and thought, and the reason why students of popular culture particularly find him rewarding is that he shows how 'ordinary' cultural practices and texts – reading newspapers, dining out, going to football matches, conversing with friends and employers at work – can carry important cultural meanings and contribute to an acceptance of certain kinds of power relations. (It must be stressed that Gramsci deals with such matters at a *theoretical* level; anyone reading him for insights into football matches or dining out will be disappointed. But he enables us to see the importance of such everyday cultural behaviour in an overall social order.) These power relations might be, for example, that of the boss over the worker, or the teacher over the student, or the man over the woman. They involve a moral authority, regarded by those involved in the relationship as natural and legitimate. Gramsci called it 'hegemony'. Its roots are in culture. A warning though: since Gramsci compiled much of his theory while a prisoner, in a collection now known as the *Prison Notebooks*, he had to write in a somewhat coded manner in order to evade the attention of the censor. His work is not easy to read, but it is certainly worth the effort.

Case Study Discussion 1

Jeffrey Hill, 'Cocks, Cats, Caps and Cups: A Semiotic Approach to Sport and National Identity', *Culture, Sport, Society*, 2, 2 (summer 1999), pp. 1–21.

I have chosen to illustrate some points about theory, especially related to Gramsci and Geertz, with an article of my own. It also brings together in a historical analysis ideas from subjects other than history. The rather odd title alludes to other writing on similar themes, and is meant to denote a continuum in anthropology and cultural history concerned with the reading of 'signs'. It focuses on Wembley Stadium and one of the most celebrated activities associated with it – the FA Cup Final – mainly in the 1920s and 1930s, in an attempt to show how the place and the event might have been understood as a particular expression of national identity.

Wembley stadium was completed in 1923 as part of a larger complex designed to house the British Empire Exhibition, which was held in 1924 and 1925. The stadium itself outlasted this event, but was known officially for many years after as the 'Empire Stadium'. Though privately owned, the name gave it grander pretensions.

The first event staged there was the 1923 Cup Final, which immediately acquired legendary status in football folklore as a result of the overcrowding that accompanied the event. The pitch had to be cleared by mounted policemen before the game could begin. Pictures of this in the press featured what appeared to be a policeman on a white horse (dirty grey in reality) doing a lone job (in fact there were others) but successfully. The story of the 'White Horse Final' was thus created, and retold for many years. Wembley therefore began its life with an instant myth. The moral of the white horse and the crowd was about English people behaving in a calm, orderly manner when directed by the forces of law (which implicitly made comparisons with the supposed irrational behaviour of hot-headed foreigners). Wembley's development thereafter is contrasted with previous sites of the FA Cup, notably the Crystal Palace in south London, which staged the Final between 1894 and 1914 and which was remembered with some fondness in later years for the good-natured holiday atmosphere that had prevailed there. By contrast Wembley, by the mid-1920s, had become much more of a state occasion. Military bands and community singing were complemented by the presence of the monarch (or high-profile members of the royal family), the singing of the national anthem, and the broadcasting of the proceedings from 1927 onwards on the BBC. Most significant of all, perhaps, was the singing before the start of play, of the hymn 'Abide With Me'. This might seem strange to twenty-first-century readers. 'Abide With Me' was a popular hymn – at funerals. It dealt with the subject of death. Why sing it at a football match? The answer is that it was popular, it was felt that it fitted well into the community singing, and it was an easy tune to follow for an untrained and vast (100,000) audience; above all (and this was perhaps not foreseen by the organizers of the event) it seemed to catch the mood of the times. It related strongly to the feelings of loss among members of the crowd and the listening public, many of whose loved ones would have perished in the Great War that had come to an end only a few years before. It is hardly surprising that the singing of 'Abide With Me' was experienced as a deeply moving event, a moment of remembrance that summed up the shared grief of a nation.

This case study therefore has both methodological and conceptual relevance, and might also be related to the points discussed in Chapter 3 on national identity.

Close to Gramsci in certain respects (though very different in others) is the French social theorist **Pierre Bourdieu (1930–2002)**. For anyone interested in ideological influences Bourdieu's work is important, for what he describes as 'symbolic power' is at the heart of his theory. Bourdieu wrote from a radical political perspective, with evident Marxist influences present in his insistence upon classes and the conflicts between and within them providing much of the motive power of social action. Moreover, he sought to place ideas within a definite materialist context, and unlike some practitioners in the field of cultural studies objected to the study of texts as autonomous entities in which an essential meaning is present. Bourdieu's historical sense placed everything in a totality of economic and social power relationships. One of his principal concepts was that of the 'habitus', a difficult idea that is somewhat akin to the Marxist notion of 'class consciousness' – a set of historically learnt experiences that broadly define particular class-related ways of life (lifestyles) and which offer a route to individuals for navigating their way through particular situations: '[the habitus is] the strategy-generating principle enabling agents to cope with unforeseen and ever-changing situations'.[8] In the habitus reside cultural standards and expectations that can be translated into cultural (symbolic) power, different from but no less real in its social significance than economic power. In attempting to establish and perpetuate certain social distinctions, and to understand why they are regarded as legitimate, cultural power is a key instrument. It advances the life chances of some and marginalizes those of others. In Bourdieu's thought it therefore serves a similar purpose of defining *moral* (rather than physical) authority to that of the concept of hegemony in Gramsci.

Case Study Discussion 2

Pierre Bourdieu

The following comments on Bourdieu are based on his paper 'Pratiques sportives et pratiques sociales', given at the International Congress of the History of Sports and Physical Education, held in March 1978 in Paris. A translated version in article form, 'Sport and Social Class' (trans. Richard Nice) can be found in *Social Science Information* 17, 6 (1978), pp. 819–40, and an edited version is included in Alan Tomlinson ed., *The Sport Studies Reader* (Abingdon: Routledge, 2007), pp. 237–41.

Of all the major modern social theorists Bourdieu is the one who has devoted most attention to sport. This is not to say that he is a theorist of sport, but that he recognizes more than most the important part performed by sport in social relations. In this paper, which opens with a polite rebuke to historians of sport for having overlooked some obvious questions about the nature of their subject, he turns his attention to the issue of why certain people acquire a taste for certain sports rather than others, either as spectators or as participants. The problem causes him to apply an analysis similar to that applied in his studies of culture generally; that is, there is no 'natural' involvement in sport related to basic human needs, rather sporting taste is socially conditioned. Bourdieu argues that a particular mentality of sport characterizes what he calls the 'elite' (upper or dominant classes). That mentality makes of sport a non-utilitarian exercise – 'sport for sport's sake', so to speak. In the modern period sport for such groups has none of the functional uses of pre-modern societies, where it is performed in order to call upon favours from deities. Sport is a 'gratuitous exercise', purely an end in itself, seen in its most sublime form in the great public boarding schools of the elite, where sport exists, like art, separate from material considerations. Bourdieu sees in the principle of amateurism, firmly rooted in the elite schools, an ideology of sport that emphasizes character building, manliness, fair play and the will to win – but to win by fair means and certainly not 'at all costs'. Bourdieu attributes many of these characteristics to Pierre de Coubertin, the inspirer of the modern Olympics, whom he sees as an apostle of a certain kind of bourgeois business ideology grounded in an educational style that is neither overly intellectual nor academic. It exists to school future heads of business, and its curriculum cultivates a sense of individualism and private enterprise. In this way a distinctive educational ethos emerges in sport that characterizes the aspirations of a particular group with Bourdieu's 'dominant class', setting it apart from other groups ('fractions') within the dominant class, and from other (subordinate) social classes. The place of sport in the bourgeois mind is given fuller meaning when Bourdieu contrasts it with sport's uses among other social groups. For working-class or petty-bourgeois groups sport provides a route of upward mobility, and is thus taken up in a professional manner with a view to maximizing efficiency in a particular sport and earning a living. Rather than an end in itself, sport becomes a means to an end, a form of physical capital to be invested wisely for profit. This is one reason why sports are maintained longer, often into old age (e.g. golf), among people of higher educational attainment, than they are among working-class men and women, for whom interest declines rapidly after youth when the utility value of sport diminishes. In essence Bourdieu is talking about different conceptions and social uses of sport; differences that, in turn, bring about a great deal of social exclusiveness in sport. '[M]ost team sports', he says, '... and also no doubt the most typically working-class individual sports, such as boxing or wrestling, combine all the reasons to repel the upper classes'. These exclusions are only too familiar to sport historians, but Bourdieu helps us to understand why they occur.

There are doubtless many objections that might be levelled at this brief outline of Bourdieu's thoughts on sport. For one thing it has a rather old-fashioned feel to it: is the contrast between the amateur and professional ethic so stark – was it ever quite so rigid as he appears to think? Were bourgeois sportsmen so disinterested in the uses of sport? After all, their sporting 'taste' was an important part of the symbolic power exercised by the bourgeoisie – surely something with significant 'use' value. And are working-class spectators quite so utilitarian – is there not at least some sheer *pleasure* in the spectacle involved in watching others play? The obvious Anglo-French bias in this piece might lead us to wonder whether it has relevance to other places. Historians, too, will always find specific exceptions to the general assertions that serve to undermine the theory; the assumption, for example, that there are such clearly identifiable social entities as a 'dominant' class (with its various 'fractions') and a 'subordinate' is surely questionable when set against the complexities of modern social stratification. In some respects Bourdieu, though respected as a sociologist who sought out empirical detail to sustain his theories, nonetheless looks like the classic sociological generalizer whose laying bare of the workings of society seems to have an overall tidiness that demands a little too much suspension of our disbelief. On the other hand, and bearing in mind that the text in question here was based on a short conference paper, inevitably reduced to the bare essentials, one cannot but admire the grand sweep and the bold attack. For all its shortcomings it gives us a way of theorizing sport, something that we should not neglect and by no means abandon.

In his excellent short introduction to the study of cultural history, Peter Burke has identified three other theorists whose ideas have relevance to understanding sport.[9] **Mikhail Bakhtin (1895–1975)** is perhaps of most interest to those working in literary or linguistic studies, where his ideas on 'voices' have been very influential in textual analysis. He has not been greatly taken up in the mainstream areas of sport study, though one of his other great innovations – the study of the role of carnival in society – might yet provide a way in to understanding 'pre-modern' sporting rituals and pastimes. **Norbert Elias (1897–1990)** was a German social theorist who worked for a long time in England at Leicester University. His studies of the 'civilising process', the subject of a book published just before the outbreak of war in 1939 but not translated into English until the late 1970s, have had considerable influence among historians of everyday life. By 'civilising process' Elias meant the social and cultural changes in manners that gradually had the effect of placing certain forms of behaviour beyond the pale of acceptable norms; this results in a society with interpersonal relationship that are more restrained and 'civil', less characterized by violence and cruelty towards both human beings and animals than was the case in former times. England, because of its particular political and social development in the form of a constitutional monarchy, was considered to have been a clear early example of this process. These changes are not attributed by Elias to improvements in the inherent personal sensibilities of individuals but to changes in economy and society, and in this way Elias did what many other theorists have done, namely make a connection between culture and society. More than most leading social theorists, Elias took a close interest in sport, though this was communicated principally by one of his colleagues at Leicester University, the sociologist Eric Dunning. For many years from the 1970s, Dunning was the leader of a group of sociologists of sport often referred to as the 'Leicester School'. They carried out much work on topics such as football hooliganism and the bureaucratization of sport, applying some of the ideas originally elaborated by Elias in relation to the civilizing process. Dunning's work has been criticized by historians of sport for lacking a sufficient sensitivity to the empirical historical record and for viewing the past too much from the standpoint of the present. Particular criticisms have been levelled against the applicability of the theory to sports such as rugby and cricket.[10] These are, to be sure, important charges against a work that seeks to interpret *historical* developments. As yet, however, they have not assumed a proportion that should cause us to dismiss altogether the Elias model. It is not, and, as Elias and Dunning have made clear, was never intended to be a universal theory; the model forms, as Dunning admits, a 'first working hypothesis [...] to be tested in the crucible of systematic, *theory-guided* [my italics] empirical research'[11] – a fitting summary on the whole relationship between fact and theory.

Connections with some of the Eliasian ideas can be made if we consider the third theorist referred to by Burke, **Michel Foucault (1926–84)**. The work of this French writer is notoriously difficult to place in conventional academic categories. It has been valuable, however, in a number of fields, and in particular to those working on the changing nature and perceptions of the body, a topic of central importance in sport. One of Foucault's chief concerns was with processes of control in society, and especially on the question of how agencies of power exercised forms of control over individuals. Prisons, hospitals, schools and factories figured in his work on disciplinary regimes, which commanded much of his attention in the 1970s. Sport can, of course, be viewed as an area of control through the regimes of exercise, training, coaching, consumption and general body awareness that are an essential part of it. The ubiquitous advertisements in the electronic and print media that address their target subjects on body culture – the 'proper' forms to be cultivated in personal hygiene, diet, stature, look, and fitness through the use of a vast commercial range of essentially cosmetic products – frequently make use of sporting contexts and images to deliver their message. They are but one part of a Foucauldian vision of body control that has been extensively employed in academic studies of sport. The particular insight Foucault brings comes from the analytical value of terms such as *discourse, knowledge* and *power*. Thus, when Foucault writes in the early 1960s about madness it is not a simple medical or psychiatric condition that he investigates, immune from historical circumstances; rather, it is the product of a particular discourse (form of knowledge) constructed by doctors and scientists whose power enables them to categorize certain kinds of behaviour as being abnormal. Their knowledge acquires an institutional power and is reproduced through it, until challenged by a new discourse. In this way Foucault sees influential forms of knowledge not as a value-free, neutral corpus of information but as a power structure. There are some links here with Elias's civilizing process and its sea-change movements of thought, and also a bold challenge to some conventional notions about 'truth'. Historians might take note of the implications of this for the relative and conditional nature of their own subject. Similarly, in his work on punishment, Foucault traces changes in ideas about criminality and how it might be dealt with, that brought about the new regimes of penal incarceration introduced in the nineteenth century, and which operated on correctional rather than punitive lines. Historians have on the whole been sceptical of Foucault's approach – to many his methods seem miles away from history as generally understood, while Foucault's own criticisms of conventional historical method have further alienated him from many members of the profession. Nonetheless, when taken up with skill and insight, as for example in the work of the Canadian scholar of gender and the body, Patricia Vertinsky, the approach can yield valuable perspectives and findings. At this point, therefore, we should pause to consider a particular piece of research conducted by Vertinsky and colleagues at the University of British Columbia (UBC).

War Memorial Gym, University of British Columbia. Opened in 1951 to commemorate British Columbia men killed in the two world wars, the Gym also stands as a symbol of the changes that have taken place in University sport and Canadian society since that time. It is a reminder that historical understanding can be gleaned from the built environment as well as from written documents. (University of British Columbia Library Archives).

Case Study Discussion 3

Patricia Vertinsky and Sherry McKay, *Disciplining Bodies in the Gymnasium: Memory, Monument, Modernism* **(London: Routledge, 2004).**

This is a fascinating compilation of research studies that all relate to a single place: the War Memorial Gymnasium at UBC, Canada. In spite of its seemingly local focus the book is in fact an outstanding example of how 'micro-history' can bring to our attention methodological, theoretical and empirical issues of great importance. To begin with it demonstrates very clearly the methods and value of an *interdisciplinary* approach of the kind I referred to earlier. The book offers us perspectives from a series of disciplinary angles – cultural history and geography, human kinetics, educational studies, sociology, architectural history, women's studies and anthropology. It also underlines the worth of exploring new sources; while the book deploys ample material from the historian's familiar range of *primary* sources (from, for example, the University's archives, or from architects' designs and correspondence) there is, at the same time, an emphasis on 'reading' the visual – that is, the physical subject of the book itself: the War Memorial Gymnasium. This building, completed in 1951 as a memorial to those former members of the University and the province of British Columbia who had lost their lives in the two world wars, is a structure that many people no doubt pass on a daily basis without ever registering its meaning. It is just 'the gym'. But Vertinsky and her colleagues have approached it as a text, bringing out its manifold significances in relation to race, gender, nation, education, architectural theory and intellectual/philosophical movements such as modernism. In this way the book is informed by (rather than slavishly follows) some of Foucault's ideas about the formation and disciplining of the body through institutional practice – in, for example, prison, barracks, school or gymnasium. The creation of gymnasia attached to colleges of higher education began in North America during the nineteenth century, with establishments such as Amherst, Harvard and California giving public approval to physical exercise and education by the building of impressive spaces for such activity. The UBC gym follows in this tradition. It is an attempt, argue Vertinsky et al., at controlling physical exercise by providing educationally approved activities that create the proper form of exercise to produce healthy and responsible citizens: to create, as Vertinsky puts it, 'regularity, efficiency, respect and obedience, as well as engendering health' (p. 3). This project is, they claim, essentially a political one, bringing into play power struggles involving, among other things, notions of gender, race, class and nation. For example, the authors show (chapter 2) how in the design of the gym the underlying architectural aesthetic of modernism reflects a pursuit of progress, rationality and absolute truth that produced a basis for a 'male' gym. It is, at the same time, a building enshrining a euro-centric philosophy, while at the same time standing upon the ground of indigenous First Nation peoples. This is followed up (chapter 3) with a penetrative discussion of the 'power geometrics' of the building, to show a space where female athletics, especially in the twenty or so years following the Second World War, were marginalized. The centrality of the gym on the UBC campus not only served to emphasize the importance of sport in the University's curriculum but also to prioritize the conventional wisdom that held the ideal sporting body to be that of the (heterosexual) male. Increasingly the new gym became a place dominated by men's sports, and the recipient of resources needed to sustain them. The women were effectively excluded (except as spectators) by their activities being removed to the old gym, renamed the 'women's gym'. Thus the War Memorial Gym, with its military connotations, became known as the 'men's gym'. This notion of a 'separate sphere' for men and women is examined by Ross and Bentley (chapter 3); it was underscored in various cultural practices and media on the UBC campus – the student newspaper, the cadres of female cheerleaders and beauty queens, the portrayal of UBC women students in the local press – which worked to reproduce conventional gender roles of 'active' male and 'passive/subordinate' female. While the focus in this aspect of the study is on the late 1940s and early 1950s, Ross and Bentley conclude by pointing out that half a century later traces of such gender relations are still evident on the UBC campus.

Like all texts, the War Memorial Gym has no fixed meaning. The intentions inscribed in it by its creator(s) are contested and worked over by others, and thus it becomes a kind of palimpsest, a text bearing layers of meaning from many hands. The Gym acts as a history of UBC over the past 60 years, showing the changes that have been wrought not only in gender relationships but also in the academic curriculum, with the decline of physical education and its replacement with the more scientific practice of human kinetics, and the financial imperatives that have brought about the removal of non-profitable snack bars to make way for computer labs (though Coca-Cola machines remain). The Gym, though, still fulfils its original function, as a war memorial. But quite what it memorializes in this respect is ambivalent, as are all war memorials. In all, then, this building can be viewed from many vantage points to reveal a multitude of tensions and stories. It fits very well into the Foucauldian idea of the interrelationship between discourses and disciplinary practices, power and knowledge.

Finally, on the matter of theory, we should consider a writer whose work has been very closely concerned with sport. Whether he ranks as a theorist in the same way as Gramsci, Bourdieu and others is open to question, but he certainly brought a new way of thinking about sport into the open, and his work has been greatly admired, not only by sport historians but also by those interested in the field of postcolonial studies. I am referring to the Trinidadian writer **C. L. R. James (1901–1989)**. James was certainly a theoretical thinker in relation to politics, to which his life was chiefly dedicated. A Marxist, the son of a schoolteacher, he spent much of his middle age in the United States working alongside activists in the civil rights and trade union movements, and disputing with American leftists on communism. In later years he moved back to the West Indies to campaign with the Trinidadian political leader Eric Williams and others for independence. He also spent much time travelling to

Africa to work with members of the Pan African movement. Eventually he settled down in England, where he lived in Brixton, south London. James's work is noteworthy for the intellectual and geographical interconnections it achieves. The word applied by the Barbadian historian Hilary Beckles sums it up: 'fusion'.

Among his many writings the best known is probably his book on one of his great passions, cricket: *Beyond a Boundary* (1963). It reflects much of the fusion theme, though reading it almost half a century after its original publication some might wonder what all the fuss is about. The book seems, at first sight, rather lightweight yet at the same time long-winded. It has a string of anecdotes about cricket and cricketers, especially those of the West Indies, together with reminiscences of a personal nature on James's life and friendships. There is a good deal of comment on the influences wrought on him by classic European literature and art, and some rather odd comments towards the end about the deleterious effects of what James calls the 'welfare state mentality' in cricket. Is this something we should take seriously? In what sense might it be 'Marxist'? Consider it, though, in a historical context. In the early 1960s it was not only one of the very few books to open up the subject of cricket in the Caribbean – and not only test cricket but that organized and played by ordinary people – it also was probably the first to set cricket within a broader political and social framework. James's treatment of W. G. Grace was years ahead of its time as history. James simply could not contemplate how such an immense figure of the Victorian world, who was not only (in Ranji's term) 'the maker of modern batting' but through whose exploits cricket had been elevated into the national game, could be omitted from history books. Consider also the implication of the title, and remember the question posed in the Preface: 'What do they know of cricket who only cricket know?'

Case Study Discussion 4

CLR James, *Beyond a Boundary* (London: Stanley Paul, 1969 edn).

The book's historical coverage is more or less James's own lifetime up to the book's publication (*c.* 1900–1960s). His description in the early chapters of his upbringing in Trinidad marks out very clearly the experiences of a black child in a colonial society. Two important influences stand out: his education in a strictly British/European curriculum, and his family's insistence on respectability (the figure of Matthew Bondman represents something they did *not* wish to become). In many ways James is the classic 'black Englishman' whose educational and intellectual success was made possible through colonialism. His love of the essentially English game of cricket, which he played to a high standard, seals his apparent subservience to the colonial system. Cricket has taught him to 'play the game'. It is, however, through these very mechanisms of 'social control' that he is awakened to an anti-colonial mentality. In one important passage he describes the class, status and racial hierarchies that prevailed in Trinidadian cricket (patterns similar to which were to be found in the other islands of the British West Indies). Recounting his own dilemma over which cricket club to join, James reveals the nuances that existed in island cricket; of those exclusively for white people, or reserved only for Catholics, or which only accommodated better-off black people 'I would have been more easily elected to the MCC...' says James (p. 56). Both off and on the field of play, cricket seemed to confirm the political, social and above all the racial status quo. Yet it also provided a means of challenging that state of affairs. 'I haven't the slightest doubt', he writes, 'that the clash of race, caste and class did not retard but stimulated West Indian cricket. I am equally certain that in those years social and political passions, denied normal outlets, expressed themselves in cricket (and other games)' (p. 72).

James's conversion from the respectable, lower middle-class black man to radical anti-colonialist comes through his friendship with one of the cricketers featured in the book who (James avers) altered not only James's own life but also the course of West Indies cricket as well. This is Learie Constantine, the first international star of Caribbean cricket, who rejected the discriminations inherent in his native land and sought his future as a cricketer in England (in Nelson, Lancashire to be precise). Constantine was political: an anti-colonial nationalist and an opponent of racism. In helping Constantine to write an autobiography (*Cricket and I*, 1933), while at the same time composing his book about anti-colonial protest in the West Indies (*The Life of Captain Cipriani*, 1932, alternatively entitled *The Case for West Indian Self Government*, 1933), James was himself impelled to leave the West Indies and embark upon his international political career.

In the final section of the book James turns our attention to an issue that brought to the forefront of Caribbean politics all the racial and class prejudices that had hitherto lain, for the most part, dormant. James returned to Trinidad from the United States in 1958 to work with the local People's National Movement as the editor of its newspaper the *Nation* in the cause of political independence. The problem that chiefly exercised him on arrival, however, was the captaincy of the West Indies cricket team. In spite of having several talented and experienced players, all of whom were black, to call upon, by the 1950s the cricket board persisted with the policy from which it had never deviated of selecting a white man to lead the team. By the late 1950s this practice had become palpably outmoded, and was seen by many in the islands not only as an affront to skilful black players but also as a symbol of anti-nationalism. In the political context of the times the issue of the 'black captaincy' possessed an inflammatory quality. James took the issue up as a political campaign in the *Nation*. His persistent editorials arguing in favour of Frank Worrell, the leading black player of the era, were based not so much on racial grounds as on having the *best* man for the job, and on this James differed somewhat from Constantine, whose position was more straightforwardly to have a black man as captain. The effect, however, was the same. The success of the campaign meant that Worrell was appointed after much argument, and led the team with great success for years. On his retirement he was succeeded by Garfield Sobers whose appointment began an unbroken sequence until the present day of black captains.

C. L. R. James Plaque is honoured with a plaque in Brixton. James (1901–89) wrote extensively on cricket and politics, and the interrelationships between the two. His place in the history of cricket is assured by his book *Beyond a Boundary*, but James was no mere cricket writer. He was a radical exponent of Marxism and a founding father of postcolonial studies. He was born in Trinidad, lived for some twenty years in the United States, and in later life took up residence in Brixton, South London. Here he is commemorated by a blue plaque and the naming of his old house in his memory. (Timothy J. Hill).

Much of the theoretical orientation we have been discussing is not inherent in the traditional study of history. It has been imported from outside; not just from countries outside Britain but from other disciplines. The emergence in the later 1960s and subsequent rapid growth of cultural studies, a multidisciplinary site through which flow currents of thought from numerous areas of study, has had a major influence over the development of new directions in sport history. Therefore, a historian embarking upon the study of sport must be prepared to include a variety of tools in her/his kitbag: anthropology, political science, economics and business studies, sociology, geography, literature and film studies are some of the disciplines to be explored in making up a composite picture of sport. In the final analysis, however, it is the historian's traditional concern with the issue of continuity and change that, for most people, will predominate.

What all these things have in common is a concern to understand the place of sport in society; to explain, in as convincing a way as possible, how sport has originated and developed, and the purpose it fulfils in our lives. It does not begin from the premise that sport is necessarily a good thing, and it certainly does not concern itself with helping people to become better at sport. Those are problems for other people to resolve. One area of academic enquiry that has blossomed in recent years is worth briefly mentioning because it performs both these functions: that is, standing back from sport to analyse it and also operating within it to improve performance. It is the subject of sport psychology. We hear far more nowadays than we ever did about the experts employed to advise elite athletes in 'psychological' and 'scientific' matters as a means of enhancing their performance. These changed attitudes are very clearly illustrated in the emergence of a new kind of manager in association football, probably best epitomized the manager of Arsenal FC, the French coach Arsène Wenger.[12] We are also more likely to hear about the 'psychological' problems encountered by sportspeople themselves, which have become a topic for discussion in a number of recent sportspersons' autobiographies.[13] The 'users' of sport psychology, therefore, are more likely to be found outside the fairly confined academic zones occupied by users of social theory.

The emergence of sport psychology itself presents an interesting historical process, reflecting some of Foucault's ideas about discourse. In both of its manifestations – the 'academic' and the 'applied' – sport psychology is a relatively recent development. To be sure, examples can be found in the distant past of athletes using 'psychological' techniques to motivate themselves and demotivate their opponents (and such tricks of the trade certainly became part and parcel of the professional sportsman's repertoire from the late-nineteenth century onwards). Equally, there has been a long-standing recognition of the benefits likely to accrue to society from having a system of organized sport, without this necessarily becoming as obsessive as it was in ancient Sparta. However, as a scientific, or quasi-scientific, practice sport psychology first came into being as a by-product of the discipline of psychology as it became established in the late nineteenth century. Even then it experienced an uneven growth. Work carried out in the 1920s by the American psychologist CR Griffiths promised to establish a settled sub-discipline, but it was followed by some forty years of relative neglect and it is not until the mid-1960s that we may speak of 'the genesis of organised sport psychology in the Western world'.[14] At this point, in the United States, sport psychology started to acquire the academic focus, methodologies and organizational structure that defined it as a 'discipline', albeit one marked by strong tensions between its academic and applied sectors. Its chief themes are motivation, competitive anxiety, individual differences, motor skills, motor learning, aggression, psychological skills training/interventions, social cognition and team dynamics.[15]

In much of what follows in this book there is an acknowledgement of the place of theory (sometimes referred to as 'models') in the study of history. This will not, I hope, be slavish obeisance to abstract thinking. Theory is not an end in itself, but a means to an end: that of achieving a plausible understanding of the historical process. There should, I believe, be a willingness to apply theoretical and conceptual tools in the study of particular historical situations, but equally a willingness to discard those tools if they do not seem to accord with what the evidence is telling us. The balance between theory and evidence is crucial; too much of either one or the other and the whole enterprise becomes unseaworthy. There is a danger, as many empirically-minded historians have pointed out, of making the facts fit the theory. But at the same time we should not think that we are ever going to achieve absolute truth simply by recovering facts. History is not like that, and it is a misconception to think that 'the facts' in themselves will yield 'truth'. Without interpretation, which is what theory assists us in, there is no history, only an undifferentiated assemblage of information about the past. The historian who said that 'each generation should re-write its own history' understood very well the relativism of the subject. What we are looking for in theories is not a picture of the absolute reality of a situation or event, but a set of ideas which have a reasonable explanatory value. To illustrate this point, let us take as an example of something from outside sport. Since its original publication in 1859, Darwin's theory of the evolution of species by natural selection has generated a great deal of discussion and criticism; there are people who will not accept its argument, preferring to place their faith in a literal reading of religious texts or, more recently, in something called 'intelligent design'. In the last analysis, however, if we wish to approach the question of evolution from a rational standpoint (which is the starting point of all academic work) Darwin's thesis is the best we have. It might not give us the absolute truth, but it does carry a high explanatory value, and no other theory has so far matched it in this respect.

Throughout this book we will have recourse to various theories and models about history and change. The main ones are as follows:

- Marxism – a general theory of social relationships and how they relate to change, that is applicable in most areas of sport history, especially (as in Chapter 3) where emphasis is placed upon social class.

- Modernization theory – which informs much of the discussion in Chapter 2; it owes a lot to Weber, and thus to the 'debate with the ghost of Marx'.
- Gender – which importantly covers some of the 'gaps' in Marxism and Weber, and an appreciation of which is so important in a subject like sport (Chapter 4).
- Globalization – which has been approached in different ways, but is important in considering the increasing international dimensions of sport (Chapter 5).
- The 'linguistic turn' – which is also applicable to a number of aspects of the history of sport, as well as to history in general; it places emphasis upon how the world is *represented* to us, and is concerned therefore with the analysis and understanding of what are sometimes called 'texts', meaning not just written documents but a range of means of communication (e.g. advertisements, plays, novels, films, the spoken word, maps, statistics etc.). It brings into consideration a range of theorists (Chapter 6).

Case Study Discussion 5

Douglas Booth, *The Field: Truth and Fiction in Sport History* (London: Routledge, 2005).

We may distil many of the issues raised in the present chapter by considering the work of the New Zealand-based historian Douglas Booth. His book has stimulated a good deal of controversy within the ranks of sport historians. It is a lengthy and quite difficult study, not to be recommended for the fainthearted who might wish casually to extract a few choice quotations. But for those keen to learn something about history and how it is fashioned, and who are prepared to tackle issues of epistemology, Booth's book will amply repay close attention. In one sense it is a history of sport history, chronicling some of the notable achievements in this branch of the discipline over the past half century. This, however, is not the book's sole, or even main, purpose. The principal aim is to present a critique of much that has been produced in the field from the standpoint of a historian who regards the orthodox method of creating a 'true' image of the past through a factually based analysis of the evidence as being beset by philosophical flaws. For Booth history is a far from 'objective' practice. It is artful and fictive in many respects, closer to creative writing than it is to science.

As may be imagined Booth is influenced by a repertoire of critiques sometimes known as 'postmodernism'. Following particularly on the work of Alun Munslow (*Deconstructing History*) he identifies three 'models' of history:

- 'Reconstructionism': this, in Booth's view, is an attempt to reconstruct an accurate picture of the past – 'as it really was' – using a varied range of sources. These sources it is felt give the historian a window, so to speak, on the past. This is probably, in spite of criticisms levelled against it in recent years, still the method most favoured by historians. It involves careful archival research in an attempt to get at the truth, though few would nowadays expect the history constructed in this way to be *definitive*; new sources will always lead to new interpretations, and the best we can expect is that our history achieves a *relative* degree of truthfulness.

● 'Constructionism': this does not differ greatly from the method described above; what Booth emphasizes here is a willingness on the part of 'constructionists' to use theory and concepts as a way of enhancing their analysis of the evidence, and also an acknowledgement that the content of history depends on the histor- ian's own predilections – formed out of influences such as nationality, social class, age, religion, gender and so on. In the final analysis, however, constructionists are at one with reconstructionists in the belief that what is produced as history must be bound by evidence.

● 'Deconstructionism': this method parts company with the previous two approaches; it abandons, says Booth, 'all pretexts of objectivity' (p. 12). To do what, we may ask? To take further the idea that history as a process of narrative and story- telling, and to examine the nature of that process. 'Proceeding from the premise that nothing written can be read as a true meaning, deconstructionists attempt to discover the intentions of the author of each and every source and text' (p. 12). Thus, we might say, deconstructionists are interested in studying the making of history rather than in attempting to give a 'truthful' representation of particular historical events and situations. The term 'linguistic turn' has often been applied to such historical work, and through deconstructionism's attention to the text and how it might be read we can perhaps begin to see why this term has been adopted.

What, in practical terms, this leads to is sometimes less easy to understand. Is it chiefly a case of theorizing and musing on the shortcomings of others? Not entirely. Booth, for example, points to the work of Australian historian Murray Phillips as a case of good deconstructionist practice. Phillips draws upon the American theorist Hayden White for literary analytical categories that help us to interpret particular texts. Thus Phillips has produced distinctive critical analyses of research by Booth himself and the historian Ed Jaggard on Australian beach cultures.[16] The upshot of this approach is to reveal that the historical narrative is as much *invented* through the literary forms employed to create it, as it is *discovered* by an evidence-based analysis of the past. This represents a fundamental shift in both philosophy and method from mainstream historical practice, and might lead us on to an axiom held dear by all those who subscribe to postmodern methodology: that language is not the medium by which prior ideas are expressed, but the structure that itself enables and creates ideas.

Such principles are relevant to any study of sport that involves texts, and this might mean not simply written texts; works of art, buildings, films, the spoken word, open spaces – all these things form part of a terrain with the potential to be explored by deconstructionist historians. One of the most interesting (and to some, curious) examples can be found in work done by the American historian Synthia Sydnor on synchronized swimming. Some might question whether synchronized swimming is a sport, while others have doubted that Sydnor's approach constitutes 'history'. Her inspiration is the German philosopher **Walter Benjamin (1892–1940)**. Benjamin felt that the idea of 'how it really was' is a chimera, and that the pursuit of it was therefore a useless activity. When we look back at the past, he claimed, all we can do is 'seize hold of a memory as it flashes up at a moment of danger'. Following this line Sydnor has produced a history that is a collection of fragments and memories – a poem almost, though substantiated by numerous footnote references that connect her work with that of 'orthodox' history. She prioritizes her role as narrator, putting herself into the text, and invites readers to 'dive into *my* narrative.' It is certainly not something that historians have become accustomed to regarding as history, with evidence, argument and interpretation.[17]

Gaps

Although the history of sport has come a long way in the past 30 years there are still many areas that await full exploration. On the whole, attention has been given to the period since 1800 and to 'the West' (i.e. Europe, North America and Australasia). Even within these confines coverage is uneven. Some of the areas and topics about which we still know relatively little are the following:

- medieval and early modern sport, and sport in Asia, Africa and South America
- the place of voluntary associations, rather than commercial or state-related initiatives
- sport in the workplace, whether that be people whose work is sport production, or work as a site of play
- sport and certain forms of media (the press and television are relatively well covered, but radio and certain kinds of literature such as novels have been overlooked)
- European sport as *European* sport (rather than the history of sport in individual European countries)
- comparative histories
- sport autobiographies
- sport as consumption, such as the sporting goods industry, sport-related merchandizing (by, for example, football clubs), and other consumer products sold in the context of sport (e.g. cosmetics, fashion wear etc.)
- sport and race/ethnicity (these areas have been opened up, appropriately, by the American *Journal of Sport History* in its summer 1999 and fall 2000 issues)

- sport and disability
- 'extreme' and 'new' sports
- and, as explained earlier in this chapter, a resistance to moving out of an ingrained *empiricist* methodology

This is not meant to be a definitive list; merely an indication of areas where further work in the field of sport history would be welcomed. Nor should we wait for the world's leading historians to take on the task of filling the gaps. Some of these topics are perfectly suitable for third-year undergraduate dissertations. While in some areas the secondary literature might be limited other source material is readily available, often in the form of oral testimony from senior family members and friends; local sports clubs and their secretaries keep minute books of historical value; local libraries frequently have excellent collections of autobiographical works by sportspeople, in a central repository if not on the open shelves; a local school (your own?) would make an excellent case study of the changing nature of sport and games in the educational curriculum; and the archives of local administrative authorities (usually accessible through the library or sometimes at the mayor's office itself) can be a fruitful source of information on leisure provision in the more recent past. Has anyone written a history of the main leisure/sport centre in your neighbourhood? If not, why not have a go yourself?

Study Questions

1. In what ways might sport be considered to be an *important* part of modern society?
2. What, in your view, are the most economically significant aspects of modern sport?
3. Why is it important to see the history of sport as part of the wider history of society?
4. What is the value of theory in studying sport, and which theorists would you find most helpful in relation to your own work?
5. In what ways might your own studies (e.g. for a dissertation) connect with existing work in sport history, or help to fill some of the 'gaps' identified in this chapter?

Further Reading

Anthony Bateman and John Bale, *Sporting Sounds: Relationships between Sport and Music* (Abingdon: Routledge, 2009).
Simon Barnes, *The Meaning of Sport* (London: Short Books, 2006).
Peter Burke, *What Is Cultural History?* (Cambridge: Polity Press, 2004).

Richard Giulianotti ed., *Sport and Modern Social Theorists* (Basingstoke: Palgrave Macmillan, 2004).

Grant Jarvie, *Sport, Culture and Society: An Introduction* (Abingdon: Routledge, 2006).

David Lavallee, John Kremer, Aidan P. Morgan and Mark Williams, *Sport Psychology: Contemporary Themes* (Basingstoke: Palgrave Macmillan, 2004).

Martin Polley, *Sports History: A Practical Guide* (Basingstoke: Palgrave Macmillan, 2007).

Alan Tomlinson ed., *The Sport Studies Reader* (Abingdon: Routledge, 2007).

CHAPTER 2

The Transition to Modern Sport

When asked to describe the game of cricket to a visitor from overseas, an Englishman with a keen line in irony said: 'Well, you see, these 22 people gather together at a large ground, stumps are set in the ground 22 yards apart, the two captains toss a coin to decide who shall bat first, the fielding team takes the field, followed by the two opening batsmen of the other team, the bowler measures out his run up...and down comes the rain.'

It's an old joke, but a good one because it reminds us not only that English summer weather can be very unkind, but also that sport has its rituals, and indeed that its origins were often to be found in the fertility and rain-making ceremonies of ancient times.

The study of history is about change, and sport is no less affected by change than are all other areas of society. There are two ways in which the process of change is important to sport historians. First, simply in the way the institutions and practices of sport change over time; the way, for example, that in cricket the MCC lost its position as the effective governing body of world cricket, to be replaced by other organizations. This point should remind us that the *status quo* of the present is a transient state of affairs, and will change in time. Second, the ways in which the legacies of the past influence how we experience sport today. In a small and local way, for example, the death in 2008 of Jimmy Sirrell, a former manager of the English football club Notts County, stirred fond memories among many residents of the city of Nottingham of a rare occasion when Notts were briefly in football's top flight. His funeral became something of a civic event that helped to stimulate a collective local memory. Equally, however, the past can work in other ways, coming to seem an oppressive legacy that gives rise to false expectations in the present. Many managers of sports clubs have discovered to their cost that it is not always a good thing for their club or association to possess a glorious past.

These two issues – historical change and our sense of the past – can sometimes merge to produce a curious notion of history. This is the way in which change often becomes synonymous with 'progress'. The standard of athletics, we are told, is now better than it has ever been: just look at the times, distances and heights now recorded and compare them with the past. Even in less quantifiable sports, like, for example, rugby or association football, it is assumed that players are now fitter and better, and would easily beat their predecessors, if only a match could be arranged across the boundaries of time. The contemporary player is seen as, in Roy Hobbs's fateful phrase from *The Natural*, 'the best there has ever been'.[1] In this way the history of the particular game becomes one long transition to the perfect state that now exists. This kind of thinking, which I term 'present-mindedness', can simply stem from an ignorance of history; not only an ignorance of facts, but also an inability to see sports in different historical contexts and to judge them according to how well sportspeople faced the challenges present in those contexts. Some observers may convince themselves that, for example, Shane Warne is a better bowler than Clarrie Grimmett or Bill O'Reilly (just look at the figures) without considering the different conditions and circumstances in which each played. Greatness is a relative concept, framed in history. Linked to the tendency to see historical change as progress, 'present-mindedness' also inclines us to focus only on what happens now. The implicit assumption of much television coverage of association football in England and Wales is that the history of the game began with the Premier League (established in 1992), and that what happened before it was a mere 'run up' to the main event, with little relevance for contemporary viewers.

That sport has changed is undeniable. But quite how the process of change occurred, and when its greatest impact was felt, is far more difficult to determine. The 'sportsman' of the early nineteenth century would generally have defined his activities around the famous trinity of 'huntin', shootin', and fishin'' (the missing 'g' denoting their aristocratic provenance). These were *participant* field sports, not spectacles to be watched by passive observers. A century later a 'sportsman' might be someone who merely paid up, stood and watched, like Danny the riveter in George Blake's novel *The Shipbuilders,* taking his place at Ibrox alongside thousands of other working men to watch Rangers.[2] Danny did not himself play the game. A century later we speak of 'sportspeople', because sport is no longer the special domain of the male, and the range of activities available to all has greatly increased (even though all do not necessarily avail themselves of them; sport is still something more likely to be practised by the young white male than the older black female). The Dutch historian Johann Huizinga, writing in the late 1930s, identified another form of change. He thought that 'sport' was a peculiar modern distortion of an older social activity, 'play'. Play, according to Huizinga, was a fundamental feature of European society. It was not confined to physical activity, and could, for example, also be seen in politics and the law. In games its essence was a spontaneity that gave pleasure in itself, rather than being a means to an end. Allen Guttmann has described this quality as 'autotelic' – *intrinsic* to the pleasures of play.[3] This is an important distinction, worth bearing in mind in the present age when the 'value' of doing sport is usually related to an ulterior purpose (health, well-being, employment, the economy). It is also worth recalling a famous fictional athlete of recent times – Alf Tupper, the 'Tough of the Track' – who ran not because of glory or gain but because he simply enjoyed it and relished its competition. For Tupper, however, the physical *contest* of athletics was what provided the thrill of games, and it was the contest element that made games into sports. Huizinga noted that the professionalism, organization and competitiveness that characterized modern sport was but a pale reflection of what had been: 'with the increasing systematization and regimentation of sport something of the pure play-quality is inevitably lost.'[4]

These distinctions, while perhaps helpful in plotting basic changes in the perception and content of sport, can also mask a number of important continuities. For example, Peter Radford's study of the early nineteenth-century sportsman Captain Barclay reveals a man with a very 'modern' approach to sport who saw it as an opportunity to employ his considerable skills and stamina to make money.[5] Commercialized sport, which in association football arrived in the late-nineteenth century, was already well established in the eighteenth century, especially in and around London, whose market provided capital and spectators for both cricket and boxing, and the all-important betting that accompanied it; in the supposedly amateur phase of cricket the game's leading player, W. G. Grace, was the very model of an entrepreneurial businessman who knew how to exploit cricket for money. So we must not assume that the characteristics that we associate with contemporary sport have only come into being in the recent past. 'Modern' features can be found wherever sporting activities are conducted in a money economy; and money economies have a very long history indeed.

Modernization

One of the most influential and much-quoted interpretations of the fundamental changes in sport has been that formulated by the American writer Allen Guttmann in his book *From Ritual to Record: The Nature of Modern Sports* (1979).[6] The book has two chief aims. The major one is to identify the quintessential nature of modern sport, its defining characteristics, so to speak, which Guttmann sees as largely coming into being in a period of some 150 years, from the early eighteenth to the late nineteenth century. This is done by contrasting the characteristics of this period with sport as understood in primitive (e.g. pre-Columbian America) and ancient (Greek and Roman) societies. The argument of Guttmann's chapter 2, from which the book takes its title, is that sport in these earlier times was usually a sacred enterprise, and something that existed for the moment of its performance;

for the moderns it had become an activity by which human achievement was measured. Modern sport is thus a manifestation of a process that some sociologists might describe in a term taken from the great German theorist Max Weber: 'rationality'. Guttmann's analysis is suffused with Weberian insights. The other aim, which Guttmann himself notes has received far less attention, is to offer some comparisons and contrasts between American and European sport. Both aims require a degree of systematization, which Guttmann certainly gives; one of the book's distinguishing features is its propensity for categorizing. The general patterns are what stand out, not so much the exceptions to the perceived trends. There is, in other words, rather more of a sociologist's method at work here than a historian's. Inscribed within its considerable learning is an exercise in model-building (or 'paradigm' creation, as Guttmann would prefer to call it).

Guttmann has listed seven distinguishing characteristics of modern sports. They are as follows:

- **Secularism**: modern sports are distinguished by concerns that are entirely secular, that is, related to human society and human achievement; they might have an ulterior motive (prestige, fitness for warfare) but they do not have religious meanings, that is, they are not performed in order to please a divine being. In this modern sport is different from that of primitive and ancient societies; the turning point came with the Romans.
- **Equality of opportunity to compete and in the conditions of competition**: in principle, modern sports are open to all, whereas ancient sport operated on the basis of all manner of exclusions; once in competition participants in modern sport should expect equality of competition (e.g. men do not compete against boys or women). In practice both these notions are confounded in many sports, and as we shall see in Chapters 3 and 4 considerations of gender and race have put up barriers to equality.
- **Specialization of roles**: defined roles, based on individual skill and strength, are a characteristic of modern sport, in which also a specialization in one sport is common; this feature was less common, though not absent, in Greek and Roman sports and it is something in which the boundaries between the 'modern' and the 'ancient' are somewhat blurred.
- **Rationalization**: this has to do with the rules that pertain to the playing/ performing of the game; modern sports do not differ from ancient ones in having rules but rather in the nature of the rules – in modern sports they are means to an end, devised and changed in order to permit the fulfilment of the objectives of the game. Rationalization is also to do with the perfecting of sports technique; it is therefore closely linked to specialization, and to what now follows.
- **Bureaucratization**: when rules acquire universal application, a bureaucracy is needed to oversee and administer them; modern sport bureaucracies, with their elected officials and staff with specific functions, are one of the major characteristics defining a modern sport. Such organization is

completely absent from primitive sport, but discernable in Roman times, and essential in modern sport, where it has grown from local to national and eventually international proportions (see Chapter 5).

- **Quantification**: the recording of times, distances and quantities (e.g. of runs in cricket) is a quintessential feature of modern sport but scarcely recognizable in pre-modern times; the Greeks did not record the times of races, not because they lacked efficient means of measuring but because, as Guttmann observes, 'man was still the measure of all things, not the object of endless measurements.'[7]

- **Records**: the idea of the record (a contrivance of modern sport rather than, as we might imagine, a 'natural' accompaniment to all sport) results from the insistence upon human achievement and its quantification; records were not unknown in former times – medieval Turkish archery, for example – but nowhere did they assume the degree of emphasis reached in modern sport.

Because of Guttmann's insistence on systematization we have to recognize that some historians have always approached *From Ritual to Record* with a degree of scepticism. The focus of contention has been 'modernization', a concept which Guttmann did not mention by name though it is implicit in the text and he has since affirmed his faith in its explanatory power. There is no need here to rehearse all the *pros* and *cons* of modernization theory, except to say that for historians, with their concern for the particular and the empirical, it has presented some especial difficulties. Historians do not always seek to establish *general* trends in the manner of sociology. There has been, for example, a tendency for 'modernization' to be used in the 'present-minded' way I alluded to above, resulting in what is sometimes referred to as a 'teleological' perspective, reading the past from the vantage point of the present, as if history is actually leading somewhere along a meaningful path of development. Guttmann quite rightly rejects the tendency, at least in any sense of moral improvement or 'progress'. Equally, though, there is the practice of creating paradigms such as 'modern sport'. The historian might ask, is the world really so neat and tidy? A favourite charge of historians against the sociologists is that they make the facts fit the model, and Guttmann is not entirely absolved of this. *From Ritual to Record* gives us two snapshots of history – ancient (traditional) and modern – without much sense of how we got from the one to the other. 'Modern' sport might acquire a particular characteristic when compared *in general terms* with ancient sports, but how applicable is the modern typology for all the sporting activities – elite and recreational, local and national, commercial and voluntary – that occur in the 'modern' period? In other words there are several sports, games and pastimes in the 'modern' period that we would be hard put to describe as 'modern'; though to be fair, Guttmann does not claim that *all* sport in the modern world necessarily has to conform to his typology. Another, and probably more important, concern among historians is: once the 'modern' form has come into being, is that it? Does it remain in that form for evermore? Guttmann has since regretted his own failure to discuss the sports of the Renaissance, and there is no doubt that with a stronger chronology the process of historical change would have received closer scrutiny. Changes in the form and ethos of sport since the 'birth of modern sport' (a favourite historians' phrase, incidentally, referring to the period *c.* 1850–1900) are important, and have been overlooked; it would have been valuable if, when Guttmann's publishers decided to re-issue his famous book in 2004, they had asked him to reflect on substantive developments since the end of the nineteenth century, to see whether the idea of 'modern sport' still applies. We must accept, however, that no academic book is without shortcomings, and Guttmann's has fewer than many. It remains an outstanding contribution to our understanding of a difficult process, always provided that (and on this Guttmann himself would surely concur) it is read *critically*.

Historical change

A critical posture must be assumed on the question of historical change. Although we are all inclined to speak of 'modern sport' as against 'traditional' games there are few historians who would now accept the idea of a finite period of change, even one as long as 150 years (*c.* 1750–1900, if we are talking about Britain). The process is seen as far slower and, equally important, far more *uneven* in its impact than is suggested in the 'traditional' to 'modern' notion. We also have to acknowledge that there are whole areas of the history of sport and leisure that we know little about. These gaps are both chronological and geographical, the latter explained by the fact that much sport history and sociology has been, if not 'euro-centric', at least 'occident-centric' (i.e. written from the point of view of 'the West'). In other words, the model of transition we employ might not fit large areas of the world.

Partly because of an ingrained 'present mindedness' few historians (myself not included) have expressed much interest in the sports of ancient times and places. They have seemed too unconnected with what we understand sport to be today. Yet even a cursory glance at this neglected past is enough to dispel such thoughts. In the vast arc of time that preceded the nineteenth century – the almost four thousand years from the third millennium BC – there were many phases through which sport and games passed. Throughout this time, however, there was a constant 'ludic' (i.e. games) presence in most parts of the world, and it served numerous social, economic, political and religious purposes, whilst also existing purely for the purpose of physical and mental pleasure. It is true that, for the most part, sports seem to have possessed a strong religious purpose (to honour the gods) often linked to fertility rites (to bring sunshine, or rain, and therefore good harvests, to ward off ill-health and ill-luck), and to have been performed by men. But there is too much variety displayed in the fragments of archaeological and literary evidence available to us simply to delimit physical contests to religio-male activity.

Greeks. As we know, in part from the depictions on vases, the ancient Greeks held athletics in high regard; they also created gymnasia in major cities as places for both physical and cultural pursuits. Whilst this leisure might have originally been confined to an upper-class elite, by the time the games at Olympia were established in the eighth century BC (they were to last for a thousand years) participation was open to a much wider mixture of social groups. While retaining their essentially sacred purpose, affirmed in the temple dedicated to the god Zeus that dominated the landscape at Olympia, the games had developed a range of disciplines including running, throwing the discus and javelin, boxing, wrestling and chariot racing. With the notable exception of Sparta, where a well-develop curriculum of women's sports existed,[8] probably

Ancient athletics imagined: Edgar Degas, *Young Spartans Exercising*, 1863. Degas (1834–1917) was a popular French painter, best known for his portrayal of ballet dancers. This early work, *c.* 1860, is not among his most famous canvasses, but it offers a good illustration of the contemporary bourgeois enthusiasm for all things Greek, as well as a defiantly honest image of sexuality, free of the prudishness of the day. Its French title is historically more precise than the English one: 'young Spartan girls challenging the boys to wrestling (la lutte).' (National Gallery, London).

with a fertility purpose, athletic contests seem to have been a mainly masculine pastime. Though few records of performance were inscribed and prizes of a material nature were not awarded, athletes were nonetheless often rewarded by their communities for their prowess, and might in a sense be regarded as 'professional' stars similar to those of today.

Romans. The Roman republic took over many of the attributes of Greek sports, but tended to play down the aesthetic appeal by endowing them with a greater military emphasis and what seems like a stronger commercial orientation. It was during these times that more obviously 'modern' sporting practices began to appear. If the centrepiece of Greek sport was the Olympics, Rome's was the gladiatorial contest, which featured an array of different bouts, both between humans, and between humans and animals. The commercial nature of much Roman sport is underlined by the completion of the Colosseum in Rome towards the end of the first century AD; it accommodated as many people as present-day Villa Park (50,000) in a design that we are still familiar with some two thousand years later.[9] The Colosseum was the hub of considerable business activity, and also fulfilled an important political function, allowing the powers-that-be the opportunity to take the pulse of public opinion by observing the temper of its crowds. With Roman sport, then, there is a clear indication of features we associate with the 'modern' sporting world.

The East. To underline the point about uneven development, in other parts of the world sport manifested different characteristics. Hindu and Buddhist religious influences shaped sport in India in both physical and spiritual forms, resulting in purely physical activities such as wrestling, but at the same time creating more intellectual endeavours that today we might describe as 'mind games'. Is what the British football manager Sir Alex Ferguson seems good at ('out-psyching' opposing managers) a sport? The main athletic consequence of the Muslim conquest of northern India in the eighth century AD was the intensification of physical games, especially polo playing among the ruling elite. Chinese sport similarly veered between the physical and spiritual, with archery particularly popular as a pastime that combined physical energy with stylistic achievement. More rugged sports increased in prominence after the fall of the Ming dynasty in the seventeenth century AD when the new Manchu rulers favoured equestrian sports. In Japan, sumo wrestling had a long history of development from at least the eighth century AD, and various forms of archery and swordplay also maintained their hold on the popular imagination. Women participated more extensively in many of these games than was the case in the ancient European world. After the Meiji 'restoration' (1868) the trend towards the modernization of Japanese society saw a demand for western sports.

In what Guttmann describes as the 'pre-literate' societies of the Americas and Africa the predominant sports appear to have been based on running activities, sometimes combined with a ball as in the stickball game of the Choctow Indians. Here the many variations in the practice of the game all seem to have had in common the religious and environmental (fertility) purpose that is such a recurring element in early games. Thus, who 'won' was not the point of the exercise; it was the performing of it, and what the performance signified for the people who staged it, that mattered. The point that used often to be heard about sport in the earlier twentieth century – 'it's not the winning that counts but the taking part' – harked back to one of the main defining features of 'traditional' games.

Medieval and early modern Europe. The upper-class and military leanings in early sport continued into the medieval period in Europe. Most of what we know about the sports of this time, roughly between the tenth and the fourteenth centuries, relates to the pastimes of the rich and is concerned with hunting or jousting, sports that needed the expensive commodity of a horse. This is not to say, however, that the sphere of 'popular' sports is a complete historical vacuum. Sports such as football, of a rough and disorganized kind, and those involving cruelty to animals were performed, usually on holy days (Easter, Shrove Tuesday, Whitsuntide). Such pastimes were simple in form, locally based, and communal in the sense that they involved the participation of large groups of people rather than being pursued singly. A good example might be the games of rough football still to be found in some parts of England in the early twenty-first century (see Chapter 4). Occasions such as this were rowdy and were expected to produce a temporary suspension of normal order, usually tolerated by the authorities, though there are several instances in the medieval period of official bans on football, either because the disorder caused was excessive, or because the game interfered with what were considered to be more important pastimes such as the militarily necessary practice of archery. After the middle of the fourteenth century, with changes in the labour market in England following the Black Death, labourers benefited for a time from higher earnings and might have gained rather more freedom to play, with the result that there was more evidence of sport for its own sake (instead of being linked to religious festivals); in urban centres such as London some of these activities acquired a more 'modern' form, with both spectating and gambling (bowls, cock-fighting). Popular sports of this kind did not necessarily exclude members of the upper classes, although by the sixteenth century the educational effects of the Renaissance were prompting a refinement of manners among the upper class in England. Henry VIII is an example. He was devoted to all the older physical sports in the hunting curriculum but, at the same time, as a Renaissance prince he displayed skills in such arts as courtly dancing and the composing of music. His daughter, Elizabeth Tudor, carried on this dual interest, tempering her passion for the chase with intellectual pursuits that befitted a woman tutored by the renowned scholar Roger Ascham.

The long-term process of change in sporting culture is expertly dissected in the work of the historian David Underdown, whose subject is the game of cricket in southern England in the eighteenth and early nineteenth century.

One of the outstanding features of Underdown's analysis of cricket's development in this place and at this time is his placing of it in a clear economic and social context, showing how cricket evolved in a particular agricultural environment that shaped both the way in which the game was played and those who played it. His study provides a master class in how good sport history should be done.

Case Study Discussion 6

David Underdown, *Start of Play: Cricket and Culture in Eighteenth-Century England* (London: Allen Lane The Penguin Press, 2000).

The main points in Underdown's argument are as follows:

1. The origins of the game of cricket are obscure, but there were many stick and ball games played in various parts of England [as elsewhere in the world] and cricket was one of them; alongside them developed a host of other rural sports and pastimes, including football – some of it very organized and rule-governed by the eighteenth century, though apparently in decline in the southern counties – stoolball, cudgel playing, bull baiting, cock fighting and horse racing.

2. By the later seventeenth century a form of cricket had become well established in the 'forest counties' of Kent, Sussex and Hampshire, in particular in that area known as the Weald between the North and South Downs. Agriculture in the upland Downs was both arable and pastoral, with many nucleated villages that retained some old farming practices and a strong tradition of communal life. In the Weald the settlements were smaller and more scattered, with less of a communal focus than those on the Downs. Wealden life was more individualistic, economic activity being based more on family units.

3. Cricket had originated as a 'peasant' game, that is, it was played by those closest to the land, not by the upper gentry and aristocracy. Many early cricket teams originated in the Weald, though the cricket was often played on the Downs where open space was more readily available. The interaction between Downs and Weald was a prime feature of the game's development, as was a political, economic and cultural tension between those prospering from the Whig political settlement of 1688 and the agrarian changes of the eighteenth century, and those who looked back to a 'golden age' of communal farming and social paternalism. The old game of cricket might have been a sporting form of this rural conservatism and nostalgia, though during the course of the eighteenth century it was being invaded by the upper classes in the interests of commercial gain and gambling, and some of the forest county clubs were being drawn into the orbit of London.

4. One of the many places which became strongholds of cricket was a village on the very eastern edge of the forest counties: Hambledon, on the South Downs in

Hampshire, just to the north of Portsmouth. By 1756 its club was a force in the game, with wealthy backers and matches played for high stakes against other leading clubs, often at the leading commercial venue for cricket, the Artillery ground in Finsbury, London. Hambledon, however, retained until the later years of the century, an identifiably *local* position as a club, in its members, its play-ers, its supporters and, to a degree, its backers; its successes at cricket against other, aristocratic-backed teams were a source of local pride and independence, 'a symbol of country virtue' (p. 151).

5. It is important to remember that the Hambledon club was a voluntary associ-ation, with a strong representation of local gentry in its membership and with a wide range of sociable activities besides cricket playing. Nonetheless, by the end of the eighteenth century influence was increasingly passing to the nobility, in particular the Duke of Dorset and, from 1786 when he was elected president of the club, George Finch, Earl of Winchilsea. Unlike Dorset, an old-fashioned aristocrat, Winchilsea was a modernizer who, among other things, sought to profit from the London leisure industry and therefore moved the Hambledon club increasingly into that commercial orbit. The White Conduit Club, precur-sor of the Marylebone Cricket Club (formed 1787), invaded Hambledon for its players and drafted them into an all-professional metropolitan circuit of matches which became mired in a murky world of gambling and corruption. Hambledon itself went into decline; the election of Winchilsea had been 'a disaster for the Hambledon Club' (p. 155). The withering away of the club was synonymous with the disappearance of an old rural way of life in the face of new commercial economics. The greatest chronicler and critic of these general economic and social changes was the Tory radical William Cobbett in his famous *Rural Rides* (1830).

As illuminating as Underdown's work on cricket is, it is equalled by a fascinating study of the modernization of sports and pastimes in the same period in America. Nancy Struna's ambitious survey of seventeenth- and eighteenth-century sport and leisure in colonial America is a brilliant account of historical change and cannot be overlooked in our consideration of the transition to 'modern' sport.

Case Study Discussion 7

Nancy L. Struna, *People of Prowess: Sport, Leisure and Labor in Early Anglo-America* (Urbana: University of Illinois Press, 1996).

Struna's is an innovative and important contribution to the history of both pre-Revolution America and sport. Though its main focus is restricted to selected regions – Chesapeake and Massachusetts in particular – it provides a fascinating account, drawn from an extensive range of primary and secondary sources, of the leisure activities of men and women in the colonies. Moreover, it goes far beyond a simple chronicling of the development of indoor and outdoor pastimes. It offers us an incisive historical interpretation of the continuities and changes that took place in the two centuries between the early seventeenth and late eighteenth centuries, and stands as a powerful addition to the discourse of leisure and modernization shaped by historians such as E. P. Thompson, Robert Malcolmson, Dennis Brailsford and others.

Struna is ground-breaking in various ways. Here are some of its chief features. Firstly in stressing the export of sporting practices from England to the colonies: 'Anglo-America' is a significant term underlining the trans-Atlantic processes involved. Secondly, the book provides a re-consideration of what we might mean by the slippery concept of 'sport', as this changed profoundly in the American territories under scrutiny. Thirdly, and related to this, Struna seeks to connect sport and labour, showing how many sports were developed out of workplace routines and, in the early stages of the period, were performed in workplace venues by people drawn from particular trades and occupations. Fourthly, there is a persuasive argument about why this fusion of work and sport changed, so that by the early years of the nineteenth-century 'sport' to many had come to mean activities conducted in a specialized sphere *separate* from work. Fifthly, and as the book's title states, there is an emphasis on sports that displayed physical prowess; not all did, but the predominant ones – horse racing, hunting, foot races, wrestling – involved contests in which victory of individuals or teams depended on physical strength. They were thus *participant* activities, not mere spectating. Sixthly, as part of her interpretation of the long-term changes evident at this time, Struna notes the gradual separation by *social class* of sports and sporting style; in particular she observes the emergence of an upper-class culture of sport, with its own rules, conduct and sense of honour, that characterized the rich landowning groups of Virginia (their economy increasingly underpinned by slave labour in the eighteenth century). Finally (at least as far as my list extends) there is a welcome refusal to view this period as a 'prelude' to the War of Independence, in which those forces leading to the revolt against British rule are highlighted.

These general features are illustrated by a wealth of local examples. John Dutton's description of a football match in Rowley, Massachusetts in 1686, for instance, provokes the thought that the game's form (Dutton observes an unusual feature of bare feet and no tripping of opponents that he had never encountered in England) might be an adaptation of English customs, or perhaps a borrowing from native-American forms of football. There is a rich profusion of such examples in Struna's discussion of taverns (or 'ordinaries' as they were usually called) in the rural and urban areas of colonial society. Benjamin Berry's tavern at Battletown, Virginia (the place subsequently became known as Berryville) was situated at a strategic point for both travellers and local residents and is a striking example of the taverns whose multifunctional nature gave them the appellation 'public house'. It provided drink, board, lodging and stabling for all – rich and poor – and a range of games and sporting contests (known as 'battles' – from which the settlement derived its original name): wrestling and fist fighting gave opportunity for men to display 'prowess', and these sports sat alongside bear baiting and cock fighting. Cock fighting, in fact, seems to have been one of the most popular sports of the eighteenth century, and most taverns aspired to have a cock pit on their premises. Berry, more than most tavern keepers, had a reputation as a sports impresario on account of the range of contests he staged, but while perhaps exceptional in this respect his 'ordinary' was not dissimilar from hundreds of such establishments throughout the thirteen American colonies. Like English pubs they were in many respects the cornerstone of communities. Also like their English counterparts taverns aroused the suspicions and the invective of opponents who saw in their contests, drinking and gaming a source of idleness. The taverns represented 'uneconomic' behaviour; they were not part of a 'rational' pursuit of leisure. In other words, they expressed a commitment to a life of play, and were thus an obstacle to work. As in England sports, the habits they encouraged and the institutions that sustained them were subjected to a fierce campaign of controls in the interests of work discipline. As may be imagined much of this was directed against the poor, though upper-class gaming and drinking was by no means unknown. The campaign met with mixed results; it certainly did not succeed in eradicating tavern culture but at the same time, Struna suggests, it encouraged sports associated with sobriety and prudence. It also widened class distinction in American sport, by causing the upper classes to look at their sense of honour and prestige: gaming in particular, undermined status – 'gaming countered gentility and refinement' (p. 161).

At roughly the same time that rural cricket was under threat in England, a new form of football was beginning to emerge. This process provides a good example of how 'present-mindedness' has affected our understanding of sport history. What we now call *association* football (and which Americans and the Irish call 'soccer' – a public-school contraction of 'as*soci*ation') derives its name from the Football Association founded by former public-school pupils in London in 1863. Historians have attributed its origins to games played in British public schools such as Eton, Harrow, Winchester and Marlborough, whence it was disseminated to other parts of Britain, and later the world, by former pupils of such institutions in the form laid down by the Football Association. The role of the FA has been regarded as crucial in the codifying and standardizing of the game, ensuring that the many different variations of football played before the 1860s were orchestrated into a single commonly understood form. Those who rejected the association football model kept faith with a code that allowed handling and physical contact, and which was associated with a public school from which this alternative form of football took its name: Rugby. The history of this game as a separate entity distinct from the association game began in 1871 with the formation of the RFU. Thus many historians have interpreted the origins of football by taking its present-day configuration – association football/soccer, as against rugby – and reading it back into the past to locate the bifurcation of the two codes at a particular point in time. The process appears to confirm two of Guttmann's characteristics of modern sport – rationalization and bureaucracy. Not all historians, however, have interpreted developments in this way.

Case Study Discussion 8

Adrian Harvey, *Football: The First Hundred Years. The Untold Story* **(London: Routledge, 2005).**

Harvey has questioned whether the process of historical change is quite so straight-forward. His careful examination of 'football' in the eighteenth and nineteenth centuries suggests that it is not. Harvey's detailed researches have posed a number of questions that cast doubt on the received wisdom. At the risk of simplifying a number of important aspects in a wide-ranging study we might suggest that the following points represent Harvey's key findings:

- Football of various kinds was a well-established sport in Britain by the eighteenth century, with particular concentrations in East Anglia, Lancashire and London; it was often well organized, with rules and referees, increasing in popularity in the mid-nineteenth century, though compared with other sports (especially cricket) we should not overestimate its importance; [as we have seen from Underdown, it appears to have been declining in the south east in the eighteenth century].
- The form of 'rough' football associated with Shrove Tuesday (and still commemorated in Ashbourne, Derbyshire) was neither as long established nor as dominant a form as is often imagined; nor was it always a violent sport.
- In the public schools football was played *within* schools (house matches) rather than *between* them, and according to a variety of rules unique to the particular school; before *c.* 1860 there is no evidence of this football being exported outside the public-school system.
- In the later 1850s and 1860s the town of Sheffield emerged as an important football centre, with the middle-class Sheffield FC devising a set of rules that were applied throughout the local area and expanding the game geographically and socially; the formalizing in 1868 of the Sheffield Football Association was a landmark in the further development of the game in England.
- The forming of the Football Association in 1863, by contrast, was an event of limited impact; the new organization's rules were not universally adopted, and in 1867 it was on the point of disbanding; it was the impetus provided by the success of football in Sheffield that stiffened the resolve of the FA to enforce its own rules.
- Until the late 1860s 'football' included a number of different rules and it was not beyond the bounds of possibility that a compromise might have been reached under the auspices of the FA, between those favouring a 'kicking' game and the supporters of a handling (Rugby School) code; the FA's determination to exclude handling, and the coordinating of rugby-type rules by the RFU in 1871 effectively sealed the division, but the process had been a protracted one with a far from inevitable outcome.

Harvey's research raises interesting points about the so-called transition from the 'traditional' to the 'modern' in sport. For one thing, it is continuity as much as change that has to be taken into account. One of Harvey's main points of contention is that the cultural changes accompanying industrialization, to which historians following Malcolmson[10] gave such emphasis, were in fact less radical than has been supposed. Another important consequence of Harvey's approach is to show that there was no predetermined form of development in sport; the possibility that, even in the late 1860s, a hybrid form of football might have developed with the FA as its governing body provides an intriguing perspective on the whole process of change. Finally, in terms of how change was initiated, Harvey has challenged the traditional 'top down' interpretation of dissemination; by emphasizing continuing grass-roots forms of football, and the formation of rules and practices outside the sphere of the public-school network, he has put forward a strong case for seeing the entire process as a 'bottom up' one. None of this is to suggest that Harvey's work passes without criticism. As with all historical research there is room for some doubt, and historians may well find fault, for example, with his revisionist approach to cultural changes in the late eighteenth and early nineteenth centuries. On the whole though Harvey's is a challenging book that clarifies with painstaking research a topic that had previously attracted only some rather impressionistic conclusions.

One of the problems with modernization theory, whether applied to sport or to other economic and social developments, is that it has tended to focus on key phases of change. Thus, it attributes change to an interaction of influences that occur in relatively short and dramatic phases, such as industrialization in nineteenth-century Europe, or the period of independence from colonialism in the developing world. One of its weaknesses is a neglect of the *continuing* dynamic of change; in short, a tendency to assume that once 'modernity' has been installed the big changes are over. The history of sport in Britain between the late nineteenth and the early twenty-first century provides an illustration.

Commercialization

At some point in the third quarter of the nineteenth century conditions in North America, Britain and some parts of continental Europe began to crystallize to allow a largely localized and fragmented sporting culture to be transformed into a national leisure market with patterned regularities in its financing, organization and morality. This was the process that historians refer to as 'the birth of modern sport', and it has been extensively documented in numerous books.[11] It assumed its most concentrated form in parts of England, South Wales and lowland Scotland. Briefly summarized these conditions were: the concentration of an increasing proportion of an expanding population in urban settlements, with a growing civic culture and identity (which sport contributed to as well as benefited from); the general rise in the real and therefore disposable incomes of most of the population, though important regional, class and gender variations persisted; the general reduction in hours of work, making spare time on Saturdays possible for men; improvements in transport, both within and between towns, which allowed for the existence of organized league fixtures such as those in cricket and football, as well as the large-scale movement of bloodstock, people and equipment for a national calendar of horse-racing events; and, of crucial importance, the developments in printing, telegraphy and distribution which enabled information to be transmitted quickly: the Saturday evening sports paper, the *'Pink 'Un'*, which for much of the twentieth century brought the afternoon's results to the British fan by early evening, was in many ways the archetypal symbol of this communications revolution in sport. Clearly such conditions did not apply universally. Some areas gave themselves more readily to commercialized sport than others. London and the North West were the leading examples, with Lancashire the paradigm: the world's first industrial region and also the cradle of its commercial sport. Nor, when the conditions did apply, were all people necessarily drawn into the market that was created. Women, for example, were scarcely part of the 'people's games'. This was in part, as historians of women's leisure have shown, because of differential economic opportunities in the sexual division of leisure. But it also had to do with ideologies of gender communicated through the leisure pursuits themselves. There is no *prima facie* economic reason why sport should have been regarded as a male pursuit while the cinema, by contrast, often repelled (older) men because it was seen as the 'woman's sphere'. In other words, there are explanations for these differences to be pursued outside the realm of the economic (see Chapter 4). Even in the world of men, there were notable exclusions from commercial sports – age, class and status being important determinants. Thus, for example, rugby union (except in South Wales, Devon and Cornwall, and parts of the Scottish borders) worked to preserve a middle-class, amateur clientele which kept commercialism at bay. On the whole, however, these demographic, economic, social and political changes produced an identifiable body of commercial sports practised by a cadre of professional players and governed by a set of commonly accepted rules, sometimes administered by international bodies such as FIFA (Federation Internationale de Football Association), founded in 1904. FIFA's game was played across the world, whilst the pre-eminent example of a 'modern' sport in the United States – baseball – remained more or less confined to North America. Its *World* Series, the competition that rounded off the long baseball season each October, was something of a misnomer.

At this point it is worth pausing to comment on a feature of modernization that sometimes escapes attention: namely, the *variations* in sporting patterns between countries that are similar in their structural make up. Allen Guttmann has drawn attention to some of the differences between the United States and Europe in relation to the development of team and individual sports,[12] but the enigma that many have doubtless observed is the failure of association football to acquire any significant following in North America. It is part of a broader issue. When, at the beginning of the twentieth century, the German sociologist Werner Sombart asked 'Why is there no socialism in the United

States?' he raised the question of American *exceptionalism*. Here are two case studies that address themselves to this particular issue, and which reveal some differences (and some similarities) in the development of sport in America when compared with European countries.

Case Study Discussion 9

Andrei S. Markovits and Steven L. Hellerman, *Offside: Soccer and American Exceptionalism* (Princeton: Princeton University Press, 2001).

Within a wide canvass of American and European sport the authors focus upon attempts to establish association football ('soccer', as it is always called in America) as a national game. There have been a few during the course of the twentieth century, though none has met with any great success. Certainly none has challenged the predominance in American sport of the three great team games – baseball, American football and basketball (with a fourth – ice hockey – in the North East and Great Lakes regions). Together these sports constitute what Markovits and Hellerman describe, in a valuable phrase, as the 'hegemonic sports culture'. This refers not so much to the games played as to what people are interested in, what they *follow*: '... what people breathe, read, discuss, analyze, compare, and historicize; what they talk about at length before and after games on sports radio; what they discuss at the office watercooler; and what comprises a significant quantity of barroom (or pub) talk ...' (p. 9). A readily accessible register of the hegemonic culture is the coverage given to sports in the popular daily newspapers. What Markovits and Hellerman are concerned to understand is how the predominance of certain sport is acquired, how they (rather than other sports) come to occupy the leading position in (another felicitous phrase) a country's 'sport space', the size and capacity of which is always limited. In many countries the leading position is taken by association football, but in America soccer is crowded out. The reasons, this book asserts, are to a large degree *historical*. Markovits and Hellerman argue that the sports able to establish a following in the crucial period from the 1870s to the 1930s – the period that is often referred to as seeing the 'birth of modern sport' – were able thereafter to retain their hegemony, in part by legitimizing their position by reference to their history. Thus, the historical associations of stadiums, team histories, famous players and museums bestowed on these sports an appearance of being a natural part of the sport landscape. As much as their innate athletic attractions they possessed a *moral* authority rooted in history. Hegemonic sports therefore acquire a wide following, albeit mainly male, within the population and are further able to secure their position through assuming a *national* status. More specifically, America's leading sports developed a series of distinctive operational characteristics that proved inimical to the methods and traditions with which soccer was bound up. In America these included the widespread influence (far greater than in most other countries, including Great Britain) of university and college sports, particularly gridiron football; the business nature of American sporting models, with unabashed market economics that produced closed leagues, moveable franchises and a hostility to any form of international regulation such as that exercised in soccer by the FIFA; and a devotion to statistics and quantification – notably in baseball – to which soccer does not easily lend itself. In this climate, therefore, America (including Canada), while appearing to be structurally similar in its modernizing society to many European countries, developed a significantly different sporting culture. Markovits' and Hellerman's work reminds us that we cannot simply 'read off' from a given economic and social process of development a predetermined cultural outcome.

Case Study Discussion 10

Charles P. Korr, *The End of Baseball As We Knew It: The Players Union, 1960–81* (Urbana and Chicago, University of Illinois Press, 2002 pp. xviii + 336).

British readers, perhaps accustomed to believing that American sports, and baseball in particular, have been more advanced commercially than their European counterparts will find much interesting material in this book, which tells the story of a trade union: the Major League Baseball Players' Association (MLBPA). To be sure, baseball has displayed certain features of capitalist initiative which have no place in major British team sports with a large following, such as association football, cricket and rugby. It was, for example, Korr himself who reminded us, in his earlier book on West Ham United (*West Ham United: The Making of a Football Club,* London: Duckworth, 1979), of the case of the Brooklyn Dodgers baseball team. When faced with declining spectator support in their city of origin, the Dodgers decamped to Los Angeles in search of spectators and profit. Nothing like this had happened, on this scale, in football. In baseball, on the other hand, though not common, such movement was nevertheless not unusual; other clubs have followed the Dodgers' example. And yet the game represents a strange case of uneven development. For in contrast to its often 'advanced' business acumen, its industrial relations remained rooted in a paternalistic regime developed in the nineteenth century. Its bedrock was the notorious 'reserve' system, a means of controlling players' freedom of movement not dissimilar to the 'retain and transfer' system that operated for many years in the Football League. What Korr does in this book is to trace both the decline of paternalism and the simultaneous emergence of a labour consciousness among elite baseball players in the 1960s and 1970s. It is interesting to note that this occurred at very much the same time as the strengthening of union power among British footballers, although the longer-term consequences were different.

Baseball was not easy ground for trade unionism. Owners brooked no opposition to their rule, the game's Commissioner offered little hope of neutral treatment to players, being in effect an employee of the owners, and players themselves grew up in an atmosphere of intense competition for places on the major league roster. In this dog-eat-dog environment – 'it's basically a selfish business' said one player 'not really a team sport' (p. 27) – solidarity was difficult to foster. It was easy for owners to target individually any player who sought to challenge the status quo. It mattered little how famous they were; even the famous Joe Dimaggio suffered at the hands of his employers. Attempts at forming unions had historically met with scant success. Then suddenly, in the early to mid-1960s, things changed. A labour economist from the Steelworkers' Union, Marvin Miller, was brought in to replace the moderate Judge Robert Cannon as leader of the recently formed MLBPA, and from that point and over the course of the next 15 years the power previously wielded by the owners became a thing of the past. It was, as one owner put it, 'the end of baseball as we knew it'. All the old instruments of owners' control – especially the reserve system and individual contracts in wage bargaining – were progressively dismantled through the application of a tough negotiating stance which included the use of the strike weapon. When the opening games of the 1972 baseball season were cancelled by industrial action, all America became aware that power relations in the game were shifting. Nine years later the players stayed out for almost four months against the owners' demand for compensation for free agency, won a major victory, and showed by their solidarity that the old relations of power had shifted decisively.

It is Korr's contention, amply demonstrated by reference to the Association's records, that this state of affairs came about through rank-and-file action among baseball players themselves. Only their determination to subscribe to and stand by their union could have accounted for its success. In spite of attempts by owners and the press to portray Miller as a manipulative evil genius who was turning players away from their true course Korr makes it clear that what Miller achieved was only possible because of the backing of the players, and in particular the efforts of the player representatives from the clubs, who seem to have acted almost as a shop steward movement bringing union leaderships and rank-and-file together. Such solidarity is a laudable thing, and to keep the union solid in the long term required considerable organizational skill. But the question remains: why, at this particular time, did these qualities manifest themselves when they had been notable by their absence for almost a century? Korr's answer is twofold: the clear determination of players, and the short-sightedness, not to say stupidity, of the owners – an *ancien regime* who surely learnt nothing and forgot nothing during this entire period. These factors, when taken into consideration alongside the radicalizing effects in US society of the civil rights movement and the protests against the war in Vietnam, help us to understand the success of a labour movement in sport at this particular time.

Notwithstanding the durability of baseball, football and basketball, both studies show a capacity for change in established procedures: in the system of industrial relations, and even in the position occupied by the sports in relation to other games. Markovits and Hellerman contend that the prospects for soccer in the United States are not necessarily gloomy. Important steps were taken in the last 20 years of the twentieth century to establish a participant soccer following, particularly among schoolchildren, and the work of, firstly, the North American Soccer League and subsequently Major Soccer League to build an elite professional network of teams from the 1970s onwards greatly helped to raise the profile of the game. The staging of the 1994 World Cup in America further strengthened this profile, and whilst there was a to-be-expected downturn in the nation's attention to soccer once the World Cup had ended, Hellerman observed a nonetheless positive response from the American media by the time of the next World Cup in France. Events since, especially the winning of the World Cup in women's football by the United States and strong performances by the men's team in Japan/Korea (2002) and Germany (2006), have done no harm to soccer's cause. Markovits' and Hellerman's conclusions are therefore less pessimistic than one might suppose. There are, to be sure, still serious obstacles in the path of soccer in North America, but the expectation by many in soccer that their game might one day soon achieve the status enjoyed by ice hockey (sometimes described as the 'Big Three and One Half' sport) seems not unrealistic.

Britain was well ahead of other European countries in developing commercial sport, closer perhaps (in spite of its differences) to the United States than to countries such as France and Germany until the interwar years. What is interesting in this respect, however, is the relative lack of American influence on the development of British sport. Not only did few American sports succeed in penetrating the British sporting culture (and this was not for the want of trying by American entrepreneurs such as A. G. Spalding, who sought to introduce baseball before the First World War), but American business models also seem to have exerted little influence. Compared with the hard-nosed capitalist attitudes displayed in sports such as baseball the main British sports retained a curious mixture of gentlemanly restraint, localism and loyalty to supporters. Clear links with distinctive communities were cultivated. Thus developed what some business historians have called the 'peculiar economics' of many British sports. It was only late in the century that these traditions began to dissolve, and opportunities for commercial development that had lain dormant for many years were seized. All of these sports changed considerably during the course of the twentieth century, though not at the same time or in the same ways.

Rugby is one example, highlighting the often variable patterns of change. For over a hundred years those who controlled the Union version of the game showed little inclination to alter the basic social and ludic form they had adopted from the 1870s. They shrugged off the breakaway northern English variant of 1895 which eventually came to be known as Rugby League, and which permitted the open payment of players, and maintained a stern hostility towards it for a century. Then, quite suddenly it seemed, the Union game was transformed in the mid-1990s. Faced with the competition of both rugby league and association football, confronted by countries in the southern hemisphere that were adopting a more professional approach to the game, and tempted by the money of television companies looking for dramatic sporting action, rugby union emerged by the end of the decade as a professional game with all the attendant media exposure that sports fans had come to expect from association football. Perhaps the most striking feature of all this was the way rugby restyled its form of play. A game that had often made for a rather scrappy spectacle because of the frequent stoppages for line-outs and scrums (albeit, no doubt, an enjoyable one to play) had its rules adjusted to allow for more continuous action and, it was assumed, spectator excitement. It became, ironically, more like its arch-enemy rugby league. And, also like rugby league, the sport's long-standing international associations, bred of empire, were developed into a new form of commercial sporting globalism.

Similar changes happened to other sports at different times. Cricket, whose resistance to all-out commercialism was coming under pressure after the Second World War, was pushed into new game forms in alliance with new kinds of sponsors in an attempt to raise income. In 1963 a one-day competition, initially funded by the men's cosmetic manufacturer Gillette, was introduced; its immediate success ensured that this form of the game proliferated to such an extent that by the end of the century it seemed to dominate. In 2006 its governing body, the England and Wales Cricket Board (ECB), sold its copyright to televise test matches to the highest bidder, BSkyB, which was permitted exclusive rights; in the same year a yet more spectator-orientated form of limited-duration cricket – the Twenty/20 – was brought in; by 2008 the main months of the domestic season (June and July) were virtually cleared of other fixtures to give the new competition pride of place. In the same year, sensing a possible decline in revenues from test matches, the cricket authorities in India were experimenting with new Twenty/20 leagues, with the strong possibility that a southern hemisphere version would be organized by Australia, New Zealand and South Africa. The English authorities even supported a 'winner takes all' international match between the England XI and a West Indies 'all stars' team in Antigua (West Indies), sponsored by a Texan billionaire. To the purists this event seemed like a Faustian pact with the devil over the soul of the game.

Athletics underwent similar changes. In spite of bureaucratization and a concern with records the sport had set its face against many of the commercial aspects of modernization. In the 1860s the more plebeian variants of running, which had become associated with betting, race-fixing and professionalism, were taken over and cleaned up by university men from Oxbridge. Though professional athletics continued to exist they were pushed to the margins, with the mainstream activity shaped and controlled by the Amateur Athletics Association (AAA) after 1880. It permitted no professionalism, nor even, until 1899, the payment of expenses for athletes attending meetings. Pocket money for athletes representing the AAA was not allowed until 1956. As in rugby union the amateur ethos was firmly entrenched by the early years of the century, embodied in Oxbridge figures such as Harold Abrahams, Eric Liddell, Douglas Lowe and Lord Burghley, all commemorated in Hugh Hudson's award-winning film *Chariots of Fire* (1981). The advent of television in the 1950s helped to sustain and gradually expand the sport's popular appeal, and the opportunities it offered for commercial sponsorship introduced a financial element which athletes themselves sought to exploit. Under pressure from the athletes, and sensitive to the poor international performances of British teams in the 1970s, the authorities recognized that an effectively financed elite squad was needed. By 1982 the trust fund principle of placing income from appearances and from commercial sponsorship and contracts into a fund to provide for athletes' training and subsistence, as well as for income in later life, had become an established feature of remuneration in athletics. Champion athletes such as Linford Christie, Daley Thompson, Denise Lewis, Jonathan Edwards, Paula Radcliffe and Kelly Holmes were earning sums similar to those of top sportspeople in other fields.

A number of other sports – horse racing, motor racing, golf, tennis and rugby league – could point to similar important adjustments to new commercial opportunities. Association football, probably the most popular national sport, experienced its transformation in the final quarter of the twentieth century after a long period of relative calm. The pace of change was rapid, if less so than in rugby union. Football's revenues had come traditionally from 'gate' receipts, and its main overhead costs (labour) were kept down by a draconian form of labour relations epitomized in the 'retain and transfer' system. It was only when falling attendances coupled with a stronger players' organization force forced the game's leaders to rethink their economic base that changes happened. The peak levels of attendance of the late 1940s had virtually halved 30 years later. By the early 1980s, many clubs had sunk desperately into debt and were only kept going through the good grace of their bankers. Only a few clubs were able to climb out of the morass. In the main they were those which formed in 1992, under the auspices of the Football Association, the Premier League. Their financial salvation came from selling to large media companies the rights to televise their matches. In 1997 BSkyB paid the Premier League £670 million over four years. For the 2007–10 period the same company paid £1.3 billion, with Setanta paying £392 million for its share of the rights. Television exposure triggered other forms of sponsorship, and enabled the 20 clubs that made up the 'Premiership' to invest in a host of overseas players, whose availability was now made certain by the easing of work restrictions by the European Union. The ruling of the European Court in the case of the Belgian footballer Jean-Marc Bosman in 1996 permitted players, once out of contract, to move without the requirement of a transfer fee. Thus, in a short space of time, while most soccer clubs continued to find existence a struggle, a few entered a land of riches that their predecessors could scarcely have dreamed about.

The creation of this new plutocracy, it was claimed, produced new social relations in soccer. The 'working-man's game' now became 'middle class'. Admission prices for Premier League matches have soared. The introduction of foreign players has brought a new cosmopolitanism to the game, reinforced by the increased dominance of clubs from the big conurbations, traditionally powerful but now threatening to erase altogether the localism which had always been a part of the game, especially in the FA Cup. Increasingly, too, the leading players have acquired a cult status as nouveau riche celebrities whom the press lauds for their lifestyle and conspicuous spending. This trend, which began with the idolization of George Best in the 1960s, reached its climax in the late 1990s with the beatification of David Beckham. In company with this came a new, literary interest in soccer, prompted largely by the success of Nick Hornby's autobiographical memoir *Fever Pitch*[13] and attractive magazines such as *When Saturday Comes* and *Four Four Two*. In their wake a succession of books and magazines, often written by celebrity fans or, in some cases, players themselves, combined to give soccer a fashionable, quasi-intellectual image as a subject for lively debate and comment among a readership of relatively prosperous, young-ish males. It contrasted with the stale sensational tabloid reportage and 'ghosted' autobiographies that had been the stock-in-trade accompaniment of the game for many years.

Many of these changes had been encapsulated in the Taylor Report, sponsored by the Home Office to enquire into the causes of the disaster in 1989 when 96 soccer supporters lost their lives as a result of overcrowding at the Hillsborough ground in Sheffield. The report produced a series of practical recommendations to improve safety standards at football grounds, the chief one being the removal of the perimeter fences that had been installed at all leading grounds to prevent invasions of the pitch by unruly spectators. In other respects, however, Taylor's tone and assumptions were those of the modernizer who regarded the football stadium as a rational business enterprise which should be presented as such. Such thinking provoked derision from those fans who saw football grounds as being in essence different from multiplex cinemas and supermarkets. They actually *liked* (or at least claimed they did) the very ambience that Taylor was condemning. In resisting the sanitizing of football grounds with all-seating arrangements and wholesome food 'outlets' the opponents of Taylor were rejecting a vision in which the soccer club became a rational business and the fan a 'customer'. It was a vision that lacked the atmosphere of the crowd, especially its male sociability, and which did indeed appear to have as its principal aim the casting out of the troublesome working-class fan who was giving soccer its bad name: 'a slum sport played in slum stadiums' as the *Sunday Times* described it in 1985. The idea of soccer with the spectators left out is not entirely fanciful, at least when the Italian club Juventus was reported to be considering building a new stadium in Turin to hold only 32,000 spectators. The 'real' audience was out in television-land.[14]

Commercialization is one of the defining characteristics of 'modern' sport. It means that sport exists as something bought and sold, a commodity available in the market place. Though such a feature is not absent from sport in earlier times the emphasis that has been placed on it in the past two centuries is greater than in any previous age. Whether 'modern' features have penetrated sport played at the club and recreational level is far less certain. It is of course true that even at this level a commercial imperative has intruded. As every member of an amateur sports club knows, the raising of funds by selling raffle tickets, organizing social events, seeking sponsorship from local businesses, and grants from local government is an essential part of keeping voluntary associations afloat. But the process is far less developed than in the higher reaches of spectator sport. I noted in a book published in 2002 that 'The life of the club is one of the untold stories of modern British social history' and I have no reason to revise that statement now.[15] There are, to be sure, countless histories constantly being produced by enthusiastic secretaries and members of local sports clubs. Unfortunately, however, most are celebratory and uncritical, and do not raise the kinds of questions that historians should be asking. But the material from which they are drawn is usually freely available, and all it needs is an effort of will on the part of sports historians – amateur as well as professional, undergraduate as well as postgraduate – to turn their attention from commercial provision to the neglected field of voluntary association. What Holt and Mason rather poetically describe as the 'quiet harbours of casual exertion and sociability' still remain to be explored.[16] They remain one of the many gaps in our knowledge of the history of sport.

As it is, one senses that the gap between recreational and elite sport is growing wider than ever. The explanation for these shifts is to be found in forces present both inside and outside sport, but one profoundly influential process was what has become known as 'globalization'; namely, the operation of economic and cultural interests and activities on a global rather than a national scale. For much of this century, although international sporting competition was commonplace, power in sport radiated for the most part from national and even sub-national sources. By the end of the century this was no longer the case. It was global influences that shaped many of the instances of modernization that we have looked at in this chapter. Media sponsorship, the acquisition of leading football clubs by foreign businessmen, the changing of the rules of sports to create a better spectacle, the focus upon achieving success in international competitions – all these developments are indications of high-level sport outgrowing its national boundaries and structures and entering into a global sphere of operations (see Chapter 6).

Conclusion

Sport has a long history. It has been present in many different types of society at different times. It has also possessed important social functions related, for example, to religion, economic life, military preparedness, commerce, health and fitness, aesthetic pleasure and moral well-being. These functions have changed, as has the conception of what sport is and what it exists to do. Some of the practices found in ancient societies might (with a little stretching of the imagination) be thought to correspond to sports we know today. In other cases, however, there is no connection; what we term 'sport' had no counterpart in the past. Thus, we cannot think of sport as an ever-present 'constant' in human society, which is why fixed definitions of 'sport' are of limited value unless they take into account precise historical and social contexts. It is better to think of it as historically specific, something created to suit the particular needs of people in particular situations. Moreover, a long perspective on the history of sport shows that what has been recorded and recalled is mostly the activity of the wealthy elite in society. To this has been added, in the recent past, the history of high-profile sport organizations, often with a commercial orientation. We should not be surprised by this emphasis. To an extent, sport and games require resources – primarily money and time – that are often beyond the reach of the poor. In addition, the act of making history has been a conscious part of the intellectual repertoire of the rich; it has been their power, their influence and their taste that 'history' has been devised in order to record. Consequently, we know a lot about the activities of this group in society, and relatively little about people who were not part of the elite. For much of our history of sport, therefore, our vision is necessarily a limited one, and when we speak of such processes as 'modernization' we have to acknowledge that these concepts often rest upon fairly flimsy foundations. There is less excuse for this, however, when it comes to the history of the more recent past. Here, the gaps that exist are less the result of there being no records, and much more a reflection of what modern historians have considered important to study. Much of what now constitutes sport history is to do with commercial sport. But of course this level of sport is practised by only a small minority of the population, and in spite of the desire by social historians to reveal what has previously been 'hidden from history' – to unearth a 'history from below' – this has happened only to a limited extent in the realm of sport. Considering that much sporting activity takes place within the framework of clubs it is surprising that this sphere of sport has not been more seriously investigated by historians. Only when such investigation has been done can we talk with real certainty about such matters as 'modernization'.

Study Questions

1. Why should we beware of seeing history as a record of progress, and being too 'present-minded' in our study of the past?
2. List some of the objections that might be made about theories of 'modernization' as applied to sport?
3. To what extent did sport (especially sport in Britain) resist commercial pressures, and why?
4. Thinking about your own studies, how might you develop a research project looking at *voluntary* sporting activity?
5. What main changes would you foresee affecting sport in the course of the next 50 or so years?

Further Reading

Denis Brailsford, *British Sport: A Social History* (Cambridge: Lutterworth Press, 1997).

Emma Griffin, *England's Revelry: A History of Popular Sports and Pastimes, 1660–1830* (Oxford: Oxford University Press, 2005).

Allen Guttmann, *Sports: The First Five Millennia* (Amherst/Boston: University of Massachusetts Press, 2004).

Jeffrey Hill, *Sport, Leisure and Culture in Twentieth-Century Britain* (Basingstoke: Palgrave, 2002).

CHAPTER 3

Sport and Identity

In recent years historians studying sport have been much exercised by the issue of 'identity': that is, how a sense of both self and group have come into being through the agency of sport. In this they have contributed to one of the main interests of what is sometimes called the 'new cultural history'. In this project identities such as social class, gender and caste are regarded not as something genetically given or fixed, but as essentially cultural constructions that produce ideas about who we are, and which arise from living and interacting in society. The forces and influences that serve to constitute both individual and collective identity are complex. They have much to do with the 'languages' (in the broadest sense of that term) that help us to think and communicate (see Chapter 5), but can also be found in other processes and organizations. It is not difficult to see how sport can fulfil a major role in all this. It has the capacity to stimulate identity at various levels of social activity. Some of these will be territory-related – locality, town and city, region, nation, supra-nation (Europe, for example, when the golfers are contesting the Ryder Cup with the United States), and even the world when at the time of the Olympic Games or the FIFA World Cup we are asked to think of ourselves as members of a world sporting family. In a different sense, identities form around entities that might seem less tangible, but which can acquire an immense emotional power: an ethnic group, a nation, a religion, an age group, a gender group. Thus, at the very simplest level, people might acquire a sense of identity by following a particular football team or, more subtly, they might through an admiration for an individual sportsperson develop a sense of what they see as 'proper' masculine or feminine behaviour. In this respect we talk about the sportsperson as a 'role model' or 'style leader'. What that person means to her/his admirers can change considerably depending on who is viewing the person or the time at which s/he is being viewed. The complex changes that have overtaken Muhammad Ali as a symbolic American hero would be a case in point. Since many such identities and allegiances co-exist in any individual or group – we all experience 'multiple allegiances' – we are talking about some quite subtle processes when we consider identity formation.

In this chapter we will be concerned with the place of sport in identities formed at the collective level, where I have selected three areas for analysis: nation, social class and race.

Nation

This is one of the main collective identities of the modern period. The study of national identity and rivalry has consumed a great deal of historians' energy, especially in relation to the period between 1870 and 1914 and the origins therein of the Great War. Nationalism, indeed, has often been seen as the major by-product of the modernization process we referred to in Chapter 2. Guttmann's concept of 'modern sport', which we suggested can be linked to the development of national economies and markets in the later nineteenth century, might also be intimately connected to the rise of nation states at this time in a quite complex way. To illustrate this we may briefly refer to the case of France. Eugen Weber's mighty study of the development of French national consciousness in the period after 1870 highlights a series of initiatives in central administration, education, communications and military service that brought about changed perceptions of 'France' and what it meant to be 'French'.[1] Within such a context occurred the efforts of the French aristocrat Pierre de Coubertin to revive the idea of olympism in sport; one of de Coubertin's chief concerns, however, was to fortify French youth through the manly pursuit of 'English' games and build a new national pride in the aftermath of France's defeat by Prussia in 1871. At roughly the same time, and in the context of competition for newspaper readers, the Tour de France was conceived.[2] Thus a putative national identity through sport was situated within a broader field of changes and at the same time borrowed from perceptions of another nationalism in order to make itself.

The identity that is formed around the idea of 'Britain' provides a useful focus for this discussion. 'Britain' is a slippery concept, in itself fairly meaningless. Geographically the 'British Isles' include the entire archipelago of islands off the north-west corner of continental Europe. 'Great Britain', since the Act of Union in 1707, is England, Scotland and Wales. It is part of the state known officially as the 'United Kingdom of Great Britain and Northern Ireland'. Thus the concept of 'Britain' is difficult enough for those who live there; for those who live outside, the difficulty of grasping the term is greater still, largely because, as Linda Colley has pointed out, it has been a typically English habit to make 'Britain' and 'England' synonymous terms.[3] Where four countries (England, Scotland, Wales and Ireland), each thinking of itself as a distinct nation, are joined together in one state it is perhaps understandable, if not excusable, that the most populous and economically powerful should attempt to embrace the other three. Moreover, for at least part of this period, English/British hegemony extended to large areas of the overseas world (the Empire, later Commonwealth) through the system of colonialism. In political life the identity of Wales, Scotland, Ireland, and many other places has until very recently been subsumed into that of an English-based polity. To varying degrees national identity within the British/English umbrella has been preserved within the official structures of the legal, religious and educational systems. These have allowed the Scots, with a distinctive system in all three, a reasonable degree of identity which was strengthened by the creation in 1999 of the Scottish Parliament. But the Welsh, on the other hand, until the arrival of the Welsh Assembly (not Parliament), have had to content themselves with a set of institutional symbols (museum, university, dual language) created with English acquiescence, and since 1964 a secretary of state for Wales who has not always been Welsh. In Ireland and other former colonial areas the issue of identity has been so complex that some have taken up arms to proclaim their national allegiance. In this context the cultural marker of nationalism has, not surprisingly, often been provided by sport.

Sport, indeed, has been responsible for maintaining some sense of Britishness, though by stressing the 'unity in diversity' of the British Isles rather than any substantial commonality. Apart from athletics, which sponsors a team representing Great Britain in the Olympics, few sports have moved beyond a limited national field as the basis of their organization. Association football typifies this, with separate associations for each country. The result is fierce competition between them. Sport's capacity to express an anti-English feeling is unsurpassed. In Wales, the vehicle has been rugby, the sport housed for 30 years after 1970 in the National Stadium in Cardiff, contradictorily the most cosmopolitan of Welsh cities where the contiguous university and civic centre, with its statue of Lloyd George – all ostensibly icons of Welshness – can serve as a continuing reminder of English hegemony. The National Museum of Wales was opened in 1927 by King George V, who came down from London to perform a ceremony that could be interpreted as confirming the subordinate position of Wales within a British state. The Museum formed the last part of an urban development, begun in the late nineteenth century, based on outside capital, initiated by a Scottish nobleman, and to an extent dependent upon imported English labour. Rugby, however, has unambiguously articulated the populist pride of Wales, through its heroes from Arthur Gould to Barry John to Shane Williams, and through its victories, the sweetest of which historically was the celebrated triumph of 1905 over the mighty All Blacks. A similar landmark came in 1999. Playing a 'home' match at Wembley, because the National Stadium was being reconstructed as the Millennium Stadium, Wales defeated their arch-rivals England with a score in the last minute to win the Triple Crown and, equally important, come out of a long trough of rugby adversity. Welsh rugby, as its leading historians show, had been an intrinsic element of Welsh nationalism since the 'golden age' that followed the burgeoning of the South Wales coalfield in the later nineteenth century, its fortunes closely linked to the changing economic fortunes of the country.[4] Alongside rugby players were the world-renowned boxers of Wales – Freddie Welsh, Jimmy Wilde, Jim Driscoll, Tommy Farr, and more recently Howard Winstone and Joe Calzaghe – whose triumphs 'continued to seize the imagination of its working class'.[5] During the Depression of the 1930s clubs declined with the economy, players migrating to safer havens such as Torquay or Weston-super-Mare, or, if they were very good like Jim Sullivan and Gus Risman and several others, to the rugby league clubs of the North – 'the road to Wigan Pier' as Gareth Williams has splendidly described this process.[6] The most sustained period of rugby success came in the 1960s and 1970s, a time when the rugby world in Wales was revitalized by a new affluence and modernization similar to that of the earlier 'golden age'. Rugby helped Welsh people at this time to identify themselves as a nation, perhaps more than they were able to through politics. After all, in 1979, devolution was rejected by a large majority.

Rugby exercised its hold because of the place it occupied in Welsh male society, a place the same game never captured in England. On the other hand association football, in spite of occasional pulsations, failed to claim the popular mood in Wales to anything like the same extent that it did in Scotland, where it has articulated class and nation more than any other popular cultural form. In a country where, since the Act of Union of 1707, there have been ever-present fears of economic subordination in an Anglicized empire, the development of football in the late-nineteenth century provided in itself evidence of this English dominance. Football existed in a neocolonial relationship to its English neighbour, being financially dependent upon transfers to England for its clubs' continuing existence. It has been this subordination that has accounted for the different soccer culture of Scotland, which created a particular kind of 'repressed nationalism' exhibited in a number of forms: in, for example, a hostility to England that resulted in Scottish supporters siding with anyone playing against England; in a long-standing if idealized desire to see a Scottish national side which did not include 'Anglos' (i.e. Scottish players from English clubs); and in a sense of superiority that sprang from the view that, in spite of exporting so much talent to England, Scotland still managed to keep its own leagues afloat and to produce good football. The mark of this last point was a belief in the existence of a certain Scottish 'style' of play – clever football played on the ground to players who switched positions intelligently. The myth, for such it often was, depended on an accompanying belief in a cruder English 'other', depending on muscle, speed and aerial brawn – 'kick and rush'. The results of Scotland-England international matches sometimes supported these views, as at Wembley in 1928 and 1967; on the latter occasion Scotland defeated England – now World Champions – with a display that was held to epitomize Scottish soccer panache ('gallus'). Such events and ideas expressed a certain kind of Scottishness, but one which since the 1980s, with the discontinuance of the annual match against England, Scotland's relative failures in international competition, and the increasing dominance of the Scottish Premier League by foreign players, it has been difficult to perpetuate. In 1992, shortly after the British general election, the Nationalist politician Jim Sillars was led to despair of Scots as 'ninety minute patriots', unable to extend into the political arena the sense of nationalism they displayed for rugby internationals at Murrayfield or football matches at Hampden Park. Since then, however, the tide seems to have turned; sport has ebbed while politics has flowed. In the early 2000s, with a government of Scottish Nationalists now installed in Edinburgh, Sillars's despair of 1992 might seem to have been unwarranted.

Case Study Discussion 11

Robin Jenkins, *The Thistle and the Grail* (Edinburgh: Polygon, 1994 edn; originally published 1954).

Jenkins, a prolific Scottish novelist not well known outside Scotland though highly regarded in his own country, published *The Thistle and the Grail* in 1954. A study of football and its place in Scottish society, it is based upon the exploits of a local team – Drumsagart Thistle – and its quest (eventually achieved) to win the Scottish Junior Cup. There is a certain irony in the novel's title. The 'thistle' could be read as 'Scotland', and the 'grail' could be translated as a mission to seek the country's future, or even its soul. The passion for football shown in the novel amounts to a pessimistic comment on a perceived shallowness of Scotland's social and cultural life; and there is further irony in the fact that, at the time of writing, even football – the nation's once-great source of pride and achievement – was going downhill. The national team's performance in the 1954 World Cup finals (the first time Scotland had appeared in this event) was awful.

The national preoccupation with football is of course primarily a male obsession through which Jenkins attempts an analysis of the 'mind' of Scotland, though he shows that it is one that might affect women as well through its pervasive influence in the life of the community. The narrative covers a season in the life of the club and its supporters. During this time a miraculous transformation from sporting despair to the pinnacle of success takes place. Starting as a team of no-hopers the Thistle proceeds to win the cup, the club's exploits provide a source of growing interest and eventually pride in the community it represents, and a sense of achievement – however transitory – is bestowed on the people of Drumsagart. Football success appears to have brought the community together and provided it with a sense of purpose.

Nowhere is the dependence of the community on the outcome of the football better illustrated than in the elaborate arrangements made to communicate the result of the fifth round tie. The Thistle are drawn away in far Aberdeenshire to Forgie Bluebell, a powerful team with three internationals. The fare to go and watch the match was 'too much for dolemen' (p. 189) especially coming as it did only two days after the Hogmanay celebrations. Since the torment of having to wait to learn the result on the return of those fortunate to have journeyed to Forgie is too terrible to contemplate, the stay-at-homes devise a plan. It is decided to pay for one of their number, Archie, to travel to the match on condition that he leaves the ground at intervals of fifteen minutes to telephone reports on the state of play back to the others. A committee is formed to orchestrate a scheme. They commandeer a kiosk, appoint a former bookie's runner, Jock Saunders, 'an expert with the telephone' (p. 191) to occupy it, and on a 'filthily, scandalously, brutally wet' afternoon (p. 191) assemble to await the call. At one point the scheme appears to have foundered through the intervention of the local police sergeant, who insists that the kiosk be kept clear for 'general use' (p. 195). A little later, approaching full time in Forgie, a moral dilemma is posed when a widow woman needs to telephone the hospital about her sick daughter:

'If she phones', muttered another to his friend, 'do you see what's going to happen? Archie will be told the number's engaged, he'll not wait because he'll be in a hurry to catch the bus hame, and we'll not get the result at all.' (p. 202)

The policeman is unimpressed with the men's urgent requests that, since the 90 minutes are almost up, the woman should wait: 'Five minutes of this poor woman's worry causes me more concern [...] than if you'd been waiting ninety years to hear how many times a chunk of leather was kicked between a couple of posts' (p. 202). But, to general applause, the woman agrees to wait, and after further delays that stretch the collective patience almost beyond endurance the necessary information is passed on – a win for the Thistle.

To Jock's disgust the men cheer as the woman, whose news about her daughter has been less uplifting, makes her way home. On this juxtaposition of joy and sadness one of the novel's great comic scenes ends, in pathos; the temporary elation brought by a football result contrasted with the enduring misfortune and poverty suffered by many of Drumsagart's inhabitants.

In spite of the eventual glory enjoyed by the club, *The Thistle and the Grail* is not in any sense a mere fable of success. Through the people of Drumsagart it presents a jaundiced view of Scotland and its inhabitants. The publisher's blurb of the Polygon edition (1994) describes the book as 'one of the finest comic novels produced in Scotland this century', but Jenkins has a depressing tale to tell in an atmosphere which, in the last analysis, is gloomy. To be sure the matches are finely reported – nowhere more so than in Thistle's contest with Carrick Harp, 'a memorable and historic game...[t]he Angel of Football, in which all believed but few had ever seen, was hovering over Tara Park that afternoon' (p. 172)[7] – and the characters richly drawn with, in many cases, a surface comic appearance, but on reflection there is little to admire in the human landscape portrayed. Alec Elrigmuir, the centre-forward whose signing sparks the club's revival, is a dream of a footballer but as a person he is dim-witted and dominated by his bossy girlfriend Mysie. Turk, the centre-half who alongside Alec provides the backbone and inspiration of the team, is a repulsive drunkard who beats his mother. Two of the club's loyal supporters are aged and infirm, the diseased Tinto and a cripple, Crutch Brodie. The local publican, Sam Malarkin, is a predatory homosexual with designs on the star centre-forward whom he attempts to proposition: '"I am not understood in Drumsagart" said Malarkin wistfully, and put his hand on the young man's shoulder' (p. 110). The novel is peopled by such characters.

In Ireland, the relationship between sport and politics has operated along quite different axes. To begin with, the context was different; the sense of nation, and of being a *colony*, was stronger. The location was also different. Whereas in Wales and Scotland popular sport was largely concentrated in the industrialized, working-class regions of the country, in Ireland this was true only of parts of Ulster, and Dublin. Elsewhere the country was agricultural and un-modernized, but at the same time dominated to an extent unknown in the rest of Britain by a single institution – the Catholic Church. Social elites, which in England had often championed the cult of sport among the masses, were far less dynamic in Ireland. The early life of the playwright Samuel Beckett, scion of a middle-class Anglicized Protestant family from Dublin, illustrates this feature very well; at school and later at Trinity College, Dublin, Sam played cricket, the English game, among a restricted circle of like-minded Anglo-Irish schoolboys and students. Beckett is still the only Nobel prize-winner for literature to be cited in the pages of *Wisden*, the cricketer's almanac. The popular Gaelic games of Ireland, with which Beckett had no contact, had been established in the late-nineteenth century by promoters such as Michael Cusack and Maurice Davin, using English models of sporting codification.[8] The contradiction in this stems from the political purpose of Irish popular sport. As inspired by the Gaelic Athletics Association (GAA) since the 1880s sport was a weapon in the struggle against British domination in Ireland, a vehicle for the articulation of Irish national feeling. GAA sport not only generated a nationalist sociability and consciousness; it did so by being a *different* sport from that of the enemy. The GAA's nationalist mission was plain for all to see, most evident in the unique naming of its sports grounds after martyrs to the cause: Croke Park, Pairc Mhic Dhiarmada, Casement Park, Davitt Park and many others.[9] But sport can never entirely encompass a nation. Just as Scottish soccer has its rivalry between Rangers and Celtic, which plays upon pre-existing religious and political traditions of the Orange and the Green, so in Ireland itself the inclusive effect of the GAA and Gaelic Games must be set against the continuing loyalties of some sports to the rest of Britain. Even after the creation in 1922 of the Irish Free State, rugby union was reluctant to fly the new tricolour at its Landsdowne Road stadium in Dublin, and continued to select its international XV, which played in the 'home nations' tournament, from both south and north of the country. Curiously rugby united Ireland in a way that politics did not. On the other hand soccer (as the Irish tend to call football), popular in both the Republic and in Northern Ireland, was divided by two competing Irish associations. In the North, moreover, it has been organized along largely sectarian lines, thus helping to maintain conflicts. In the Republic, the success of Ireland's international team in the early 1990s produced contradictory effects. The national side enjoyed a longer period of success and support than it had ever known, but it was achieved by a manager

(Jack Charlton) who was English and a team of talented players whose Irish lineage was often spurious. Their success was as much to do with globalizing forces as with indigenous Irishness. A different kind of division was to be found in athletics in the Republic, where until the late 1960s the Catholic Church implacably opposed the participation of women.

The Irish example, however, has a uniqueness in the British context; it shows a political connection between sport and nation of colonial dimensions, which makes it closer in some respects to that of overseas areas of the former British Empire than to the mainland. The role of the GAA reveals, albeit in somewhat sharper form, a resort to sport as an instrument of colonial liberation that has been evident in varying forms in other places. Cricket, originally a means of bonding the Empire, as often as not became the means of prising it apart. Success at cricket helped Australians to throw off the inferior status assigned to them by the English, and the rows generated by the 'Bodyline' series of 1932–33 went deeper than the issue of fast leg-theory bowling. They signified tensions of both a political and economic nature between the industrialized metropolitan core and its primary-producing periphery at a time of falling world agricultural prices. In this context Australia produced its first truly national hero, the respectable petty-bourgeois Don Bradman, whose extraordinary exploits on the field provided the inhabitants of Australia with a focal point of unity to override the ethnic and religious conflicts that beset the country's white immigrant society. At a rather later stage, by the 1970s and 1980s in fact, cricket became the agent for the assertion of national pride in India and Pakistan, especially once the game there had shed some of the elitism inherited from colonial days. But it was in the Caribbean that cricket became most closely associated with colonial nationalism. Cricket exercised an important symbolic meaning in this part of the world, where national identity was fragmented and black people subordinated. For them, as the Trinidadian radical C. L. R James observed, cricketers filled 'a huge gap in their consciousness and in their needs'. In its club organization cricket in the Caribbean developed a subtle hierarchy of race and class status. Until well after the Second World War, however, although its leading performers were black men such as George Headley, Learie Constantine and the three 'Ws' (Weekes, Worrell and Walcott) the representative team of the West Indies was firmly controlled by white captains like the patrician H. B. G Austin and, later, J. D. Goddard. In the 1930s Constantine had begun to hint at the unfairness of this system, but it was not until the 1950s that any significant changes occurred. The triumphant West Indies team in England in 1950 was still led by the white Goddard. His mantle passed to a succession of light-skinned men during the course of the decade, when not only were there far better and more experienced black cricketers to choose from but anti-colonial sentiments were also gathering strength in the Caribbean. Black national consciousness brought to prominence, and in some cases to political power, leaders of the stamp of Cheddi Jagan, Forbes Burnham, Norman Manley and Eric Williams. Two tours of the region by the English national team – in 1953–54 and

1959–60 – were affected by demonstrations which, while sparked by incidents on the cricket field, revealed feelings in society over decolonization. Following a campaign in Trinidad by C. L. R. James in *The Nation*, the newspaper of Eric Williams's People's National Movement, a black captain – Frank Worrell – was eventually selected. The decision marked more than a recognition by the West Indies cricket establishment of Worrell's sagacity as a tactician. It was an acceptance that the balance of power in the Caribbean was shifting, that cricket had played its part in that shift, and that white supremacy in cricket, as in society generally, could no longer be sustained.

The end of Empire placed Britain in a changed international position. Adapting Arnold Toynbee's verdict on Europe after the Second World War, we might say of Britain that it became a centre on which external international influences converged rather than, as it once had been, a centre from which influences radiated to the outside world. This change was particularly acute in sport, which the British liked to think they had invented and exported to others. The impact in the 1950s of defeats by apparently 'lesser' countries – the West Indies (1950) and Pakistan (1954) at cricket, and most dramatically by Eire (1949), the United States (1950) and the Hungarians (1953 and 1954) at football – underlined the fact that sporting excellence was diffused throughout the world, and that there was much the British could learn by lifting their gaze and looking abroad. In doing so it became apparent that neither 'Britain' nor the national sub-units within it were any longer quite as distinct an entity as they once had been. In fact, the whole process produced something of an identity crisis. Just as the rise of multinational corporations and the European Union has thrown the idea of a national sovereign identity into confusion, so in sport it was no longer possible to cling to old certainties. The English cricket team, for example, was not the lodestar of nationality that it had been in the interwar years.[10] Changes in both the team and the country it represents have undermined the site of morality and nationality on which the cricket team was once firmly based. It has not been composed entirely of English players for some thirty years past, it has certainly not lived up to its old position as one of the 'masters' of the game and it cannot necessarily count on the natural support of many English people. Multiculturalism has produced conflicting loyalties, so that for many residents of Britain it might seem more natural to follow the fortunes of the West Indies, India, Sri Lanka or Pakistan in international cricket.

Social class

There has always been a close connection between sport and social class in Britain. Some sports, notably rugby league, have been strongly working-class in character, while others (hunting and field sports, motor sports, and aviation) have been the preserve of the rich. Association football, though played in many of the leading public schools, acquired by the end of the nineteenth century the reputation of the 'working-man's' game. Cricket, in spite of its upper-class leadership, was able to bring together people from various social groups, which is why it was known as the 'national game' in the nineteenth and early-twentieth centuries. The same might be said of horse racing, popular among working people not as a participant sport but as an occasion for a bet, 'a bit of a flutter'.

It is at the local level where many of these social differences are best investigated.

Case Study Discussion 12

Margaret Stacey, *Tradition and Change: A Study of Banbury* **(Oxford: Oxford University Press, 1960).**

Margaret Stacey's study of the Oxfordshire town of Banbury is a classic piece of observational sociology that reaches deep into the 'ordinary' life in Britain in the late 1950s. It has an especially close focus on the clubs and associations that made up much of the town's social and cultural activity, and from which marked social class divergences in membership were evident. Stacey sums this up, and simultaneously illuminates what is possibly the central function of voluntary association, when she remarks of Banbury's sports clubs: 'Banbury people do not engage in sport as an exercise in competitive athleticism but as an occasion for social intercourse': as a competitor remarked of a tennis tournament in which he was playing, 'these do's are 75 per cent social and 25 per cent tennis' (p. 88). Students of electoral behaviour have noted that voting preference is dictated less by what people vote *for* than by whom they vote *with*, and we might adapt this observation to the study of sports and leisure clubs: they have existed to preserve social identity as much as to purvey athletic activity.

Stacey's examination of the complex interplay of voluntary association membership in Banbury brings us to a point which takes the discussion of sport and leisure into a different sphere. Stacey traces the 'connexions' and 'networks' that came into being between different elements of Banbury's voluntary associations. What is equally important, she makes the connections between voluntary association and the town's political life. To give a small illustration of her otherwise lengthy and detailed deconstruction, we might take the example of Banbury's sports clubs, of which there were several, though none, significantly, which bore the town's name. Stacey found two levels of clubs, which she named Sports I and Sports II. The first was composed of rugby, cricket, tennis and hunting clubs. It had two distinctive characteristics. One was the high proportion of committee members who lived outside the borough, which showed that these clubs served to bring farmers from the outlying districts into contact with the social life of the town. The second was the high occupational status of the group's members who either owned above-average size farms or were professional and business people from the town itself. Freemasonry was present in this group, and while they did not have any formal links with political or religious organizations, the members of Sports I were 'overwhelmingly'

Conservative and Anglican. The other category of sports clubs – Sports II – was made up of a different cricket club, the table tennis league, Post Office sports and the Comrades' Club; all sports requiring little in the way of expensive equipment, and all therefore accessible to the less-well-off. Societies such as the Foresters, Oddfellows and Buffaloes were represented. Stacey included Sports II in the 'lower part of the Conservative connexion'. Conservatism thus emerged as the centre of gravity of much associational life, with Liberalism acting as the focus for a second but much less powerful network. Except for trade union activity, Labour possessed scarcely any network of its own, and what it did have was made up of low-status, immigrant (non-Banbury) workers.

The Banbury case study brings out important points about the function of club life in class formation, and has been used by Ross McKibbin to illustrate profound shifts that were taking place in British society in the middle years of the century.[11] Clubs of the kind found in Banbury were central to a social process in which the middle classes were re-formed into a more homogeneous though certainly not monolithic grouping, over a period that stretched from the 1920s to the 1950s. Crucial to this process was the fashioning of an a-political consciousness that enabled some of the continuing fractions within the class – principally those connected with religion – to be overlain with shared values. Some of these were supplied by the sense of 'other' arising from the growth of Labour as a political force at this time. The haste with which hitherto opposed elements of the middle class, their political allegiances previously divided between Conservative and Liberal, conjoined in anti-socialist alliances during the 1920s testifies to the influence of external forces in shaping these shared values. But internally, so to speak, middle-class consciousness also depended upon the existence of an ethos which voluntary association provided. The strictly hierarchical world of local clubs and societies generated this ethos. As McKibbin puts it, the clubs operated on a set of conventions about 'proper' behaviour among the 'right sort' of people, who would not be 'embarrassed', and qualities such as 'niceness' and 'humour' could be encouraged.[12] It was a code that eschewed violent or impassioned commitment, and in which politics was in effect depoliticized. The Conservative Party under Stanley Baldwin in the 1920s aligned with it perfectly, making Conservatism the 'natural' home for all 'neutral' opinion. 'I give expression', proclaimed Baldwin on one occasion, 'in some unaccountable way, to what the English people think'.[13] In literature there is no better example of this Conservative mentality than Warwick Deeping's novel *Sorrel and Son*, published in 1925 and reissued fifteen times within two years.

Sports clubs fitted the ethos perfectly. It is McKibbin's contention that within a middle-class milieu sport existed to promote sociability and minimize the disruptive consequences of competitiveness. At a local so at a national level this credo applied, sustaining outmoded conceptions of amateurism and ultimately doing much harm to the international competitiveness and standing of British sport. There is certainly much evidence that a gentlemanly, clubbable atmosphere prevailed in British sports (brought out well in *Chariots of Fire*). It was responsible, most obviously, for the maintenance until the 1960s of a social divide between amateurs and professionals in cricket. Much of the public display of social difference (separate changing rooms and points of entry onto the field of play for amateurs and professionals, for example) had disappeared by the late 1940s, though some conventional markers of class remained: the granting to the amateur of full initials *before* the surname (thus P. B. H. May) in press results of matches, as against the designation of professionals either by initials *after* the surname, or simply by surname, was the chief example. Amateurism was discontinued in 1962 mainly because it was becoming increasingly difficult for amateur players to play the game in an unpaid capacity. Many were having to resort to covert professionalism by taking paid sinecures on the staff of the county clubs. As may be imagined, however, it took some time for old social habits to die out, and even in the 1970s the selectors of the England test team were looking for a captain who displayed amateur characteristics, which chiefly meant being 'the right sort'. It was doubtful whether Ray Illingworth, a Leicestershire and former Yorkshire cricketer who enjoyed some success as England's captain between 1969 and 1972, really lived up to this image, and the selectors probably favoured the counter claims of the Glamorgan player Tony Lewis. He had made his first appearance as an amateur (A. R. Lewis) and had been educated at Cambridge University, where, moreover, he also played rugby.

Even in the more commercialized game of soccer the amateur spirit prevailed for a long time. It manifested itself both in the Football Association, which had an upper-class, old-school-tie atmosphere reflected in its elegant headquarters at Lancaster Gate opposite Hyde Park, and in the more provincial and down-to-earth world of the Football League. Football had accommodated professionalism without suffering the splits that affected rugby, but the professional players were treated without much respect, and there were a number of ways in which 'professionalism' in the sport was resisted; club shareholders placed a ceiling on the dividends they paid to themselves, betting and the football pools were opposed, radio and television were regarded as threats to attendances at matches and therefore held at arm's length, and overseas developments in the game were largely ignored. It was in this last respect that the amateurism of British football was most starkly exposed, for it contributed to the decline of British teams in international competition, a fact made plain by the England team's mediocre performance in the 1950 World Cup competition, followed by its humiliation by Hungary at Wembley in 1953. This match, astounding to most football supporters as much for the manner in which Hungary's victory was achieved as for the margin (6 goals to 3), called forth a torrent of criticism from the popular 'modernizing' press. Roy Peskett of the *Daily Mail* captured the mood of reform which seized most sports correspondents at the time when he saw in the match an implicit contrast between a dynamic European continent able to learn, adapt and innovate, and a moribund England in danger of being left behind in the world.[14] The target of much press criticism was the gentlemanly and outmoded attitudes of the Football Association, now clearly overtaken by the rational planning evident in the Hungarians' approach to football. One incident drew down hoots of derision; Stanley Rous, the FA secretary had, in an unguarded moment, told the press that England should not fear losing to Hungary because 'losing can be fun'. Such a Corinthian attitude seemed weirdly outmoded, and the cartoonist Roy Ullyett of the *Daily Express* took up his pencil in excoriating manner at Rous's expense. Bob Ferrier in the *Daily Mirror* felt equally outraged, urging:

We must sweep away those plumbers and builders and grocers who select national teams, and give the responsibility to men who have played and know the game. And above all, our League set-up must make sweeping and immediate sacrifices to our international game.[15]

One of the problems had been, and remained, the priority claimed by League clubs over the requirements of the national team. The modernizing Alan Hardaker, who took over as secretary of the Football League in 1957, achieved many things during his stewardship, but few in this area. Changes, less radical than those suggested by the press and by many football supporters, were set in train by both FA and the League during the course of the 1950s and early 1960s. England, of course, won the World Cup in 1966, though as host nation without the need to qualify, and ultimately with the benefit of a much-disputed goal. Some of this singular success can be attributed to changes at the FA in the later stages of Walter Winterbottom's period as national coach, and to the tactical insight of his successor Alf Ramsey. Perhaps, in the final analysis, gifted individuals with a rare coaching acumen are the key to it all. England has yet to repeat its achievement of 1966.

Rugby union was the sport most imbued with a middle-class spirit, indeed rather defiantly so. Its hostility towards those clubs which had broken away from the Rugby Football Union in 1895 over the 'broken time' issue to form the Northern Union (later Rugby League) was unremitting. Rugby Union's great expansion in the interwar years was linked to that process of class formation which, as we have seen, so benefited the Conservative Party. The local rugby club, patronized by its *nouveau riche* membership of dentists, solicitors and estate agents, became a pillar of anti-socialism in many British towns, complemented by the embracing of rugby by so many of the private schools, together with a host of the new grammar schools established in the municipalities in the 1920s. It was a reaction to the increasing association of football with the working class – its 'Woodbine' image as some called it. East Lancashire was one enclave of immunity in this national trend; its leading grammar schools – both the old-established and the newer creations – kept faith with football, a sport that they, alongside the big public schools, had helped to create. Wales, as we saw earlier, together with Cornwall and parts of Devon, were the only places not to manipulate rugby for social exclusiveness.

Golf, a game of 'relentless amateurism and petty snobberies',[16] might have outshone even rugby in this respect. John Lowerson's account of the game's development makes clear that its expense confined golf to an affluent middle class, though it was probably never just the 'suburban' game often imagined. Its late-Victorian expansion – a spectacular one when in the 1890s alone over 500 clubs were founded in England and close on 200 in Scotland – is explained by the game's fitting into a middle-class mentality which demanded a relaxation from work suited to all ages and all seasons. It also possessed a practical relevance in that business contacts and deals could be pursued at play. In reading golf club histories such as those of Richard Holt and John Bromhead[17] little doubt remains that golf was a game in which class and status was a major consideration in every aspect of its organization, from the appointment of the right kind of person as the club secretary, to the admission of new members (where ethnic as well as class factors sometimes applied), right down to the proper dress code and the maintenance of a correct relationship between members and the club professional. Even famous international tournament pro's like the American Walter Hagen were refused entry to clubhouses in the 1920s because their very presence offended the spirit of amateurism. Golf was the only game which created separate clubs, or sections within clubs, for working people (or 'artisans' as they were quaintly described). The social tone of a place might be set by its golf course, which was important in attracting the right class of visitor. This was especially so at seaside resorts. Southport's links at Birkdale, for example, secured the cachet 'Royal' and the club became a key force in defining what was a very middle-class town. This emphasis on decorous behaviour probably retarded the development of golf as a competitive sport. Though professional golf in Britain did grow after the First World War it never received the backing from the game in general that it did in America, whose golfers dominated the game's major tournaments thereafter.

McKibbin attributes the relative decline of British golf, as he does also the general decline of British sport during the twentieth century, to these essentially 'political' reasons: sport's 'excessive voluntarism and the social codes of those who governed it'.[18] In this he has no doubt touched a nerve that historians have probed only fleetingly in the past; namely, the relationship between sport and social status. Lowerson's comments on the leisure clubs that grew up around urban oligarchies in the early part of the century pinpoints both the 'club-ability' that these organizations offered for a middle class often unsure about its social role and position, and the difficulty historians have faced in plumbing the depths of social meaning contained in them. In John Lowerson's words, '[t]heir ostensible purpose was a particular sport. But often far more significant and far less easily reconstructed by historians was their role as instruments of relatively fine social differentiation and arbiters of public custom'.[19] In many cases their social role was probably more profoundly influenced than we so far realize by the presence of their female membership, as certainly happened in the rapidly developing sport of tennis in the interwar years. The tennis club, usually less exclusive in either class or gender terms than its rugby and golfing equivalents, became a central feature of middle-class communities at this time. The part played by such clubs in the production of Wimbledon champions might have been minimal, but if nothing else they fulfilled an important function in the marriage market.

Race

The concept of race is perhaps the most problematical of those under discussion in this chapter. Whilst scientists no longer find it a valid analytical tool, the idea of 'race' continues to animate public opinion. In this respect it is the opposite of 'class', which in Britain at least is still employed as a conceptual device though having apparently lost much of its force in society and politics. Race is of course a sensitive area, which partly explains why relatively little has been written on it by British sport historians. In the recent past, however, changes in demography and the wider acceptance of the idea of multiculturalism have encouraged new kinds of studies.

The situation has long been different in the United States, where sport historians have applied class models less frequently. This should not surprise us. Given the legacy of slavery and the migration of black people from the South to northern industrial districts historians have been obliged to acknowledge the issue of race in American sport. In general terms, therefore, there is a contrast between the American and European racial contexts; the former has a long *internal* history, while in the latter until more recent times the racial presence has been largely an *external* one, derived from the relationships that existed primarily in the colonies. Many of the models applied by European historians to study race – notably the ideas of the 'melting pot' and 'assimilation' – have originated in America.

In the United States racial segregation in society affected all the major sports in the nineteenth and twentieth centuries. In golf and tennis for example there was scarcely a sign of black players at the top level before the 1950s and 1960s. Boxing, a sport that came to be dominated by African-Americans in the second half of the century, traditionally kept black and white performers apart as far as possible. The victories over white opponents of the great black heavyweight Jack Johnson in the years before the First World War had provoked race riots in some American cities. In the 1920s the champion white heavyweight, Jack Dempsey, would not fight his main black rivals. The success of Joe Louis in the 1930s and 1940s brought a new respect to black fighters, especially after his politically charged fights in the 1930s against the German Max Schmeling; they endowed Louis with a patriotic aura that was embellished during the Second World War when he served in the army. After Louis, and until almost the end of the century, all heavyweight champions were black, the one exception being Rocky Marciano (1952–56). The astonishing success of Cassius Clay/Muhammad Ali in the 1960s and 1970s placed boxing firmly in the frontline of race politics and also foreign affairs, as a consequence of Ali's membership of the militant Nation of Islam and his refusal to be called up into the services during the Vietnam war.

Case Study Discussion 13

David Remnick, *King of the World: Muhammad Ali and the Rise of an American Hero* **(New York: Random House, 1998).**

At the time he first fought Sonny Liston for the world heavyweight championship, in February 1964 at the Convention Hall, Miami Beach, Cassius Clay was not universally admired in the United States. Leading white sportswriters were offended by his self-publicity stunts which involved flamboyant monologues at press conferences with Clay forecasting his imminent victory in a contest, often naming the round in which a knock-out would come. They called him the 'Louisville Lip', considering him arrogant and over-ambitious; in the racial idiom of the day he was a 'cocky negro'. Though the winner of a gold medal at the 1960 Olympic Games, Clay was not expected to beat the then champion, Liston, who himself was disliked though for quite different reasons. He was the 'bad negro'; he had been in prison for armed robbery and was patronized by organized crime syndicates. Liston, however, had defeated all the other leading contenders. He was fearsomely powerful. Other fighters had seemed incapable of hurting him. Clay by comparison seemed lightweight. Yet he beat Liston – by some margin – in a contest that became the subject of mystery and controversy. Liston, the indestructible, failed to appear for the seventh round. Was he injured, had he just quit, was it all a Mafia-inspired betting scam? Clay delighted in admonishing his critics in the media: 'Eat Your Words'. Shortly afterwards he became Muhammad Ali, a member of the radical and subversive Nation of Islam, an associate of Elijah Muhammad and Malcolm X, and a far more threatening character than 'the Lip' had ever been.

At Lewiston, Maine, in May 1965 the return match between Ali and Liston was yet more astonishing. Liston, supposedly better-trained and fitter than for the Miami fight, went down in the first round to what some considered a slight punch (though others judged it a 'killer' blow, delivered when Liston was off balance and falling into Ali's line of attack). The count was bungled by an inexperienced referee and poor communication with the ringside timekeepers. Ali was declared the winner. Immediately sections of the crowd howled 'Fix!'. Suspicions were aroused that Liston had been threatened by Ali's Nation of Islam supporters, and had agreed to 'lie down'. Controversy raged for a long time thereafter, but as with so many aspects of Sonny Liston's life mystery and uncertainty as to the true facts persisted. No evidence has been unearthed to corroborate the charge of fixing, and perhaps the outcome of the Lewiston match is to be explained simply as a better boxer, quicker around the ring and physically fitter, defeating an ageing fighter for whom this was one contest too far.

Remnick's study of Ali interweaves a number of threads that had been present in American boxing since the nineteenth century: writing and the role of the media, crime, race relations, politics and ideals of heroism. Muhammad Ali seemed an unlikely candidate for hero status. In spite of his undoubted personality and verbal felicity – he exuded far more charisma than most boxers – his behaviour irritated many whites. Unlike previous black champions – notably Joe Louis before and after the Second World War, and Floyd Patterson in the later 1950s – Ali did not conform to the white person's idea of the 'good negro'; that is, a man who deferred to white society, and (if an integrationist) a supporter of respectable and moderate movements. Ali rejected such attitudes. He despised Patterson as an 'Uncle Tom' and a 'white man's nigger', and gave support to an uncompromising black protest movement. He ranted against what he called the 'white power structure'. All this placed him, like Jack Johnson many years before him, beyond the pale of white (and some sections of black) society. Even his ability in the ring was doubted. Not until after the Liston fights, and in particular his defeat of Patterson in November 1965 and a series of wins against strong opponents in 1966, was this put beyond question. Moreover, in 1967, he took issue against the war in Vietnam. 'I ain't got no quarrel with them Vietcong' he said. Ali's implacable stance against being drafted into the army undoubtedly cost him dearly; in financial terms, for his title was taken away from him and he did not fight at all for the three and a half years from 1967 to 1970; but perhaps more importantly in moral terms, for his campaign intensified the hatred that many already felt for him. On the other hand, as opposition to the war increased and merged with black, women's and student protests in the later 1960s Ali came to be seen as a new kind of patriot. His connecting of the anti-war movement with the struggle for black power – 'Why should they ask me to put on a uniform and go ten thousand miles from home and drop bombs and bullets on brown people in Vietnam while so-called Negro people in Louisville are treated like dogs?' – politicized him in a way no previous American sports person had ever been. He refused the blandishments of those who urged him to join the army and serve his time in the National Guard, or perform exhibition bouts for the troops. He stood firm to his conviction: 'I was determined', he told one reporter, 'to be one nigger that the white man didn't get' (p. 291).

In the face of all this Ali became one of the great heroic figures in later twentieth-century America: and of the very few – perhaps the only – sport heroes to undergo the transformation from a figure hated by many to one revered by almost all. Circumstances largely outside sport greatly aided this change. Opposition to the war, a more general acceptance of desegregation and civil rights, the success of black athletes in other sports and a recognition perhaps (after Ali's retirement) that he had achieved the pinnacle of heavyweight boxing, after which the sport would never see the same skills and charisma again. As Remnick sees it 'Ali is an American myth who has come to mean many things to many people: a symbol of faith, a symbol of conviction, a symbol of beauty and skill and courage, a symbol of racial pride, of wit and love' (p. 304).

The Second World War had much to do with the introduction of more progressive ideas on race relations in the United States, just as it did in Britain in the field of colonial relationships. The conflict had been far less controversial politically than that of 1914–18, and in particular it was difficult to justify segregation by race in a war to defend liberty against the threat of fascism. Baseball illustrates this change very clearly. The national game had been starkly segregated along colour lines. Separate leagues existed for black and white, though significantly the latter were regarded as synonymous with the game and referred to as the 'major leagues' or even 'organized baseball'. Negro leagues, which developed in the 1920s, had a keen following and often strong business backing, but in general lacked the resources and publicity enjoyed by the white leagues; often the negro teams had to play in white-owned ball parks, where African-American spectators were put in segregated seating, and paid enormous sums in commission to booking agents. None of the many outstanding black ball players ever turned out for a major league club after the 1890s. The breach in this system of apartheid only came in 1945, when Branch Rickey, the owner of the Brooklyn Dodgers, signed a black player, Jackie Robinson, to his farm club the Montreal Royals, and two years later transferred him to the Dodgers themselves. Rickey's actions might well have been motivated as much by commercial as by civil rights considerations, but in making his move he was astute enough to choose the right kind of man for a breakthrough gesture. Robinson was a good player, but more importantly like Louis before him he was of 'good character' and possessed the social credentials that won approval from white people. He became immensely popular among both black and white fans. His impact in race relations was, Kathryn Jay has argued, greater even than that of Louis because Robinson's was a *team* game.[20] Nonetheless, the desegregation of baseball was a slow process – not until the late 1950s was there a significant black presence in the major leagues.[21] The same was true in other sports such a professional football and basketball, where black players recruited into predominantly white teams often had to endure what is now called 'institutional racism'. Considering that in society generally the civil rights movement did not achieve some of its main aims until the 1960s, and that in spite of this racial tension still ran deep, especially in the South, it is hardly surprising that the integration of black people into American sport did not happen overnight. By the end of the century, however, most sports could point to some African-American heroes, and in a few – athletics, professional football and boxing – they were in the majority. But as in other countries where the same process was occurring the presence of minority groups in sport was still limited; whilst on the field of play it was noticeable, in management and the boardroom it was the exception.

In western Europe similar kinds of racial issues have arisen following the large-scale immigration of peoples from former colonies in Africa, the Caribbean, and south and south-east Asia since the late 1940s. Prior to that, in the colonial period, race relations were conducted for the most part at a distance. We have seen above, however, how the subtle interplay of race and class in Caribbean cricket could produce an impact on Britain in the form of anti-colonial sentiments. In addition to this there was a regular movement of sports people from the colonies to Britain and metropolitan France. The exploits in both football and cricket of Arthur Wharton from the Gold Coast (Ghana) made him a celebrity in the north of England in the late-nineteenth and early-twentieth centuries. Numerous cricketers from the Caribbean and India made their way to the northern leagues in England in the 1930s and became local heroes in their towns. The Indian cricketers K. S. Ranjitsinhji ('Ranji') and his nephew Duleepsinhji actually played for England, though it helped that these two were from an upper-class background. Some boxers, like Len Johnson, attained fame in spite of their being prevented by the governing body from competing in British championship fights. But in spite of sporting fame, racism was never very far away. The cricketer Learie Constantine, notwithstanding his stature as international cricketer and a wartime civil servant with the Ministry of Labour, was refused a room at a London hotel in 1944 because it was said that his presence would offend white American guests. In France it was encountered by sporting migrants like the Senegalese boxer Battling Siki and the athlete Ahmed El Ouafi, who won a gold medal at the 1928 Olympics. After the Second World War a number of outstanding footballers went from North Africa to play for French clubs; between 1945 and 1962 there were over 100 such players, 8 of whom represented France. The most notable of them was Rachid Mekhloufi, who nonetheless returned to Algeria in the late 1950s to support the Front de Liberation Nationale (FLN) in the war that achieved independence from France in 1962, whereupon he returned to football in France. Outshining even Mekhloufi was the greatest of all footballers of north African origin, Zinedine Zidane, who captained the French team that won the 1998 World Cup with several players of francophone African origin. This triumph, in Paris, of 'noir-blanc-beur' (black-white-brown), was hailed by some as a victory of multiculturalism over racialism, though ironically Zidane's career ended on a sour note after an alleged slur (possibly racial) against him by an Italian opponent in the final of the 2006 World Cup. Critics have argued that the integration achieved in the national football team has not extended to other areas of French life, and an outburst of racial and social unrest throughout France in the autumn of 2005 gave some substance to these views.

The field of racial stereotyping in association football in Britain has attracted considerable attention, with the singular issue of the apparent under-representation of British Asians in the game coming under recent scrutiny.[22] In cricket, which as we have seen was a game that embraced the 'empire', racial mixture if not integration has always been apparent. Research conducted by

the historian Jack Williams in the 1980s and 1990s has been of great significance in establishing a paradigm for examining racial issues in the sport. His
Cricket and Race (2001) discusses several aspects of race in the game since the
late nineteenth century, including the international repercussions of South
African apartheid and the confrontations between England and Pakistan in
test matches in the 1980s and 1990s. However, one of his most revealing
insights is to be found in the area not of international cricket but of the
game played at a 'recreational' level in England. Here, in the local leagues
throughout the country, Williams demonstrates a strong involvement in the
game by cricketers of Asian and Afro-Caribbean descent. The pool of ethnic
talent at this level was long ignored by the white cricket establishment until
the ECB adopted a pro-active policy on racial integration in the late 1990s.
Long years of neglect had led, as Williams showed in his case study of Asians
in the Bolton area of south Lancashire, to a separation of local cricket along
ethnic lines.

Case Study Discussion 14

Jack Williams, 'South Asians and Cricket in Bolton', *Sports Historian*, **14
(1994), pp. 56–65.**

Bolton, an industrial town that had specialized in engineering and cotton spinning,
received a significant number of migrant workers from the cricket-playing countries
of south Asia from the 1960s onwards. Some 7 per cent of the town's inhabitants
were of Asian descent by the early 1990s. The town itself had a tradition of league
cricket stretching back into the nineteenth century, and in the last twenty years
of the twentieth century this tradition was augmented by a large number of Asian
cricket clubs. Unlike other areas further to the north, notably around the cotton-
weaving town of Nelson, the Asian clubs did not form their own separate leagues,
but they were restricted to a defined stratum of the local cricket world. None was
represented in those leagues considered to have the leading players. Among the
Asian clubs themselves there were many differences of religion, language, family,
clan and geography, resulting in a considerable fragmentation that made a non-
sense of glib references to the 'Asian community'. Religious and geographical loyalties were cut across by ties of caste and country. It was rare to find a club that
combined Muslim and Hindu members in equal proportion, but equally all-Muslim
clubs were either of Indian or Pakistani composition. It was unusual to find a club
with a particular religious affiliation that drew its support from across the social or
geographical range. Williams cites Deane and Derby, a leading Muslim club, as
being one of the very few to attract members from different Muslim groups. This
club had applied for membership of the leading league – the Bolton Association –
twice in the early 1990s and had been turned down, in spite of having a good
record in the Association's second division. When clubs from outside the Bolton
area were accepted it led to accusations from Asian cricketers that the Association
favoured white clubs.

Local Hero. Pride of Southport: Red Rum, three-times Grand National Winner in the 1970s. Statues to famous sportspeople in their birthplaces are now common throughout the world. Here, however, the celebrity is a horse, commemorated in the town's elegant Victorian shopping arcade. 'Rummy' was trained in Southport by Ginger McCain at his stables behind the second-hand car showrooms owned by his family in Aughton Road. He was a true 'horse of the people', much loved not only for his achievements at Aintree but because of the humble circumstances from which he came and the fact that his triumphs bestowed pride on a town that, like many other English seaside resorts, had known better days. (Author's photo).

Conclusion

Each of the areas examined above, whilst all the while remaining a key site of identity in sport, has seen significant changes over the past hundred years. The sense of nation is strong, possibly stronger in some respects than formerly, but has been overlain by other identities among which race is a major influence. This was pointed up by the notorious 'cricket test' applied by the British politician Norman Tebbit, who claimed in the early 1990s that British Asians maintained a residual loyalty for Pakistan, India and Sri Lanka in test matches against England, the country of their birth. Tebbit saw this as 'failing' the 'test' of British identity, implying that immigrants had not become properly integrated into the national society. In a different way, however, we might see this as a quite natural outcome of a multicultural society, where sport offers its followers a range of potential identities and loyalties. Is it axiomatic that people living in Britain should necessarily support England at cricket? Does a failure to do so imply some kind of disloyalty? It seems perfectly possible that the traditional 'home nations' matrix of support will not accommodate the visions of those brought up within a context of immigration and multiculturalism, which will demand new kinds of allegiances.

What this chapter has sought to bring out is the part sport plays in shaping our sense of who we are. This is a process which is, to an extent, culturally determined, and in Chapter 5 we shall follow up some of these issues. Over time the relationship between sport and people has changed, not only because certain sports have waxed and waned in their position in society but also because people, responding in part to how sport is represented to them, have interpreted sport differently, *appropriating* it for new purposes. Association football, to take perhaps the most obvious example, acquired the image of a 'working man's game' when it was first formalized as a 'modern' game in Great Britain in the late-nineteenth century; but when it was exported to the European continent soon afterwards it often took root in middle-class circles, though still retaining an attraction to men; in the United States, however, in the later part of the twentieth century, it received strongest support among white youngsters, especially girls, who were taken to matches in cars by their parents; soccer had become a suburban pastime for the junior members of the middle class. Its appeal to Afro-American sections of society, though, remained limited. Such shifting patterns of social class, age, gender and race can be traced in most sports. They remind us that nothing is fixed for all time, and that for those who work in sport a capacity to understand and manage change is crucial. History, therefore, provides an important point of reference for us all.

Study Questions

1. Test yourself: what would your own profile of identities be, in order of importance?
2. Can you add to the discussion of sport and identity by developing other areas (e.g. youth, and age generally, region, religion etc.)?
3. Why has the subject of race (and ethnicity – what is the difference?) in sport received relatively little attention in Britain?
4. What is your view of the 'cricket test'?

Further Reading

Ben Carrington and Ian McDonald, *'Race', Sport and British Society* (London: Routledge, 2000).

Mike Huggins and Jack Williams, *Sport and the English 1918–1939* (Abingdon: Routledge, 2006).

Kathryn Jay, *More Than Just a Game: Sports in American Life since 1945* (New York: Columbia University Press, 2004).

Jules Tygiel, *Past Time: Baseball as History* (Oxford: Oxford University Press, 2000).

Jack Williams, *Cricket and Race* (Oxford: Berg, 2001).

CHAPTER 4

Sport and Gender

Until quite recently it would have been common among sport historians to assume that a chapter on gender would be about the involvement, or lack of it, of *women* in sport. There was some justification for such an assumption, because traditionally sport history has been biased towards men and for a long time a more balanced approach had been needed. Furthermore, the participation of some women in sport has noticeably increased, at both the recreational and elite levels; the number of female sport heroes, for example, with outstanding achievements in international competitions to their credit, is no longer something to be counted on the fingers of one hand. When Tony Mason published his *Sport in Britain* only some twenty years ago he was able to observe many areas of sport from which women had been and still were excluded. 'Sport', he concluded, 'remains a largely masculine world both at the top and at the bottom'.[1] The situation has changed considerably since then, and even within the dozen or so years between the publication of that book and his *Sport in Britain 1945–2000*, co-written with Richard Holt, it had become possible to modify the earlier state of affairs and note important changes in participation rates for women. In particular there was the enthusiasm for female exercise, stimulated in part by 'style leaders such as Madonna and Princess Diana'. 'Sweat was sexy' remarked Holt and Mason, adding the crucial condition: 'providing it was showered off with a suitably branded product.'[2] Thus was concisely encapsulated a significant social and cultural development – a newly forged liaison between gender, sport, consumerism and femininity.

These developments in women's participation and influence in sport, which are worldwide and not confined only to western Europe and the United States, are a success story that is worthy of the celebration that has been accorded to it by commentators. In the forefront of developments has been the striking increase in opportunities for women in the United States as a result of Title

IX of the 1972 Educational Amendments legislation, which came into effect in 1976. Though not (as is commonly supposed) confined to the area of sport the provisions of Title IX have had their greatest impact there. Title IX, which was itself a product of the radical thinking that grew out of the civil rights movement and the anti-Vietnam War protests of the later 1960s, identified a number of areas in education where it was felt women had been unfairly discriminated against in the past. In sport it was responsible for significant increases in female involvement, as the act required equal funding for females in institutions in receipt of federal funding. Thus, in high school athletics there has been an almost tenfold increase in women's participation, and at college level (where in 1970 less than 30,000 women students took part in athletics compared with some 155,000 men) there has been a fivefold increase.[3] And in the Little League network of baseball for the young, where previously girls had not been accepted for team membership, one out of every seven players by 2009 was female. These changes have not come without struggle, however. The equality principles enshrined in Title IX were perceived by some to pose a threat to the budgets for male sport, and strenuous and persistent opposition to the implementation of the legislation's provision was encountered from, especially, the football lobby. Writing in 2002, some twenty-five years after the date originally set for compliance with the terms of the act (1978), a leading American sports scholar observed continuing non-compliance with Title IX in universities and colleges; little progress was made under unsympathetic administrations such as that of Ronald Reagan in the 1980s, and the tendency to see football as having a privileged position ('men's sport, women's sport, and football') was still evident.[4]

In spite of these continuing problems Title IX is nonetheless a success story, a tribute not only to those whose campaigns were responsible initially for securing such enabling legislation, but also to those who have subsequently fought to claim women's legal rights. As may be imagined, therefore, it has been a fit story for celebration, and typifies much of what has been written on women in sport, not only in the United States but also in many other countries. It conforms to what historians sometimes call 'Her-story'; that is to say, equalizing the balance in the historical record by giving more details about women's experience so that it matches up more nearly to what is already known about men. Whilst there is nothing wrong in doing this it can nonetheless become a limiting exercise if it leaves unanswered questions about the real nature of female involvement in particular kinds of activities. For example, we might show that the participation of women has increased significantly in the game of soccer by pointing to the numbers of young girls playing in the United States, the success of the US women's soccer team in the Women's World Cup, and the strength of the professional game in European countries such as Italy, Norway and Sweden. But does this help us to understand any better the power relations of the sport? More women might be playing soccer, but the game might still be administered by men according to male precepts. Have the women who are involved subscribed to an ideology of 'masculinity' in order to succeed, and how are they seen by other people in society? Indeed, how far do the changes noted in soccer relate to changes in other sports, and other parts of society? The existence of questions such as these suggests that we need to amplify the 'Her-story' account with something else.

The additional dimension has often been found in an emphasis on *gender*. In other words, to make the focus of our study not just what has happened to women, but the broader issue of the relationship between men and women in sport (or whatever subject we are specializing in). For the historian the study of gender relations must exist alongside the study of the relations of social class, race, age and so on, to form a profile of social interaction and power that better enables us to understand the working of society, how it is structured and how it changes. Thus, sport and gender is not simply synonymous with sport and *women*.

What steps have been taken in sport history to achieve these objectives? To answer this question we need first to branch out from sport itself and consider some of the historical work carried out in the wider field of leisure.

Women, gender and leisure

For a long time women's absence from sport and leisure reinforced a conventional 'common sense' understanding that leisure was a *male* activity. This perception (or, as some might have seen it, 'truth') sprang fundamentally from the economic and social experience of waged-working men. They were the family 'breadwinners' for whom leisure was a post-work privilege, provided for them by the domestic labour of their wives and, to a lesser degree, their daughters. The men operated according to a fixed calendar: (waged)-work times, and non-work times, the latter spent in various pursuits – at the pub, in the garden or the allotment, at the match, at home listening to the radio or watching the television or cultivating a hobby, and so on. Wives, and to an extent, daughters, operated according to a more fluid timetable. If they too had waged-work their 'home' time was filled with domestic duties: cooking, washing and ironing, child care, shopping. If they did not work, then they fulfilled an unwaged domestic role from dawn until dusk, managing the domestic economy. In this sense 'leisure' became something appropriated by men at the expense of women, and the very word 'leisure' took on an implicit male meaning: as a fixed period of time for relaxing activities such as was not available to women in the same way. For their part, women either had little leisure at all – 'relatively few [women] had the means or time that made much leisure possible'[5] – or, if they did, it took place in forms quite different from that experienced by the men. Taking all this into account, then, leisure becomes a social activity only fully understandable within the power relations of gender.

Historical examples of these leisure patterns are revealed in studies undertaken of British industrial towns at various times in the twentieth century.

In the Yorkshire coalfield, the mining town of 'Ashton' (the name given to Featherstone by a group of sociologists who investigated life there in the 1950s) was similar to many other industrial working-class communities studied at this time, where work and leisure possessed a strongly proletarian and masculine character. Most leisure activities were bound up with work and the pit. Leisure, for miners and their families, was very largely sensuous in nature, given to the pursuit of hedonism and enjoyment rather than intellectual improvement. It was based either on the miners' lodge (trade union branch) or on the Miners' Welfare, a cultural institution formed nationally in the aftermath of the First World War and run jointly by the coal owners (the National Coal Board from 1947) and the miners' trade union. Drinking played a big part in it, and thus the various pubs together with the working-men's clubs, of which there were six, were the centres of attention. Sport (cricket and angling), the colliery band and the St John Ambulance Brigade were the significant activities carried out in the voluntary sector of leisure; other important leisure interests, such as rugby league and bingo (tombola), were offered through the commercial sector. In Ashton only the Labour Party catered specifically for women's voluntary leisure through its women's section. In such places, therefore, the main social and cultural divisions in life seemed to hinge around gender. There was little work available for women, and marked barriers between the male (work) and the female (domestic) spheres developed. Women's leisure was far more restricted than men's, and 'for many women with young children the cinema is the sole relaxation outside the home'.[6] 'Callin' – visiting other people's houses for a chat and a gossip – was a principal means of relaxation for Ashton women. Even when the sexes were apparently taking leisure together, in, for example, the selection of the local 'Rugby League Queen', this popular ceremony was advertised as demonstrating that Ashton 'possesses beautiful women as well as strong and skilful men'. A clear distinction between the functions of the sexes was thus created. Did Ashton have no 'strong and skilful' women, or 'beautiful' men?

Another example is to be found in the Lancashire cotton-weaving town of Nelson, a community of some 40,000 people for most of the twentieth century. In one respect it was very like Ashton – strongly working-class. However, an important difference was to be found in the work available to women in textiles. Many weavers were women, and although they were rarely appointed to supervisory roles there was an equality of men and women on the mill floor. Family life was far less divided between male wage earners and unwaged female domestic workers. Nelson's more open labour market gave women a status in both the economy and social life that would not have been possible in coal mining. Thus leisure in Nelson was less rigidly subjected to the gender divisions seen in Ashton. Nelson's cricket club, for example, an institution of great importance to the town because it was responsible for much of its civic identity, drew members from across the social range and was particularly keen to include female members in its fund-raising activities. By the 1920s commercial leisure activities in the form of the cinema and dance halls had become popular for younger, unmarried women. Before this there had been several recreational opportunities available in the cultural networks based upon chapels and political movements, the latter producing women activists and espousing female causes to a greater extent than in many other places.[7]

Nelson is worth noting, though it was something of an exception. In the main, working-class lifestyles possessed an implicitly male-centred understanding of leisure. The same was true, as we know from several studies of the Victorian and Edwardian period, of middle-class life as well. The idea of the home as a haven from the stresses and strains of the office and the wife as the 'angel' by the hearth was a powerful ideological barrier to the expansion of women's intellect. By the interwar years things were improving in middle-class life, especially for the unmarried female, and it was from this social milieu that women's participation in sport largely came. The noteworthy expansion of women's cricket in the 1930s, for example, owed much to middle-class professional women. Recent efforts by the ECB to widen social and ethnic participation in women's cricket have met with some success, and the on-field achievement of England's women cricketers in winning the World Cup (2009) is one vindication of this policy. One suspects, however, that the general picture in women's sport is not vastly different at the beginning of the twenty-first century from what it was half a century previously, in spite of the availability of consumer durables that have taken some of the drudgery and time out of domestic labour. Female involvement in sport, whether of an organized or spontaneous nature, is far less likely for married working-class women, especially those from Muslim communities. Even among those known as the 'upper classes' it is worth remarking that in a recent special issue of the journal *Sport in History*, devoted to the British upper classes and sport, there was little mention of women; moreover, all the contributors to this issue of the journal were male.[8]

This is not to suggest, however, that ideas about men, women and leisure have not been subjected to a good deal of re-examination by scholars. As well as taking account of gender in the leisure experience there has also been a feminist awareness of the need to use scholarship in a polemical way – as a means of making sport and leisure more accessible to women. Thus, much feminist writing on sport and leisure seeks not only to explain that particular world but also to change it. What I might term the 'theory, enquiry, action' thrust of this scholarship has been evident particularly in sociological writing, which accounts for the lion's share of contemporary studies of sport and gender. Women, particularly married women, are shown to have created leisure, but in forms quite different from those of men. For example, a detailed survey of women in Sheffield in the 1980s reveals that many respondents did not use the term 'leisure' at all, 'seeing it as a vague and amorphous concept'. Instead of fixed periods of time, women preferred to think of those moments which produced a 'special state of mind or quality of experience'. Opportunities to be 'free', to 'be yourself', to 'do nothing' if the fancy so takes you, to rest, relax, or gossip – all these were experiences treasured by the women interviewed.[9]

In many cases they were brief moments. Constraints of both social class and gender shaped the experience of these women. Commercial leisure also played its part in fostering what Angela McRobbie has termed the 'feminine career'. Her excellent close reading of *Jackie*, a popular magazine for teenage girls, shows how in the 1970s conventional ideas of femininity, domesticity and early marriage were still being reproduced,[10] though by the 1980s they were undergoing changes of content and tone which clearly reflected the influence of feminism in encouraging a greater awareness of gender equality and 'realism' in the representation of women.[11] Such ideological constructions of 'femininity' nevertheless put up a powerful barrage against attempts to bring young women into sport, as Sheila Scraton found in her study of secondary schoolgirls in Liverpool. In a number of ways, to do with dress, discipline and physicality, the girls found physical education lessons distasteful and, to their teachers' dismay, simply 'dropped out'.[12]

To a certain extent, historical enquiry has lagged behind that of sociology. In fact the volume of work in general has been less, and the absence of a single overview book in English on the historical aspects of sport and gender, or even of women in sport, underlines the gap between the two disciplines. Historians can always point to 'gaps' in the historical narrative, but in the area of gender in sport there are rather more gaps than usual. Given the changes in attitude about gender that have taken place in recent years some of these are really quite surprising. Little has been done, for example, on the later-twentieth century development of 'feminised' sports such as aerobics, and scarcely anything at all on the traditional reliance that sports clubs, both professional and amateur, have placed on women as part of their back-room staff. The question 'who makes the tea?', a perennial item on the agenda of local cricket club committees, is one that might be broadened out to form part of an agenda for historical research. Women's supportive role in essentially male sports is one of the great untold stories of sport history and, it might be added, scandalously neglected in the displays of many sports museums that have sprung up in recent years.

We do have, however, in the work of some (mostly female) sport historians, a new critical slant on the familiar perception of the male historian – that leisure is defined by time, money and energy. The constraints of gender and social class were particularly evident in the poor neighbourhoods of large cities like London, where women dealt with the constant threat of poverty through a robust and intimate system of neighbourhood sharing. Helping each other out with money, domestic utensils, food, child care, and gathering as and when they could to gossip and drink – these were the features of daily life for women for much of the later-nineteenth and early-twentieth centuries. Monday, when goods redeemed from the pawnshop for the weekend were pawned once again for the much-needed weekly cash, was the high point in the week. It provided the opportunity for a brief meeting at a local pub, a leisure break timetabled into the endless round of making ends meet, and a time for specifically female conviviality. For most families there was a fairly rigid gender division – 'London husbands and wives lived in quite separate worlds' says one historian – and so links between women were often stronger than those between men and women.[13] Approaches of this kind, developed by feminist historians employing in an imaginative way the concept of gender, have enabled us to capture a form of leisure that has been previously 'hidden from history'.

Thus females – old and young, married and unmarried – no longer occupy quite the marginal place in the historian's vision that they did in their own contemporary social order. We are therefore better able to understand the decorative and feminized role male society sought to allocate them. Their 'socialization' into femininity, for example, is laid bare in important studies such as that of middle- and working-class girls in late-Victorian and Edwardian England, when the home and the schoolroom – but especially the home – were crucial cultural influences in preparing them for the sexual division of labour and leisure in society. The Girl Guide movement provides an interesting illustration of contemporary mentalities. Though apparently initially the product of autonomous action by young women themselves, the Guides were carefully shaped into a 'feminine' counterpart of the boys' Scouting movement. This was a process which involved, among other things, the adoption of suitably feminine names for patrol groups, and the focusing of the girls' attention on matters of beauty and appearance. Once Lady Baden-Powell, the wife of the founder of the Boy Scouts, had taken control of the girls' movement during the First World War, there developed an emphasis on the cultivation of a respectable self-reliance that taught girls to resist the lures of sex and mass culture, whilst at the same time being 'efficient women citizens, good home-keepers and mothers'.[14] Similar regimes were installed through the paternalist work programmes of some employers, such as the Rowntree chocolate factory at York and Boots pharmaceuticals in Nottingham.[15] Using oral testimony Claire Langhamer has uncovered some interesting evidence on the sporting activities of younger women in the interwar years. She found a keen interest in the more informal outdoor pursuits of cycling, rambling and camping; swimming and tennis were popular, and although team games seemed less common among working-class women than they were for their middle-class counterparts, rounders had a keen following, especially, it seems, in Liverpool. The commercially-provided sports were too expensive for many, though when the opportunity arose ice-skating had its attractions, whilst spectating at football and cricket matches was not unknown, especially for young women whose boyfriends took them to the match.[16]

I want to develop these points by examining further some individual pieces of research by historians of sport and leisure. In order, the first two are by female historians, but it is worth pointing out that, whilst women have been responsible for most of the historical work carried out on gender, there is no sex discrimination in operation. Gender studies are open to men as well as women.

Case Study Discussions 15–17

13   To begin with, then, a book by Jean Williams, *A Beautiful Game: International Perspectives on Women's Football* (Oxford: Berg, 2007).

In some ways it seems perhaps the most 'traditional' of the three approaches examined here. I have chosen it, however, because it is a combination of academic and polemical thinking, and demonstrates very well the fusing of theoretical study with social action. It has one paramount quality that much sport history lacks: it is comparative history of the boldest kind, with detailed case studies of soccer in the United States, Britain, Australia and the People's Republic of China. In each of these the game among women has become important in recent years, China and the United States in particular having produced some fine teams and skilled practitioners. Each has a rich history of football by women, embellished in recent years in the United States through the assistance of federal equal-opportunities legislation (Title IX) that has helped the attainment of some very impressive levels of participation in soccer by schoolchildren and young women. In the case of China the history is a very long one indeed, and the country appears to be regarded by FIFA as the 'cradle' of the game. By contrast, in Australia the game has a shorter history; the first national squad came into existence only in the late 1970s as part of a spurt at that time, probably precipitated by increased immigration from football playing countries in southern Europe. There is, however, evidence of extensive women's football at earlier dates, with the mid-1940s being a time of significant activity. All countries can point to successes, but lack of resources, a perceived absence of opportunities to exploit commercial openings in women's football, hostility from national organizations and sexism in various other forms, have been among the continuing obstacles to women's participation in the game.

Williams's work typifies what might be termed the 'classic' historian's method: that of collecting evidence, analysing it and writing up the findings in an interpretation. In *A Beautiful Game* she develops a story begun in an earlier book about the place of women in football, and their struggle to establish their game in the face of strong male opposition. The theme of the gender war in sport is prominent in Williams's approach to history. It is a project that, among other things, illustrates the truth of Sheila Rowbotham's famous dictum – that women have been 'hidden from history'. Using archival sources from various football governing bodies, including much from the FIFA itself, Williams pieces together the difficult and often discontinuous history of women's football. Britain offers a good warning to those who like their history to be of an 'onward and upward' kind; women's football there 'peaked' during and just after the First World War, when the celebrated Preston team based on the Dick, Kerr engineering works (later English Electric) achieved much success in publicizing the women's game, both domestically and, after a tour of the United States in the early 1920s, internationally (even though the Dick, Kerr women found themselves playing against men's teams while in the United States). Development did not proceed in a uniform fashion, however, and not until the final quarter of the twentieth century were the achievements of the earlier year rekindled. The task is made the more arduous by the fact that an international framework is Williams's chosen field in which to analyse development. Moreover, the approach is not always traditional. There is, for example, a strong emphasis on the contemporary, together with interesting discursive forays into questions of sources and of how to fill those awkward gaps faced by historians working in this field. The gaps, furthermore, extend to those under-represented areas of Africa and South America. Thus, whilst some might see Williams's work as an example of 'her-story', the book amounts to far more than simply a redressing of the balance between men and women in the historical narrative of football. It is a challenge to the cultural and historical construction of football as a 'man's game', and the inference the reader should draw from the study is that football must be seen as simply that, 'football', a game played by men and women and beset, as are all social activities, by tensions arising from gender, class, ethnic, age and other divisions.

14 Next, a piece of work which takes the analysis beyond sport itself, and in a sense also beyond the discipline of history. This is research of an interdisciplinary nature by Catriona M. Parratt on a popular festival from 'pre-modern' times: the Haxey Hood. ('Of Place and Men and Women: Gender and Topohilia in the Haxey Hood', *Journal of Sport History*, 27, 2 summer 2000, pp. 229–45.)

It exemplifies two aspects of methodology that we looked at in Chapter 2: the place of history within a convergence of cognate disciplines, and the 'survival' of older sporting rituals into the contemporary world that related to the issue of continuity and change. The subject is a form of 'folk football' similar to that which figures in Adrian Harvey's study of the transition of popular culture in the early nineteenth century (see Case Study Discussion 6). But rather than dying out, the Haxey Hood persisted against all the forces of 'modern' popular culture and is still to be found in the village of Haxey in the Isle of Axholme (north Lincolnshire). Its existence, however, is severely circumscribed in place and time. Very localized to the village and its immediate surroundings, it is played ('performed' might be a better term) once each year in the period between the New Year and Twelfth Night. The game, unrecognizable as football in any modern sense of the sport, has been a regular feature of the cultural life of this once-remote, fenland community for several centuries and nowadays serves (as well as an opportunity to consume large amounts of alcohol) principally to register the distinctiveness of this particular place. In addition to a historical perspective, Parratt's study of the Hood draws upon theory: in particular the work of the cultural geographer Yi-Fu Tuan and his concept of 'topophilia', which is concerned with how physical spaces acquire cultural meanings. In addition sociological, geographical and anthropological insights show how an identity of place in this particular case is created, through a continuing local legend that recounts a story about the Isle of Axholme, its history, its people and the relationships between them. Such popular festivals (there is a similar one in Ashbourne, Derbyshire) are often regarded by the untutored observer as spontaneous events, and so it might seem when witnessing the 'sway' that characterizes the mass of bodies contesting the Haxey Hood. In fact, these gatherings were highly organized and followed long-established customs. Parratt shows how in Haxey the game had fixed characters ('the Lord', 'the Fool' and a set number of players – 'Boggins') and proceeded according to well-understood rules. The event itself, which takes places on 6th January each year, following a week of ritualized preamble based upon local pubs, is a rowdy though non-violent affair, somewhat resembling a large and rather disorganized rugby match. In essence the winner is the man who is able to take hold of the Hood and lodge it safely at the pub of his choice.

A cardinal feature of the Haxey Hood is the display of male strength it affords. Local champions are celebrated. However, Parratt teases out subtle gender implications in the event. It is inspired by an ancient story of a local noblewoman, Lady de Mowbray, whose hood it was that some peasants retrieved when, one windy day, it blew off into a field. The good lady rewarded them with land, and gave them the names by which the players are now known. Lady de Mowbray, in Parratt's reading of the game and its provenance, becomes synonymous with the feminized land and home, central concerns in an annual ritual which is about claiming land and returning the hood to its 'home' (pub). Moreover, a number of songs ('Drink Old England Dry', 'John Barleycorn' and 'Farmer's Boy') of varying age are traditionally sung at the Haxey Hood; they self-evidently celebrate drinking, as well as male prowess, but the lyrics also relate to the de Mowbray legend in their celebration of the land and its annual re-birth. Thus Parratt can conclude that in this surviving folk ritual in which men assume the central role 'women are marginal, but nonetheless crucial' both in the symbolism of the story and its re-enactment, and in the spectators who come in large numbers to witness the event: 'without them much of its meaning would be fundamentally diminished' (p. 239).

15   Finally, work by a male historian, Richard Holt, on the late-Victorian and Edwardian period in Britain. ('The Amateur Body and the Middle-Class Man: Work, Health and Style in Victorian Britain', *Sport in History*, 26, 3, December 2006, pp. 352–69.)

This is a short but important piece of work because it represents an innovative historical approach to the question of sport and gender. Holt throws off much of the baggage that has conventionally burdened this topic; his discussion is not about women at all, and not entirely about the practising of sport. Instead, following a perspective originally sketched out by the French theorist Michel Foucault, he draws attention to notions of the male body, how it is perceived and how changes in body 'style' might come about. In essence Holt examines what we might term an 'aesthetic'; that is to say, how the questions of why people perform sports, which sports they perform, how they perform them, and how they *look* as sportspeople all come together at a particular historical moment. Drawing many of his examples from London, Holt examines the response to sport, and particularly its amateur ethos, among the growing ranks of the professional middle and lower-middle classes. This was the world not only of the successful stockbroker but also of Mr Pooter, the less successful company clerk, and the younger but aspiring boatmen of Jerome K. Jerome's classic work *Three Men in a Boat* (1886). Holt depicts a world of competitive capitalism and self-help where a strong belief in what the French called 'la carriere ouverte aux talents' (which we might term 'meritocracy') and the necessary work ethic that went with it impelled men to strive for achievement. Their labour was not especially physical; they worked in sedentary jobs based for the most part in airless offices, to which they travelled from home by bus and train. Bringing late twentieth-century notions to bear on this environment, Holt uses the idea of 'work-life balance' to illustrate a perceived need for sport and exercise as a complement and antidote to the kinds of work this new commercial revolution had brought about. It should remind us that the term 'recreation', which nowadays has an old-fashioned ring about it, was in the late-Victorian period the apt description of this activity: leisure as the means of releasing the tensions and re-charging the energies that accompanied work. Thus the office worker, like the coalminer, longed to be liberated from his confined work existence into the fresh air and open spaces. Contemporary scientific opinion held that the male body (though not the female) responded to strenuous use. 'Work hard, and play hard' was the formula for good health. The physiological thinking of the day demanded a harmony between the physical and the mental state and in turn suggested a new aesthetic of the body. The celebrated sportsman W. G. Grace, despite his triumphs in cricket, was not the idealized masculine form of the Edwardian period: another cricketer, C. B. Fry, more nearly approximated to it: slim but broad of shoulder and with an alert bearing. Fry also personified another principle of amateurism – he was not a specialist. His sports were many, and he *participated* in them. Watching (spectatorism) was frowned upon simply because it was not active. Some of the sports most committed to the amateur ethic – rugby union being a prime example – were not, apart from their big events, sports attended by more than a few spectators. The new aesthetic of sport went beyond the physical form of the male body to what we might nowadays term the 'cultural signifiers' of sport: the badges, trophies (think of the FA Cup), blazers, cricket flannels and the general demeanour of the sportsmen. The historical inflections might have been borrowed often from ancient Greece, but contemporary economic and health imperatives provided the motor for this middle-class amateurism, a significant repository of cultural capital.

In this way Holt's analysis places the development of much late-Victorian sport in a context of the contemporary structures and ideologies of work and health. It explains an idea of 'manliness' that became deeply rooted in society and which exercised a continuing influence well into the twentieth century. Moreover, in his awareness of historical discourse Holt demonstrates an important engagement with an academic debate originating outside the realms of sport history. His article implicitly takes issue with notions of a failed British 'bourgeois revolution' stemming originally from the work of Perry Anderson and Tom Nairn in the 1960s, and which has more recently been illustrated in the research of the historian Martin Weiner. Furthermore, in the particular context of Victorian sport, Holt's purpose is to draw attention away from the conventional focus on the public schools as the prime movers of 'manliness' through 'muscular Christianity', and to place emphasis upon the broader commercial and social developments that explain the take-up of the amateur ideal. We might want to register some reservations about Holt's reading back of present-day concerns into the world of the late Victorians, and about his characterization of some 'amateur' heroes: Jack Hobbs, for example, portrayed by Holt as the embodiment of the amateur principle, was in the last analysis a *professional* cricketer who owed much of his success in the 1920s (when he scored most of his many runs) to the most un-amateur practice of 'pad play'. Minor quibbles apart, however, there is no doubt that Holt's scholarship provides a model template for historians exploring gender issues in sport, in that he demonstrates with admirable clarity and persuasiveness that masculinity is not a biological given but a cultural identity constructed in particular historical circumstances; and, moreover, that interpretation of it is the subject of debate. Like everything else in history, we cannot take things for granted; nothing is ever 'definitive'.

Here, then, we have three approaches to the question of sport and gender that differ in their conception and methodology. They offer not only a model for future research but also an illustration of different kinds of history in action. Above all, they show unequivocally that studies of gender need not begin and end with the subject of women.

To round off this chapter I am going to look at an account of sport and gender that differs completely from those we have examined previously. With Parratt and Holt we have encountered something a bit different from the normal run of historical and sociological work, but in what follows I want to consider something that is not 'history' at all in the normal sense of the word, and which some historians might reject as having any validity for the project we are dealing with. It is a novel.

Case Study Discussion 18

David Storey, *This Sporting Life* (London: Longmans, 1960).

Storey was part of a group of British writers in the late 1950s and early 1960s who dealt with the theme of social class in a largely northern working-class setting. John Braine, Alan Sillitoe and Stan Barstow were other leading exponents of this school of social realist fiction. Storey's novel is probably the best known in his own lengthy bibliography, no doubt because in 1963 it was made into a film by Lindsay Anderson, starring Richard Harris and Rachel Roberts. What Storey chose to foreground in his novel marked it out from other writers of the genre. Although *This Sporting Life* has plenty to say about social class – it is essentially a study of a working-class man – it also succeeds in confronting issues of gender and gender relations. His main male character is Arthur Machin, a rugby league player renowned for his strength, but in the character of Mrs Hammond, Machin's landlady, he brings into the centre of his narrative a finely drawn female character, as he had also done in *Flight into Camden*, published in the same year. Storey places Machin in sport – after work, the main site of 'maleness' – where, increasingly throughout the novel, he comes to perceive the tensions between what is expected of him as a man and the shallowness of conventional masculinity.

It is in his relationship with a woman that Machin's masculinity is put to the test and found wanting. This has nothing to do with sex, success in which is the conventional social measure of masculine prowess. It has, however, everything to do with understanding women and being able to bridge a divide between the sexes that is created and re-created daily through countless forms of separation in work and play, driving men and women apart. The sporting life is, of course, the quintessential instrument of female exclusion, for women have no part in the football. Machin has an affair with Mrs Hammond, a withdrawn, desiccated, self-pitying woman. In her psyche is stored all the toil and pain of working-class life. She is seeking to expunge the shame of a failed marriage, ended not in divorce (an exceptional occurrence in this social context and time) but in the suicide of her husband. The circumstances are mysterious, but he seems to have lost the will to live. The event leaves her guilt-stricken and suspicious of any relationship with a man. At the same time, she is caged in a confining domesticity, caring for her two young children, taking in a lodger to make ends meet and keeping alive the memory of her dead husband through the ritual daily cleaning of his boots, which are permanently kept in the hearth. Nobody could be farther removed than Mrs Hammond from the glamorized, sexually submissive image of woman conventionally associated with the masculine gaze, which is the image featured in Machin's favourite novelette reading. Yet this is what provides the fascination for Machin. He wants to bring her back to life, to arouse in her some spark of emotion for him. But all his efforts to establish a real relationship, shorn of the customary expectations of a society in which gender roles are rigidly performed, come to nothing. The novel is a bitter critique of contemporary British society at a historical moment when old ideas and institutions were under attack and the country was facing up to modernization. By taking his analysis into sport and gender relations Storey was ahead of his time in establishing a theme that only fully came into public view with the rise of the women's movement in the later 1960s. Like other writers of fiction in other situations he captured a mood and a problem in a way that historical study cannot do, and for this reason we would be justified, I feel, in adding David Storey's novel to our list of sources for the study of sport and gender.

As a brief concluding point we may note an area that has resisted deep analysis. Even the most persistent feminist scholars have not always penetrated the experience of those women for whom class and gender relationships have been overlain by those of race. While historians of sport are gradually coming to terms with the diversity of experience that exists among women, relatively little has so far been achieved in the sensitive area of racial experiences.[17] Western perspectives, even among feminist writers, have been an obstacle to the understanding of, for example, Muslim women's involvement in sport. In an important study based on interviews with Muslim schoolgirls and young women in London, Hasina Zaman has attempted to expose some of the mis-understandings that accompany this subject, especially the notion that Muslim women are the victims of a conservative and patriarchal culture, symbolized in its gendered codes of dress.[18] Zaman shows that the women themselves are often anxious to retain an Islamic philosophy about exercise and the female body, and consequently find western-style changing provisions in schools and leisure centres offensive to their sensibilities. Religious teaching causes them to regard sport and fitness not as a secular pursuit of fitness and health for its own physiological sake, which is equated with vanity, but as an extension of their faith, a way of praising god. Zaman's interviewees were all keen to participate in sport but found western attitudes about it difficult to circum-vent from the point of view of their religion. The problem was summed up by one woman who went along to what she thought would be a women-only swimming session at her local baths:

I don't think that being a Muslim woman should prevent you from doing sports. I go to 'women-only'... because you know that my religion says that I shouldn't expose my body to men, but you know that when I went to women's night, I assumed that it will be all women and even lifeguards or the safety people would be women and I was shocked that it was men. But I tried to get into the pool as soon as I could, that is the only thing that ruined my swimming, apart from that I like swimming.[19]

Zaman's work helps to explain some of the difficulties faced by women from this religious culture, and might also begin to explain why participation in sport and other leisure activities is so uneven across the range. Gender inequal-ities in leisure, as in work, exist in part because women themselves are, so to speak, complicit in their creation. What seems like oppression to some fem-inist historians looking back into the past was not experienced in that way by women at the time. Nor are religious precepts necessarily something that 'hold back' women.

Conclusion

Two questions stand out above all others in the discussion of gender in sport history: how have historians handled gender; and what is the value of the his-tory they have produced?

There is no doubt that historians have awoken to the question of sport and gender; no longer is the history of sport implicitly assumed to be about what men do on the field or in the committee rooms. Nonetheless, it is dif-ficult to escape the feeling that much more could still be done on gender issues in the domain both of sport and sport history. Historians have tended to lag behind sociologists in this respect, not only in terms of the volume of work produced, but also in the insights offered. 'Her-story' approaches still largely prevail, with the chief purpose being to focus on women in sport rather than on the effect of gender relations in society and how they affect, and are affected by, sport. It is surprising, and also something of a criticism of the development of sport history, that there is no general work that provides an overview of the empirical and historiographical endeavours in the field of women, sport and gender in Britain and Europe during the past two centuries. The best book on this is still Jennifer Hargreaves's *Sporting Females*, written some fifteen years ago. It balances an essentially sociological analysis with a strong historical perspective, while including a broad range of topics in its discussion. Hargreaves shows clearly that 'women' are a diverse category that is complicated by issues of age, race, class, physical ability and geographical location: there is no simple 'female experience' of sport. Moreover, she works into her analysis the polemical theme referred to earlier that produces a call to action, demonstrating clearly that women have the capacity to resist and change traditional male-based notions of their role in sport. In the final analysis, however, this fine book is (as its title says) about women in sport and how gender relations have positioned them there. There is much less on the kinds of issues opened up in Holt's essay (see above), and this – the male body and the aesthetic of sport – is an area that merits greater attention.

Setting aside, however, the question of how historians have studied (and should study) gender, what can we say about the *value* of the historical perspective? In the area of gender, more so than in most other aspects of sport, there is a polemical charge to much of the historical work undertaken. This undoubtedly results from the feeling that *present-day* problems of access and inequality, which have by no means disappeared, can better be understood by opening up our field of vision and taking in the past. Gender relations would not have become the prominent issue it now is in sport without the vigorous interventions of (mainly) female historians to add the subject to the historian's agenda. We have seen in this chapter how the present and the past have interacted to change our perceptions of gender in sport. As a result of placing historical gender inequalities under the microscope we are now in a position more clearly to understand the process of marginalization in sport, and to deal with it in the present and future. The campaign to achieve a breakthrough like Title IX in the United States and then, having secured the legislation, to continue the long struggle to ensure its effective implementation provides a perfect example of the value of a historical perspective on sport. It provides an appreciation of how a combination of structural changes and human action enabled a specific event like Title IX to come about. It also creates a record of the pioneers – both athletes and activists – whose initial struggles give a stimulus to their present-day successors. In this way a sense of history can help to move mountains in the present.

Sport is only minimally about highly paid performers. For the most part it involves people who enjoy athletic activity for its own sake – for the pleasure and sense of personal and team achievement it gives. These runners, passing along Oxford's High Street in 2007, are a case in point. They are taking part in a 10K run to raise money for muscular dystrophy. In recent years this kind of event has become increasingly common, appealing to young and not-so-young as a form of charity work that also has benefits for health. It illustrates the continuing vitality of voluntary association, as people group together in a communal purpose. What is more, there is always a good representation of women. Running (or 'jogging'), alongside aerobics and other keep-fit activities, has proved very amenable for both male and female participants. Is it a sport? This kind of recreational running is not beset by problems of competition and record-keeping, and is relatively free of the tensions that plague 'elite' performance. Perhaps we should simply call it a 'physical activity' that seems genuinely to have broken down some of the barriers present of the long-standing sexual division of leisure. (Katharine M. Hill).

Study Questions

1. Briefly explain the differences between 'women's history' and 'gender history'.
2. From your own experience which sports would you say have seen the most female involvement in recent years, and how would you explain this?

3. What do you understand by the idea of the 'sexual division of leisure'? Do you find it a valid concept in contemporary society compared with the 'sexual division of labour'?
4. What main conceptual and methodological differences in their approach to sport history do the case studies of Williams, Parratt and Holt illustrate?

Further Reading

Jennifer Hargreaves, *Sporting Females: Critical Issues in the History and Sociology of Women's Sports* (London: Routledge, 1994).

Michael S. Kimmel and Michael A. Messner, *Men's Lives* (London: Allyn and Bacon, 2001).

Claire Langhamer, *Women's Leisure in England 1920–60* (Manchester: Manchester University Press, 2000).

Sheila Scraton and Anne Flintoff, *Gender and Sport: A Reader* (Abingdon: Routledge, 2002).

David Storey, *This Sporting Life* (Harmondsworth: Penguin Books, 1962 ed.).

Garry Whannel, *Media Sport Stars: Masculinities and Moralities* (London: Routledge, 2002).

CHAPTER 5

Mediating Sport

As we noted in Chapter 1, the output of sport history has increased significantly over the past 30 years. However, much of what historians have produced has tended to remain within a conventional historiographical framework of *outlook* (what we perceive sport to be) and *method* (how we should study it). Elite sports have been given more attention than those practised at a recreational level; men rather than women have been the subject of attention; 'westernized' sport in the nineteenth and twentieth centuries is more amply covered than either earlier sporting activity or that of the non-western world. In addition to this there has been a preference for thinking about sport as a series of finite activities: the games people play, and those who play, organize and watch them. Whilst this focus has produced many interesting studies it might nonetheless be claimed that there have been limitations inherent in it, and that these have led to certain omissions in our understanding. One of these relates to the way that sport is a process understood *indirectly*, that is to say, not as an activity known through direct participation – as player, organizer or spectator at the sporting venue – but as an activity reported from another source rather than being experienced at first hand. The immense growth during the twentieth century of various channels of communication – the newspaper press and related print journalism, radio, television, books, film and photography – should remind us that all of these forms serve to *mediate* ideas about sport. They are in fact the *media* on which sport is now so dependent, not only for communicating information but also for providing support and sponsorship. Where would the much-vaunted English Premier League – regarded by some as the world's leading association football league – be without BSkyB and Barclay's Bank? It is from the media in all its forms that a great deal of what we know and understand about sport is derived.

Nowadays we tend to think that 'the media' is synonymous with television; radio might possibly get a look in, though it is surprising how little attention historians of sport have given it. In fact, the media encompasses a wide range of communication in written and visual, electronic and paper forms. In addition to radio and television, the national and local daily and Sunday press, magazines and books of various kinds, there is now the internet and other advanced technological means of conveying ideas and information about sporting activity throughout the world. Nor should we forget one of the oldest methods of communication: word of mouth. People can sit for hours at home, in the workplace, in cafes and in pubs simply talking about their favourite sportspeople and events, and in this way embellish the vast collective store of 'public' sporting memory.

The press

Since the eighteenth century one of the principal agencies in the creating of this sporting memory has been the newspaper press. Until the rise of television it was the chief source of information and ideas about sport. All sections – the national dailies, the Sundays, the local newspapers and the specialist sports papers and magazines – reported it, and to extensive readerships. It was estimated, for example, that just after the Second World War each of the most popular dailies was read by over 20 million people. The Sundays had even higher readerships, with that of the *News of the World,* its coverage spiced by divorce cases and sex scandals, reaching possibly 46 million people. In their various ways all operated on a long-held assumption that sport sold newspapers. Since the later years of the nineteenth century a strong specialist sporting press had been in existence, establishing codes of sports writing either on a focused area, like *Sporting Life* which concentrated on the turf, or, like the Manchester-based *Athletic News*, on a range of sports. Their style, in company with that of most of the late-Victorian and Edwardian press, tended originally to be heavy and detailed. James Catton, who edited the *Athletic News* in its later days, was a distinguished sports journalist whose classically inspired by-lines ('Ubique' and 'Tityrus') say something about the man and his prose. Detailed narratives were the style of the local press too. When Bury won the FA Cup twice within the space of three years at the beginning of the century, the *Bury Times* first recorded the club's achievement in four columns of tightly packed reporting, and on the second occasion (a 6-0 Cup Final record) with a full six-columns page, illustrated only by small vignettes of players and officials. Changes came with the foundation in 1896 of the first mass-circulation daily, the *Daily Mail,* and in 1903 of the *Daily Mirror,* initially a paper aimed at middle-class women with plenty of pictures and advertisements for expensive shops. They departed from the dense layout of the established press to introduce a more readable page on which pictures increasingly conveyed much of the story. By the interwar years the specialist sporting press had lost some of its appeal to the national 'tabloid' dailies and Sunday newspapers, with their characteristic sports pages placed at the back of the paper and covering some

10 to 15 per cent, and in the case of the *People* just after the Second World War 20 per cent, of its entire content. Writers were emerging by the 1930s as media personalities in their own right. In the manner of the American journalist Grantland Rice, credited with the invention of a new human interest journalism – the 'gee whiz' style – they forsook the prosaic for the imaginative, the human drama, and the 'behind the scenes' story: in short, sensationalism. The sports editor of the *Daily Express* in the 1930s, Trevor Wignall, was one of the pioneers of this new style in Britain, alongside such journalists as Henry Rose, also of the *Express*, Peter Wilson, himself the son of a *Daily Mirror* writer, and Alan Hoby of the *Sunday Express*. A mystique surrounded the last two, described by their papers as 'The Man They Can't Gag' (Wilson) and 'The Man Who Knows' (Hoby).

The style of the popular press served to position its readers to sport in a number of distinctive ways.

- sport for the most part was cast in terms of popular sports. Horse racing, because of its betting appeal, soccer, boxing and cricket made up the vast majority of the sports pages. Other sports were covered only when they possessed a well-loved national event such as the Boat Race, or when a British competitor had achieved success, as with Fred Perry's triumphs at Wimbledon in the mid-1930s. Otherwise minority sports were felt to have little intrinsic appeal to readers, especially in the 1930s, a time of competition for circulation when the newspaper market was overstocked with titles.

- such a focus emphasized male interests. Though some of these sports, cricket and soccer for example, were played by women, female contributions to them were almost wholly neglected, except when they had a 'novelty' value, as in the brief flurry of women's soccer during and just after the First World War. There was no sense in which the popular newspaper press felt that it had any obligation to inform and educate its younger female readers, which in some cases made up a considerable proportion of the readership, about the possibilities open to them in sport. If readers wanted to know about women's cricket, for example, they would usually need to consult a specialist publication like *Women's Cricket*.[1] The press therefore conformed to a conventional wisdom that sport was a male preserve, and thereby helped to reinforce popular attitudes about the sexual division of leisure.

- there was a markedly insular approach to sports coverage which ensured that readers viewed the sporting world from a British perspective. In fact, that world was largely coterminous with Britain, or even localities within it. The local press continued to be an important part of sports coverage and a major force in stimulating local partisanship. One section of it in particular became a regular and well-loved feature of local life. This was the football special – often printed on coloured paper and known as the *Pink 'Un* or the *Green 'Un*. Before radio started to broadcast soccer results at five o'clock on Saturdays after the Second World War the football specials, which were on the streets by 6 o'clock, were first with the results and often with extensive match reports. At the national level developments in sport were well covered by all the major dailies by the interwar years, but developments in other countries were less prominent. They came into the reckoning only when British competitors and teams were contesting a sport with foreigners. Thus the early soccer World Cup competitions of the 1930s, in which no British teams took part, were ignored. The fourth World Cup of 1950, held in Brazil, was contested by England, though without success as the team was eliminated at an early stage. At this point, as if to emphasize their insularity, the entire British press corps took the plane back to London. This astonished the cosmopolitan journalist Willy Meisl, who could scarcely believe that British reporters would want to miss 'watching and studying the cream of the world's foremost soccer nations'.[2] Three years later, when the England team lost a home match for the first time against foreign opposition – the famous 6–3 defeat by Hungary – the popular press suddenly discovered that things had been going on abroad of which it, and its readers, were quite ignorant. The Wolfenden Report of 1960, *Sport and the Community*, sponsored by the Central Council of Physical Recreation (CCPR) to look into the apparently backward state of British sport, rounded on the press. The Report concluded that 'the outlook of our sporting Press is often as insular as the attitude of some Governing Bodies. Britain's position and problems in international sport are not generally understood because the public are rarely made aware of developments abroad until they are taken by surprise by the results'.[3] It was a fair point, but it made little difference to the basic approach of the popular press. By the closing decade of the century the sports content of the popular press was little different in tone from what it had been in the interwar years. More international competition in many sports brought an apparently more cosmopolitan outlook, though at times newspaper coverage could be very nationalistic, as the reporting of the World Cup in 2002 showed.

What are now called the 'broadsheets' (formerly the 'quality' press) – mainly the *Times*, the *Daily Telegraph*, the *Guardian*, the *Independent* and the *Scotsman* – did not always share these characteristics. For many years the *Daily Telegraph*, which in 1937 had absorbed the *Morning Post*, has been able to claim the most comprehensive sports coverage of the dailies, spanning both the popular and the minority, the amateur and the professional sports. As a paper of the aspiring middle classes of the Home Counties it was especially sound on rugby football, and was unique in maintaining a full reporting of private school sports. The *Times*, as Mason has noted, 'generally looked down its aristocratic nose at sports with large spectator followings'.[4] It did cover the Cup Final regularly, mainly because it was a national event whose significance transcended football. This became apparent to the paper in 1914, when the monarch attended the match for the first time. For the most part, however, the *Times* showed as much interest in amateur sports as professional ones. The *Times* reserved a special place for cricket, as did the *Guardian* (when still the *Manchester Guardian*). Its main writer on this sport was Neville Cardus, who significantly doubled as music critic. His reports and essays were considered to have elevated sports writing – not generally regarded in Britain as a high art – to a level and quality more usually associated with American authors such as Ring Lardner and Ernest Hemingway. Spanning the worlds of sport and literature in this way was exceptional, and Cardus's achievement was matched by few others: Henry Longhurst, Hugh McIlvanney and Brian Glanville were notable later examples. Glanville, indeed, has claim to have contributed one of the few serious English novels on association football, *The Rise of Gerry Logan*.

Case Study Discussion 19

Michael Oriard, *Reading Football: How the Popular Press Created an American Spectacle* (Chapel Hill: University of North Carolina Press, 1993).

Someone once asked me which book of sport history had most influenced me: I replied 'Oriard's *Reading Football.*' Of course, any answer to such a question involves a whole set of personal preferences and interests, and this book has influenced me because it contains a number of features that are very relevant to the trajectory of my own work: (i) it deals with the role of the newspaper and magazine press and subjects it to close reading; (ii) it is informed by theory drawn from cultural studies, yet is not dominated by it and (in contrast to the 'deconstructionists' identified by Douglas Booth, see p. 21) retains a clear belief that the historian can and should attempt to reconstruct the past; (iii) it is strong on the idea of *representations* and helps us to understand the creation of a 'hegemonic sports culture' (see p. 42); (iv) although in many respects a history book, it also draws on other disciplines, notably literature, and thus displays the enrichment to be gained by the historian in adopting an interdisciplinary method; and (v) it contains a prodigious amount of interesting and well-presented research (including the use of visual evidence) and is a joy to read. In all, it is a model of how to compose good sport history.

Oriard's book emphasizes that our understanding of sport (and, by implication, many other things in life) is a *mediated* one in which a number of meanings or ideologies are communicated. His focus is the game of American football, which had evolved as an adaptation of rugby in the later years of the nineteenth century. By the 1890s it was the big winter sport of the north-east United States, based on a network of elite universities and colleges. It was an amateur game, and not until some sixty years later did professional football begin to approach it in popularity. The press was the crucial instrument in transforming a game devised for students to *play* into one with widespread popular appeal to spectators and readers. While newspapers and magazines *reported* sporting contests they simultaneously introduced other stories into their narratives; stories, for example, about masculinity and gender relations, the social order, race, social class, violence, amateurism and professionalism and much else. By making extensive use of the vivid and dramatic illustrations that accompanied its stories, Oriard demonstrates that the press carried football beyond the confines of sport to create an ideological vision of contemporary America. An example of this is seen in the coverage of the styles of play in football. The late nineteenth century was a time of intense debate about how the game should be conducted; this devolved into two principal and opposed camps – one committed to preserving what was seen as the true amateur ethic of play, the other advocating a more 'professional' approach (while maintaining the amateur status of players) that involved a scientific study of tactics to eliminate risk and chance, and thus maximize the possibilities for winning. This, it was claimed by its detractors, led to the transformation of play into work, as well as a boring spectacle, but defenders of the professional approach pointed to the prestige that rested on competitive matches between leading colleges: do you want to play 'attractive' football, or do you want to win? The chief proponents of these contrasting philosophies were Caspar Whitney and Walter Camp, and their cases were expounded, analysed, defended and attacked in the leading magazines of the day – *Harper's Weekly, Outing, Collier's,* the *Saturday Evening Post* – as well as major dailies such as the *New York Times*. What Oriard terms 'multiple narratives' were presented to readers – often in the same magazine – that conflicted in their views as to the direction in which football should be taken, a difficult line being drawn between a desired hard manliness inculcated through rough games and, its reverse, a descent into barbarism when matches became little more than displays of open thuggery. Behind all this were clear implications for American itself. Did future national success depend on the scientific rationalism of the 'professional' school, or the innately talented leadership of amateurs with flair?

In addition to the ideologies inscribed in these texts is the question of how they were interpreted by readers. Is the scholar's interpretation in line with that of a contemporary reading the text a century earlier? This is a problem encountered in all such analysis, and the fact that it is a historical text renders it doubly difficult. We cannot go back and *ask* the reader what s/he thought. Critics have suggested that Oriard and others cannot analyse readers so much as make certain assumptions about them. Oriard would himself recognize this, though argues that the range of interpretative possibilities is not endless. The press (to continue with this example) does not brainwash its readers, who for their part are not entirely free to make up their own minds. A negotiation takes place. Both parties operate under constraints about what they can tell and what they can know. In the continuing academic debate about the power of the mass media, therefore, Oriard's historical study has much to contribute.

Radio

The influence of the newspaper press was strong in other areas of sports presentation. One of these was broadcasting, which has always drawn heavily in both technique and personnel from the newspaper office. Between 1922 and 1955 broadcasting in Britain was a monopoly of the British Broadcasting Corporation (BBC), and it was during these years that a particular 'style' was developed, initially in radio and then transported into television by both the BBC and its commercial rivals. Sport's relationship with radio had begun in 1921 in the United States, when baseball matches were somewhat crudely reported by a studio-based commentator relying on information sent over the telegraph by an observer at the ballpark. In the following year broadcasts acquired a wider audience when Grantland Rice covered the World Series for station WJZ of Newark, New Jersey. But it was in 1923 when Graham McNamee was thrust into the commentator's chair for the World Series that a new and lively style of broadcasting was born. It made McNamee one of the most popular voices on radio. The BBC imbibed many of these influences and moulded them into a distinctive cultural product of its own. The history of the BBC, especially during its monopoly phase, is often interpreted in terms of the influence of its first Director General, the Scot John Reith, who left the Corporation in 1938. Reith's rather austere vision of public broadcasting as an essentially educational service purveyed in a dignified, respectable manner (typified in the wearing by male radio announcers of black tie when at the microphone in the evening) is often parodied. In fact, it was consistent with a philosophy enunciated by the Sykes Committee of 1923 which, in its enquiry into broadcasting, had regarded the airwaves as 'a valuable form of public property' entrusted to the broadcasting authority, which was charged with administering it responsibly.[5]

In this context the broadcasting of sport in Britain was given a number of distinctive inflexions. To begin with, and to be expected, there was a notably upper-class, public-school manner of presentation. This was illustrated in the accents and demeanour of a succession of radio and television sports presenters. Starting with the commentator at the first broadcast Cup Final in 1927 – George Allison, the later manager of Arsenal FC – there is a clear lineage through Raymond Glendenning and Peter Dimmock, Head of Outside Broadcast and presenter of television's *Sportsview* in the 1950s, to Brian Johnston ('Johnners') a television and later radio commentator on cricket who invested the popular 'Test Match Special' commentaries in the 1970s and 1980s with a sense of fun influenced by public-school *mores* (Johnston had himself attended Eton College). Not surprisingly, there was maintained in the BBC's approach to sport a keen amateur ethic. The Corporation resisted too close a focus on the popular 'betting' sports such as association football and greyhound racing, although horse racing, with its aristocratic following, was more favoured. The most recent detailed study of BBC radio in the interwar years has shown that the sports most covered were rugby union and motor sports, with horse racing and football a little way behind.[6] Until forced by competition from rival broadcasting networks in the later part of the century to adopt a more 'populist' style derived from the 'tabloid' press, the BBC clung to a mode of presentation that cherished dignity, neutrality and even a degree of insouciance in the reporting of sport. In 1949 commentators at a soccer match between England and Italy were enjoined by their producer to stimulate a sense of partisanship whilst not 'groaning' every time a English move broke down.[7] S. J. de Lotbiniere ('Lobby'), head of television Outside Broadcasts in the early 1950s, developed a notably patrician style which he communicated to his commentators: identifying the two sides, and explaining the rules, techniques and context all formed part of an *informative* approach to describing play which eschewed any attempt to transform the process into a cheap entertainment. 'There's very little time', noted 'Lobby' in an internal memo, 'for any but the most memorable wisecracks'.[8]

Such an ethos ensured that the BBC maintained the traditions of the 'quality' press in covering a range of sports from an educational perspective. Attention to essentially participatory sports such as athletics, through coverage of the AAA championships, increased interest in and the esteem of such sports.[9] Radio also helped other sports, notably cricket and boxing, to acquire a wider appeal, often among a new audience of women and young people.[10] Alongside the amateur principle was another feature of the BBC's approach to broadcasting: its emphasis on the nation. The Crawford Committee of 1926 had stressed that the BBC should be a 'trustee for the nation', and in taking up this idea the Corporation became one of the principal agencies through which an identity of the British nation was fashioned.[11] This was achieved in sport by the direct broadcasting, where possible, of national sporting occasions such as the FA Cup Final, the big horse-racing events, test matches, Wimbledon and the Boat race. As Briggs has noted, these came to be regarded by the BBC as 'musts'.[12] Moreover, the Corporation succeeded in this without, at the same time, neglecting a sense of localism. Indeed, as Briggs has also pointed out, Reith always distinguished between centralization of control and centralization of content, allowing regional directors much latitude to exploit opportunities for local material in their own way.[13] Until at least the 1950s there was a strong element of regionalism in the BBC's radio output. The North Region, for example, became noted for its 'exceptionally large number of outside broadcasts'. They included many sporting occasions such as the 'Roses' cricket matches between Lancashire and Yorkshire, which allowed local rivalries within the region to be given play.

As a means of communicating sport radio was overtaken by television during the final third of the twentieth century. As the American sports entrepreneur Branch Rickey once observed: 'Radio stimulates interest. Television satisfies it.' Whether this is true of radio is difficult to say. Mike Huggins, in his recent work on radio, tends to be sceptical about it. While accepting that radio helped some sporting events to acquire a national status they might otherwise never have attained – the Oxford-Cambridge boat race being a clear example – he finds no strong evidence to support Rickey's claim that radio stimulated interest in sport. Huggins's emphasis, however, is on attendance at sporting contests; some Football League clubs certainly felt this was adversely affected by broadcasting, but Huggins seems to think that on the whole attendance benefited from exposure to radio. But whether this served to create a deeper sporting culture, with more people experiencing their sport at home rather than going to matches, is an interesting issue. It seems likely, though in the last analysis we cannot be certain. What is certain is that radio retains an important niche in communicating information and ideas about sport. The ability of radio to respond quickly to events gives it an immediacy that television lacks, and there are still many radio companies around the world depending heavily on their sports coverage to keep listeners.

Television

In the 1950s the BBC began to develop its coverage of sport on television, and, in the face of the challenge from ITV, to cultivate a stronger emphasis on 'entertainment' than had previously been evident in radio. Rugby league quickly came into prominence. It served as an excellent substitute for what had long been the most glaring omission in the BBC's sporting schedule: association football. The opposition of football's authorities, notably the Football League, to live transmissions of games on radio meant that, except for a brief spell of coverage in the late 1920s, it was not until after the Second World War that League fixtures were consistently broadcast on radio, and then only the second half of matches. The League, pressured especially by clubs in the lower divisions, opined that live broadcasts would drive away spectators, and it took the marked decline in spectating that occurred in the 1950s and early 1960s for the League slowly to shift its stance. There was, for example, a very brief arrangement with ITV in 1960 for the live coverage of First Division matches, but apart from the tele-recordings of League football matches, chiefly by the BBC, no sustained live-coverage arrangements were made until the deal with BSkyB in 1992, by which time 'first division' soccer was no longer administered by the League. The FA's attitude had, in general, been more tolerant, with the result that games within its jurisdiction – the FA Cup and England international fixtures – were frequently broadcast, especially if they did not clash with League fixtures. As television developed in the 1950s, and the BBC sought to maintain its reputation for sporting journalism with the introduction of popular programmes such as *Sportsview* and *Grandstand*, so the absence of football came increasingly to be filled by rugby league. National television coverage on the Saturday afternoon *Grandstand* programme took rugby league out of its previous regional confines and made of it a sport that viewers in all parts of the country became familiar with. No longer was it necessary, as it had been until a few years previously, for the Wembley Stadium authorities to publish an explanation of the rules of the game in the programme notes for the Final Tie for the benefit of southern spectators. The success of rugby league on television owed much to former rugby league manager and journalist Eddie Waring, who held the main commentating place from the early

1950s onwards. By the early 1970s he was established as a television 'star'. By contrast with the serious-minded approach to sports reporting still adopted, for example, by the football commentator Kenneth Wolstenholme, a disciple of the De Lotbiniere method, Waring quickly settled into a more relaxed, wise-cracking style. His jovial appearance and guttural northern speaking voice seemed to cast him in the role of music-hall comedian rather than traditional BBC commentator, a part that Waring himself was all-too-ready to exploit with a store of jokes and quips. By such a combination of words and pictures rugby league became a television entertainment. But many of its followers in the North had mixed feelings about this transformation. On the one hand they were pleased to see their game and its heroes receive recognition to rival that of rugby union. On the other they were often very sceptical of a process which, especially in the 'stage northerner' role assumed by Waring, seemed to be trivializing the game.[14]

The trivialization of sport as a consequence of increasingly sophisticated techniques of television presentation has been an idea asserted by many writers. The American historian Benjamin Rader, for example, has argued strongly that the dramatization of sport on television has resulted not only in rule changes but also in a transformation of the style and ethics of sports.[15] This idea links in some ways with the process described by Alan and John Clarke in a British context as the supplanting of the 'sporting event' by the 'media event'.[16] The traditional experience has been replaced with something manufactured in a television studio, not for a 'spectator' but for a 'viewer' and, ultimately in many cases, for a 'consumer' of advertising. Rader instances boxing as a sport where this trend is very clearly exemplified. Rugby league might, in less dramatic form, be seen as a victim of this process, especially after its takeover by global television in the mid-1990s. By this time, with the introduction of yet slicker methods of presentation to attract the viewers' attention and interest in a whole range of sports, it might be claimed that Rader's point has acquired even greater force. A number of innovations have certainly taken the experience of sport well away from what it once was for the 'ordinary spectator'. The mediating role played by the commentator has been strengthened by the development of the team of 'pundits', orchestrated by the 'anchorman', whose presence in the studio at important events is designed to tell viewers what to watch out for in the forthcoming spectacle, and how to think about it afterwards. As celebrities in their own right they also add a touch of glamour to the programme. Such production values have been clearly illustrated in recent coverage of the Olympic Games and the football World Cup. In the latter case the presentation of the 1998 competition in France even sought to bring the city of Paris into the studio alongside the experts, with the use of a huge back-projection depicting some of the city's best-known landmarks. Visually, the pleasure of the sporting spectacle has been enhanced to include such features as the high aerial shot from an airship, underwater cameras at swimming events, the 'camera in the stump' shot in cricket, the tracking shot from the touchline in rugby and football, and the ubiquitous action replay, either in slow motion or in 'real time'. Cricket, once considered to be a repository of tradition, has broken many long-established conventions in the aftermath of Kerry Packer's innovative presentational techniques in World Series Cricket (WSC) in the 1970s.

There are, however, problems with the notion that television trivializes sport. All cultural experiences and texts derive their meaning from a complex interplay of influences which serve also to change them. It is not helpful to think of the sporting experience, or any other, as being subject to a fixed, authentic 'essence' which has a prior validity. Rather, we should approach sport as a set of meanings which change according to the varied and unequal interests that are brought to bear on them. Cricket is a sport on which a good deal of such attention has been focused. Opponents of the changes in form and duration of cricket play that were introduced for commercial reasons from the 1960s onwards have pointed to what they regard as a 'debasement' of the game's essence. The idea of cricket in the late-nineteenth and early-twentieth centuries was of a slowly evolving battle of wits expressed, at its best, in the beautiful arts of batting and bowling. A hundred years later this aesthetic seemed less compelling, and there are many who will argue that the new approaches to the game since the 1960s have injected fresh life, interest and money into cricket, thus resuscitating a game that was in danger of becoming moribund. However, no matter what one's personal preference might be, there can be little doubt that these new forms were financially necessary for the game. Limited-over matches, especially of the Twenty/20 variety, represent neither more, nor less, the 'genuine' version of cricket than does the traditional form. They are simply a changed version of an evolving sport.

Fictions

One interesting source of information about sport is the stories about it found in imaginative fiction such as novels. They have a long history. One of the first major novels to have sport as a part of its narrative was Thomas Hughes's *Tom Brown's Schooldays*, published in 1857. The book and the numerous film and television adaptations of it have enthralled several generations of readers/viewers with the story of Tom, the country squire's son from Berkshire, his friend East, and the travails they succeed manfully in overcoming at Dr Arnold's public school, Rugby, in the 1830s. It is a story about the new educational curriculum being developed by Arnold, in which the religious and moral education of the boys was paramount. Sport, though it figures in the story, was probably not as prominent a subject in Arnold's plan as some subsequent admirers of the story have imagined, though *Tom Brown's Schooldays* is often taken as the classic text of what has come to be called 'muscular Christianity' – that combination of physical and spiritual virtues that defined the mid-Victorian gentleman. Though a very English story, the book was very popular in the United States where it spawned a whole school of American sport fiction, much of it aimed at a juvenile readership. In the shape of fictional schoolboy heroes such as Frank Merriwell, Chip Hilton and the Kid from Tomkinsville a noble idea of sport, fair play and the good society was purveyed to young American readers right through the period from the 1890s until the 1960s. The American sport hero, says Michael Oriard, the foremost historian of these developments, was 'industrious, persistent, honest, brave, steady, generous, self-sacrificing'.[17] In Britain the example set by Hughes has been amply followed in children's fiction. Understanding upper middle-class, public-school morality without taking the influence of this literature into account is impossible. If, moreover, it was a meaning system inspired by an elite, its effects reached down to other points in the social hierarchy. Through children's comics, annuals and cheap fiction the ethos of the public school became a subject for popular culture. The presence over many years in the children's comic the *Dandy* of 'Lord Snooty and His Pals' testifies to this. Lord Snooty, in Eton collar and silk hat, led a group of very obviously working-class boys through a weekly series of adventures, just as Snooty's real-life counterparts led the nation through its adventures. School stories, and the place of sport within them, were an ideological staple in the mediation of gentlemanly virtues to the population at large. Michael Hardcastle perpetuated some of these same themes in the setting of boys' local soccer leagues. Teamwork, dedication to sport and honesty emerge as key virtues. In Hardcastle's *In the Net* (1971) Gary's devotion to football is fulfilled when he wins the respect of his teammates and, equally importantly, that of his father in a crucial match played (a concession to the women's movement here) against a team of girls, who prove to be tough opponents. In *Soccer Special* (1978) a lucky break provides Miles, whose fussy mother has persuaded him that he is too sickly for the game, with a chance to play clandestinely for his local team. He proves his ability with some impressive displays in goal, and shows unexpected reserves of strength when rescuing the injured team captain after a serious fall. Being accepted by their fellows and achieving success at sport ensure for both Gary and Miles the transition into the realm of masculinity, following periods of uncertainty brought on by doubting mothers or strained personal relationships at new schools. What are prized in these stories are qualities not very different from those lauded in the public school verse of the beginning of the century.

Nor was it just boys who were subjected to this fixation. Popular fiction for girls also used the expensive school and its sporting activities – often exclusive ones such as horse riding and yachting – as the setting for stories of female togetherness and adventure. Angela Brazil was the leading exponent of this genre, whose heyday was the interwar period, when weeklies such as *School Friend* reached a genuinely popular readership and purveyed, as Mary Cadogan and Patricia Craig observe, 'an impeccable moral code'.[18] At the end of the century the tradition was still strong in the work of writers such as Elinor M. Brent Dyer, whose stories of Chalet School centred on winter sports, or Bonnie Bryant who featured horse riding in her successful 'Saddle Club' series.

For some reason that is difficult to fathom sport has not been seen as a topic fit for the serious novel. David Storey did well to break this taboo in 1960 with *This Sporting Life* but few writers have followed Storey's lead, and none has produced such an elegant example of the genre. In America, on the other hand, sport has often been a prominent theme in the writings of leading novelists, among whom such celebrated figures as John Updike, Norman Mailer, Richard Ford and Philip Roth readily come to mind. In Updike's series of books on the character 'Rabbit' Angstrom, for example, which essentially chronicle the changing fortunes of Middle-America since the late 1950s, it is important that Rabbit has been a notable local basketball star in his Pennsylvanian home town. Though his playing career has ended before the first novel in the series even begins, the sport nevertheless is a recurring theme in the narrative, helping to define Rabbit as a person with memories of what might have been, to the extent that it is basketball that is partly responsible for his death in the last novel of the sequence. A similar use of sport is employed by Philip Roth in *American Pastoral* to show that the world of the hero, 'Swede' Levov, another former neighbourhood hero of the baseball field, basketball court and running track, has irredeemably changed. Roth's earlier novel, ironically entitled *The Great American Novel* (1973), is entirely about baseball, which it covers in a very eccentric way. It demands of the reader some understanding of the game and its history. Indeed, the novel is partly about history, and what we can believe is history. Roth deliberately blurs the line between 'truth' and 'fiction' to confuse the reader.

Historians have not in the main been inclined to give much credit to this kind of material as historical evidence. Whether they are explicitly historical, as for example many of the novels of Sir Walter Scott were, or whether they deal primarily with events contemporaneous with the time of writing, creative writing is considered to be unreliable as source material because it is based upon the imagination. Historians of sport are no exception to this general trend. With the exception of an active group of sport literature specialists in America, who formed the Sport Literature Association in the early 1980s, few have devoted serious attention to the ways in which the subject of sport has been worked over in creative form. I think, however, this omission is mistaken. Writers of imaginative literature, while not professing to do the same job as a historian, nonetheless create historical sources simply by being part of society and the historical process that is unfolding at the time in which they write. In that sense their output is like other kinds of historical documents; it does not exist primarily for the sake of future historians but is produced to serve a quite different and usually far more immediate, often commercial, purpose. Because novels, plays and poetry have this social existence and function, historians should be willing to interrogate them for what they are saying about the society in which they were produced. No novel exists in a vacuum, nor does it merely reflect what is going on in the 'real' world. In fact, some of what we understand as the real world comes from the ideas of reality offered to us in fiction.

Alf Tupper, 'The Tough of the Track': fictional hero of a great age of British middle-distance running. Tupper first appeared in the DC Thomson comic Rover in 1949 and continued to appear in Thomson publications until the early 1990s. A great favourite with teenage male readers, Tupper rose to the highest level of performance while remaining an ordinary working man. He was an amateur in the traditional sense of running for enjoyment rather than financial gain, and his character appealed to readers because of its gruff 'ordinariness'. Tupper shunned all pretence and ostentation, and opposed snobbery wherever he encountered it. (DC Thomson & Co Ltd).

Case Study Discussion 20

Jeffrey Hill, '"I'll Run Him": Alf Tupper, Social Class, and British Amateurism', *Sport in History,* **26, 3 (December 2006), pp. 502–19.**

From 1949 until 1960 stories about the young fictional middle-distance runner Alf Tupper, the 'Tough of the Track', appeared regularly in the British comic, the *Rover.* They were continued for the following 30 years in its successor publication, the *Victor.* They, along with their companion titles *Wizard, Adventure* and *Hotspur,* were published by the D.C. Thomson company of Dundee (Scotland) for young male readers, most of whom were probably working-class youths in their teens. Until transformed into a comic strip format in the early 1960s the D.C. Thomson titles contained densely written fiction which offered a 'good read'. In the 1950s the weekly issue of the *Rover,* for example, would have some half a dozen stories, each of 3–4000 words in length, based around a particular character. Tales of heroism and adventure predominated. Alongside the perennially appealing Alf Tupper there was, for example, Matt Braddock, an unconventional but brilliant Second World War pilot constantly at odds with his superiors. Although their heroism bordered on the improbable all the stories purveyed a form of 'realist' fiction contained within strictly conventional genres. In contrast to the Harry Potter tales popular in the 1990s and early 2000s the Tupper stories eschewed recourse to the supernatural or the magical in their narrative resolutions, relying instead on a social realism rooted in the workplace and athletics track.

Tupper was a first-class worker, always keen to do a good job. As he often asserted: 'work comes first'. But he loved running and the physical contestation it presented, and spent all his spare time either training for races or running in them. He had no other hobbies, few close friends, no family he cared to acknowledge and scarcely any possessions worth speaking of, but none of these mattered to him alongside work and sport. Unlike the sport heroes of a later generation Alf made no money whatsoever from sport, nor did he expect any, because he regarded himself as a true amateur who ran for the enjoyment he derived from it. He did, however, achieve high success. In a story that ran for several weeks during 1952, and which culminated in the final of the 1500 metres at the Helsinki Olympic Games, Alf ran the race of his life and won the gold medal. His fictional achievements were equal to those of the great real-life British runners of the day – Roger Bannister, Chris Chataway, Gordon Pirie and Derek Ibbotson.

An essential element of the stories was the excitement they generated in the readers' minds. Each story lasted over some three or four weeks, and would climax in a race. The stories followed a tried-and-tested formula in juvenile fictions where the hero is confronted by a series of 'tests' to prove his worth. In Alf's case these usually came in the form of a 'rush job' at his factory, involving him for a few days in arduous tasks that often meant working through the night. It made his performance at the running track on a Saturday, when Alf would arrive tired and weary, all the more remarkable, displaying the deep reserves of physical and mental strength he was able to draw upon in pursuit of excellence. From this, it may be imagined that the stories contained a subterranean layer of moral earnestness. The Tupper character could be read as a symbol of British achievement, a tribute to hard work and resistance to the easy blandishments of the consumer society (which was developing rapidly in the 1950s when the stories were becoming popular). Alf was thus a 'moral' hero, a role model of the kind that had previously been found in similar fictions going right back to Tom Brown. However, there was an additional, and somewhat unusual, dimension to Alf Tupper. He was a rebel; not, as in many Hollywood versions of rebelliousness, against the materialism and conformity of the affluent society, but against the British class system. He hated snobbery, and the snobbish types who abounded in his sport of athletics. Much of his sporting drive is fuelled by a determination to 'have a go at the swanks', to assert the place of the ordinary man and woman and to ensure their just reward. The stories therefore make their readers think about social relationships. They pose questions about the nature of society even if answers to the questions are not spelt out.

Film

One branch of sport fiction not to be overlooked is film. There have been several memorable representations of sport in documentary film, usually considered to be a more 'truthful' art form than feature film. The Olympic Games have often attracted film makers, notably Leni Riefenstahl's film of the 1936 Games, *Olympia*, which drew upon classical Greek images of the body in its opening sequences to establish a crypto-fascist tone in the montage. In 1964 the Tokyo Games were recorded on film by a leading Japanese director Kon Ichikawa, who succeeded in drawing an immediacy and drama from the athletic events which, up to that point, had rarely been achieved on the screen. By contrast the official FIFA film of the 1966 World Cup was a rather plodding affair, though well received by viewers, especially in England for obvious reasons. Documentary technique was used to more imaginative effect recently in Douglas Gordon's film of the French footballer Zinedine Zidane (*Zidane: a 21st century portrait*, 2006). Gordon used 17 differently placed cameras during a Real Madrid-Villareal match to focus only on Zidane himself, showing his every action over the length of the match (93 minutes) which is also the length of the film. If nothing else it revealed how little possession of the ball even a great player has in an entire game. More seriously the film gave its audience a unique perspective on one man's involvement. This is never offered in the controlled gaze of televised sport, in spite of television directors' love of the close-up, nor much opted for, one suspects, in the individual spectator's vision of a match.

Bearing this in mind, whether documentaries achieve a more 'truthful' representation of sport is open to question. Sometimes, perhaps in the case of *Zidane*, their very artfulness takes them away from reality. The film has received some critical acclaim but one doubts the extent of its appeal to the football fan as opposed to the film buff. Documentaries are rarely good 'box office'. Feature films, with their huge audiences, exercise a far greater influence over the public imagination. Sport has been the subject of a great many such feature films, especially in the United States where baseball in particular has furnished some excellent representations. Among the better known are Gary Cooper's portrayal of Lou Gehrig in *The Pride of the Yankees* (1942), an archetypal example of sporting idolatry and wartime patriotism; Barry Levinson's 1984 film version of Bernard Malamud's 1952 novel *The Natural*, which transformed the dark ending of the novel into a glorious celebration of baseball; and Phil Alden Robinson's *Field of Dreams* (1989), based on a novel of 1982 by W. P. Kinsella, *Shoeless Joe*. A point of reference in both the Levinson and Robinson films is the Black Sox scandal of 1919, when eight members of the Chicago White Sox were banned from baseball in contentious circumstances for 'fixing' a World Series. The incident has provided an intriguing and enigmatic story, not to mention a fascinating source of study in cultural history and memory.[19] It is especially noteworthy that the past quarter century has seen the fascination with the Black Sox case intensify. Its associations with lost innocence and its representation in many accounts as a conflict between labour and capital, good and evil, might have possessed a particular resonance at a time when changing values brought a longing for past certainties. Kinsella's *Shoeless Joe*, for example, is a magical fiction which conjures a restoration of justice for the damned eight, as in a certain sense does John Sayles's excellent *Eight Men Out* (1988), a radical, independent film maker's sympathetic portrayal of the Black Sox as victims of political circumstances and mean-minded employers. A feature film such as this is important therefore not so much in showing us what baseball was actually like in 1919 (though the film does a decent job of reconstruction) as in providing an imaginative reworking of a historic episode and reviving the history for contemporary consumption.

It is through films and novels of this kind that we can begin to understand something of the appeal to American males of a sport like baseball. Its mythic status in American society is accounted for by a number of factors; its longevity as an organized professional game; its supposed proliferation in the great defining national moment of the Civil War, when it supplanted the 'English' game of cricket; its expansion into leagues which incorporated all the major urban centres and, by extension, many of the little leagues in the rural areas; its multiracial appeal in spite of the fact that baseball was segregated until the late 1940s; its ability to generate national heroes – Ty Cobb before the First World War, Babe Ruth in the 1920s, and his successors Lou Gehrig, Joe DiMaggio, Willie Mays, Mickey Mantle and Mark McGwire. Above all, according to Allen Guttmann, it is baseball's capacity to evoke the pastoral in American society that explains its special fascination in the male psyche: its success as the 'national game' comes from a nostalgic association with small towns and the past. 'The Gestalt is a complex one', says Guttmann, 'which includes open space, grass, warm weather, the bright sun.'[20] Like cricket in England, baseball has the power to recall a lost past, and films can help in that process of recalling as well as any medium.

Case Study Discussion 21

The Natural, Barry Levinson (dir.), Tristar Pictures, USA (1984).

An interesting film for all those keen on baseball and US history. It is based on the novel by Bernard Malamud (*The Natural,* Farrar, Straus and Giroux, NY, 1952) who set his story about the baseball player Roy Hobbs in the pre-Second World War era, a 'golden age' of the sport when legendary figures such as Babe Ruth and Lou Gehrig bestrode the ball parks. As the framework of his novel Malamud re-fashioned the Arthurian myth for modern times. The novel has many magical qualities, and he also gave his story a dark edge. The final scene, with its echoes of the Black Sox scandal of 1919, sees Roy Hobbs confronted by an admiring youngster who wants him to deny the allegations of corruption that have been levelled against him. '"Say it ain't true Roy", says the boy. When Roy looked into the boy's eyes he wanted to say it wasn't but couldn't, and he lifted his hands to his face and wept many bitter tears.' By contrast Levinson gives his audience an upbeat resolution. The highly gifted Hobbs, played by Robert Redford, unequivocally rejects an attempt by his unscrupulous employer to buy him off, and succeeds, in an impressive cinematic climax of images and music, in hitting the home run that secures victory for his team, the Knights. Though the film retains some of Malamud's sourness towards the game – in its depiction of crowds and baseball management, for example, and especially its ambiguous treatment of women – there is a pervasive warmth about it; golden sunlight bathes many a scene, bringing out the Redford image of the good guy to maximum effect. The final wordless scene is a homage to the family and the farm in American life. In many ways it presents a nostalgic look back at a time in baseball, before players' strikes and big earnings when the game, in spite of its scandals, seemed simpler and more American. It was of course a time of the *segregated* game, with separate leagues for white and black players, and *The Natural* deals unquestioningly with the white leagues as if they are the *natural* form of the game. It is undoubtedly a sentimental and conservative film whose portrayal of America seems old-fashioned for the 1980s, but it was a success at the box office and it might be that it suited a particular mentality that Ronald Reagan, elected president in 1980, attempted both to foster and exploit. Reagan was seeking to restore American 'honour' after Vietnam and the perceived failings of his predecessor (Jimmy Carter) over the Iran hostage crisis. Reagan, a well-known film actor, had also been a radio commentator on baseball in his early days, and perhaps the film just managed to catch a particular moment in American history when the president appeared to be leading the United States back to a fondly imagined 'normality'.

Non-fictions: museums and heritage

There has been a significant move in recent years to encourage what is sometimes called 'public history'. This rather vague term (isn't all history 'public'?) usually implies history purveyed through channels of public, or perhaps more appropriately 'popular', communication such a television. Thus public history is often history produced in an attractive and non-academic way by star presenters such as Simon Schama and David Starkey. Equally it might also be a historical perspective conveyed in the form of 'heritage'. This is another unnecessary term, invented to describe what is when all is said and done just another form of historical activity. In spite of its rather unfortunate association in the 1980s with certain politically inspired initiatives, however, it has a worthwhile objective. One of the major sites of heritage is in fact the museum, a hallowed institution of historical activity since the nineteenth century, but which is currently undergoing some important transformations. Let us briefly illustrate this with an example from outside sport. At the time of writing these words the Ashmolean museum in Oxford was closed for a lengthy period.[21] The reason was that its collections, including some of the finest displays to be found anywhere of ancient Egyptian artefacts and Royal Worcester porcelain, are to be 'themed' and greater space made available for special exhibitions. Many of the artefacts previously on display in glass cases will never be brought out again as the public rooms are devoted to other kinds of visitor attractions. Much of this – which could be described as a 'dumbing down' of the museum – has to do with meeting government targets and earning public funding by bringing more visitors into the building. Since, unlike many other countries, there is (at the time of writing) no entrance fee to national museums in Britain that are in receipt of public funds, the museum directors have to make their displays as attractive as possible and, what is more, raise profits through sales in the shop and cafe.

This digression points up some of the pressures facing museums of all kinds. A growing number of such places are nowadays dedicated to creating a history of certain sports. In America, for example, there have long been 'halls of fame' devoted to commemorating the history of sports such as baseball, basketball and American football, to name but a few. In addition, there are several museums related to particular teams and their stadium; a case in point is the Green Bay Packers' museum in Green Bay, Wisconsin, which among other things gives much attention to a famous former coach Vince Lombardi. Such places are well suited to the new climate of public history because they trade on the popularity of sport, and when situated in an actual stadium are presented with potentially large 'captive' audiences on match days. The Manchester United museum at Old Trafford is a good British example, attracting large visitor numbers and, being strategically placed next to the shop, ensuring a good return on its part in the club's merchandising policy. A similar function is performed at the All-England Lawn Tennis and Croquet Club in south-west London, better known as Wimbledon. At the National

Football Museum in Preston[22] the first thing the visitor sees on entering is the shop, and the museum is located within Preston North End's football ground, so that on match days spectators scarcely need to detour in order to make a visit. At Twickenham, the home of English Rugby Union, there is a similar arrangement. The commercial purpose of the sport museum is thus clearly evident, but what of its educational purpose? What kinds of history might such a museum purvey?

There is, as may be imagined, a good deal of variety. Technical wizardry that enables an 'inter-active' relationship between visitors and exhibits frequently abounds, though many museums deal only with the particular sport or club, reviving memories of famous past events. The Manchester United museum is a good example; an attractive layout, with good gadgetry and film excerpts keep fans involved for hours, but within a very limited framework of club history. It is simply Manchester United, and a very narrow conception of it at that, which is here being glorified. By contrast, the National Football Museum, whilst not neglecting inter-activity, attempts to provide a serious contextualization of English football, showing the economic and social circumstances that shaped the development of the game. It offers a far more rounded picture of sport in society, without necessarily losing the emotional and aesthetic appeal that a museum of sport can provide through moving cinematic images, colour and visual displays. The museum offers a sensuous experience that cannot be felt by reading a book. Indeed, to judge a museum against the kind of history to be experienced through reading is unfair. The museum's means of communication is more limited, less nuanced. Nonetheless, this does not acquit some museums of criticism for offering a biased approach to their history. Many are seduced into concentrating only on the glory of the sport and its stars, and thus into a neglect of the less dramatic or charismatic aspects.

Case Study Discussion 22

The Wimbledon Tennis Museum, All-England Lawn Tennis Club, Wimbledon, London (Curator: Honor Godfrey).

In February 2008 I was part of a team of historians and heritage specialists invited to visit Wimbledon. The visit had two parts. The first was a tour of the All-England Club grounds conducted by a professional Blue Badge tour guide which gave us the authentic visitor experience. Second was an academic seminar introduced by a paper from Honor Godfrey outlining the aims and objectives of the Museum. Here were two quite distinct levels of history – the one light, anecdotal, based around popular features of the Wimbledon story (the pony roller, strawberries and cream, Henman Hill, the BBC studio, Boris Becker's rented house, and so forth), with the overriding trope that Wimbledon is for *everyone*, not a rich person's preserve. This was illustrated by the fact that admission to the ground (though not to the main courts) could be had (in 2008) for as little as £20.

The seminar concerned a more serious representation of history, though in line with recent developments in museology it downplayed the strictly *educational* in the interests of telling a lively story. Whilst it retains a traditional museum display of objects rather than an 'inter-active electronic' experience the Museum is very conscious of meeting the varied demands of its visitors, for whom it provides an eclectic range of perceptions and observations, focusing on Wimbledon's *uniqueness* as a place (grass plays an important part in this); also brought out is the power and movement of modern tennis, and the Englishness of Wimbledon, reflected in the various traditions going back through 1922, when the present stadium was built, to the Victorian origins of the sport. It is nonetheless, as its curator describes it, 'a museum for the 21st century', an appellation perhaps most clearly reflected in its attempt to be inclusive – to represent 'as many voices as possible'. In a recent re-designing of the Museum various focus groups had been consulted to determine what people expected to see in a tennis museum: schoolchildren, for example, had emphasized touch screens, virtual reality, costumes and players; overseas groups had stressed the pilgrimage aspects of Wimbledon, and wanted film clips and a focus on the Centre Court; the Lawn Tennis Association (LTA) had said that the Museum should remain a museum, and not become a 'tennis experience'.

The problem, I think, with this very worthy and serious attempt to represent the sport is that Wimbledon is a difficult idea to conceptualize. It simultaneously 'means' different things.

- The **sport** of tennis, with which 'Wimbledon' is synonymous
- An event – the tournament held at Wimbledon each year for two weeks in June
- The **club** where, for 50 weeks of the year, tennis is played of which we hear nothing; and also the location for an organization – the All England Lawn Tennis and Croquet Club – that has an important political role in the sport
- A **place** – a suburb of south London, that has also had other interesting sport histories (of speedway and association football especially).

Some of these aspects are represented in the history portrayed at the Wimbledon Museum; but others are not present at all. For the historian, then, the Museum, whilst presenting a fascinating picture of tennis in which the star players inevitably, perhaps, occupy the centre of the canvas, is equally notable for what is left out of the story: the non-elite activities, the problems of sporting injuries and performance enhancing drugs; the work of the back-room staff; the place of the club in the immediate neighbourhood. If the true test of a sport museum is whether it features the ladies who make the tea, most do not pass. I do not want to suggest of the Wimbledon Museum (as I might of certain other places) that it designs a shop window only to cast tennis in its most favourable light – it is decidedly *not* a simple exercise in sport propaganda. But Wimbledon does remind historians that our subject, whether in print or in museum form, is an elusive one; that the museum's collage of words and pictures making up what the public might see as a *natural* vision of Wimbledon is in fact a very carefully *selected* series of *representations*. It is this process of *selection*, and the presuppositions and biases that have guided it, that we need to keep in mind when visiting museums, as well as when reading history books.

In the last analysis, the question is about what in literature is often called reader reception; what did you think of this book? In museum terms, what did you like/dislike about this museum, and what are your expectations of the museum's 'history'? The question is best answered by asking the reader to do her/his own fieldwork and self-analysis.[23]

Conclusion

This chapter has dealt with topics about which historians of sport often express a certain ambivalence. In some cases, for example the reporting of sports events in newspapers, historians have been eager to quarry such sources for the primary material they contain. But when it comes to analysing the *effects* of newspapers, or radio and television programmes, on their readers, listeners and viewers, many historians are a good deal more sceptical about the value of such a project. This is yet more noticeable in relation to the ways in which creative writing deals with the subject of sport. The essential problem is that effects cannot be measured according to the conventional methods applied by historians. To put it another way, how do we judge the impact of a newspaper editorial or a television presentation on the individuals at the receiving end, to whom the editorial or presentation is addressed? How can we tell whether the ideas about sport contained in a novel are accepted (or even noticed) by the reader? To be sure, these are not easy questions, especially for a historian whose readers and viewers are no longer with us. Therefore some historians would prefer to leave the material alone, or at least to leave the question of its effects alone. This chapter has therefore traversed some difficult territory, dealing with material that is without doubt consumed by a very large audience and which is responsible for conveying some ideas about sport. Or so we might assume. It seems a reasonable assumption that what we know about sport, how we react to it, whether we feel it is a good or a bad thing, is in some way shaped by the various 'media' that communicate opinion and information to us. Quite how this works we are not sure. But our uncertainties should not prevent us from enquiring and, where necessary, making intelligent guesses about 'effects'.

As an intriguing reflection on the whole question of mediating sport, there is a perceptive observation about the reporting of association football made by sportswriter Gary Imlach in the biography of his father, the Scottish footballer Stewart Imlach. Talking about the FA Cup competition in England, Imlach notes the prevalence of the 'giant-killing' narrative: that is, stories told in the media about small clubs defeating bigger ones in cup matches ('cup-ties'). Once, he says, these were reported *after* the event, if and when such a victory had occurred; but there is an increasing insistence nowadays for the giant-killer narrative to frame the entire event of the cup tie. '[...] there's too much money invested in the game for everyone concerned not to extract maximum value. So the giant-killing story is told in advance, as a hedge against it not being supported by the facts once the game begins.' Imlach goes on to conclude that, while football has always been 'full of stories' games are now 'nudged into one of a handful of narrative shapes set aside for the purpose.' They are now 'driving the game, or at least *the way we're invited to think about it*' (my italics).[24] It is a telling point, and one that has relevance for our understanding of sport far beyond simply association football.

The historical perspective mapped out in this chapter shows a long-term sequence of media forms: the principal ones are the newspaper press, radio and television. The press has been with us now for well over a century, while radio and television are more recent. Their relative influence has changed, but each still occupies an important place. What is more they have drawn on each other, and continue to do so. Television might nowadays dominate the transmission of sports news and events but it is impossible to understand the content of television sport without some knowledge of what has preceded it in radio and the press; from them many conventions about the conception and reporting of sport have issued. At the same time newspaper coverage of sport has changed in the face of the more immediate news available through radio and television. Where once the press, as the major channel of information, dealt in direct reportage of sporting events, it now concentrates more on developing stories out of the factual events, which are already known to readers. Technical improvements have of course been made in all forms of representation. The sport spectacle is transformed by television especially into a parallel *media* event using all the technological wizardry available. These developments not only serve to intensify the viewers' excitement but also have an importance for the historians. One major weakness in the historical sources available has concerned *how* games were played before very recent times; pictorial and photographic evidence gives only a superficial sense of styles of play, as for a long time after the invention of moving film only fragments of footage were available. Sustained film coverage of sports events prior to the Second World War, and even after it in many cases, is all too rare. From about the 1960s that began to change. Assuming therefore that good film and television archives are maintained by the broadcasting organizations, historians in the future will have at their disposal the means of tracing developments in sporting practice in a far more rounded way than has ever been possible before. Visual technology, however, still has its limitations. In spite of great advances in technical equipment and know-how what is filmed only reveals what is in the mind of the television producer or camera operator; if their concern is with close-ups of personalities, or the action that is perceived to constitute the dramatic or controversial 'highlights' of a contest, future historians might yet despair that a tabloid mentality has deprived them of opportunities for a fuller appreciation of the sporting event.

Thus the idea of sport is constantly being produced and reproduced in various ways through various branches of the media. It is a process without beginning or end. What we understand as sport mainly exists for us through this process.

Study Questions

1. From your own reading of sport reports in newspapers, what is your view of how they are constructed and what they tell you? What is their relationship to information provided by other media?
2. Radio is a neglected topic in sport history; how might you devise a small research project, using audio and written materials, to rectify this neglect?
3. To what extent do you consider the media coverage of sport to be over-concerned with 'personalities'? Relate the idea of a 'media' spectacle to that of an event experienced by a 'live' spectator.
4. List the novels/plays/films you consider to have portrayed sport convincingly. How did they achieve their effect?

Further Reading

John Bale, *Anti-Sport Sentiments in Literature: Batting for the Opposition* (Abingdon: Routledge, 2008).

Jeffrey Hill, *Sport and the Literary Imagination* (Oxford: Peter Lang, 2006).

Kevin Moore, *Museums and Popular Culture* (London: Cassell, 1997).

Michael Oriard, *Reading Football: How the Popular Press Created an American Spectacle* (Chapel Hill: University of North Carolina Press, 1993).

Garry Whannel, *Television, Sport and Cultural Transformation* (London: Routledge, 1992).

CHAPTER 6

Sport in a Globalized World

The idea of 'globalization' has acquired a strong currency among many academics in recent years. It has been applied to all manner of international developments and relations in a number of fields – political, economic, cultural. There is a tendency to see it as a description of the way in which we are all now members of one homogeneous world – a 'global village' – and therefore influenced by the same decisions made by the large corporations that dominate the world market. It has been regarded as the extension of capitalist relations ever wider in the world and the forms of exploitation that are a necessary part of it – hence the protests, sometimes the scene of violence, that have been staged at meetings of the G20 and which are sometimes known as the anti-globalization movement. Whilst there might be value in this notion, we nonetheless have to bear in mind that the process of globalization has equally be seen as a good thing in that it has removed some of the inequalities that formerly attended world economic relationships in an age of imperialism. One of the problems with using the term 'globalization' is that it means different things to different people, and indeed the entire process has somewhat contradictory features. As well as being a unifying force, it can also cause fragmentation and tensions. Globalization is, in fact, a problematical concept, when applied either to describe a process in the world or as a means of understanding the contemporary international relations. It is not something that can taken as a 'ready made' explanation of how the world works. In sport, there have been influential studies of the 'globalizing' process but, as the authors of an important book on labour migration have reminded us, the concept is sometimes used uncritically and in a way that takes little or no account of history.[1]

Sport nevertheless provides a rich terrain for discussing this topic. When Manchester United, a football club that not so very long ago drew its support from parts of the city of Manchester and its surrounding suburbs, can now claim to have a fan base of over 50 million people worldwide, and see its team

116

shirts (which, also not so very long ago, were worn only by its players) on the backs of adults and children almost everywhere in the world, clearly something very interesting is going on. Much of this is of recent origin, but there are aspects of it that stretch back a long way. Historically there have been examples of transnational interaction in sport that might be seen as early instances of globalization, and which when examined closely reveal the complexity of the process at work. There are various ways in which we might approach this process of internationalization. In this chapter I want to focus upon three.

- The transmission or 'diffusion' of sports
- Player movements and the opening up of labour markets
- The development and influence of international sport organizations

Sport and diffusion

The process of cultural diffusion contains several examples of practices that have originated in a particular place and been either successfully or unsuccessfully exported to other countries in the world. In non-sporting terms the history of the Hollywood film industry provides an excellent example of successful cultural export to other countries, not all of them anglophone. In sport, however, American practices have not always travelled well, baseball being a case in point; outside the United States it has met with success only in certain Latin American countries (Cuba and the Dominican Republic) and Japan. Basketball has fared better. In a broader sense, however, some European publics responded enthusiastically to American influences in sport, especially after the First World War when the idea of 'modernity' was strong. In Weimar Germany, for example, boxing attracted the avant-garde who embraced its honest vulgarity and naked commercialism in preference to the cultural legacies of the despised old regime. America had much to do with this. But no sport, no matter where it has originated, has met with greater success on a global scale than association football. Quite what determines the success or failure of these initiatives is sometimes hard to pinpoint. Is it related to the intrinsic nature of the sport itself; or to the environment into which the exported sport is sent; or to the response of entrepreneurs and opinion shapers in the recipient country?

   The case of cricket, an English game that has been successfully exported to a number of countries, provides an interesting case study, revealing among other things that the idea of 'globalization' involves a far from straightforward process of the international transmission of cultural practices. Presently (2009) the world governing body of cricket – the International Cricket Council (ICC) – accords membership to 104 countries, albeit separated into three different categories depending upon the stage of development of the game. Ten of them are granted top status ('full members') as countries entitled to participate against each other in international fixtures known as 'test' matches.[2]

All are former members of the British Empire, and several retain a place in the Commonwealth. An early example of cricket as a 'global' game is provided if we examine a book by a leading cricket player, writer and administrator from the period just before the First World War

Case Study Discussion 23

P. F. Warner ed., *Imperial Cricket* **(London: London and Counties Press Association Ltd., 1912).**

Pelham Warner was an influential figure in world cricket for many years. This book, which deals with a variety of aspects of the game, commemorates the spread of cricket through the British Empire to become, by 1912, the game with the most extensive global reach. The timing of its publication acknowledges the hosting in England of the first (and for many years the only) multinational cricket event – the Triangular Tournament between England, Australia and South Africa, which Warner saw as a fitting climax of the game's imperial development. In fact, the event was something of a flop, marred to a large extent by bad weather. *Imperial Cricket*, however, is more than a public relations exercise for the tournament. Fundamentally it extols the virtues of cricket as a national game in England that has been exported to the colonies and dominions to forge a worldwide union: '... a brotherhood of cricket which neither time nor distance can obliterate' (p. ix). The undercurrent of optimism that works through the book, suggesting the British Empire as a force for stability and good in the world, a source from which 'civilized' influences might radiate, has an ironic quality for the later reader, aware of what was to follow soon after the book's publication.

Several contributors deal with various cricket topics but the main content of *Imperial Cricket* is a series of descriptions of the state of the game in all the various parts of the Empire; from countries such as Australia and South Africa, where it was well advanced, to those (such as the East Africa Protectorate and Malaya) in which the game had scarcely begun to establish a foothold. The arrangement and tone of the content creates a metropolitan-centred perspective on the game's development: early chapters deal with England and the evolution of cricket there, attention devoted to institutions such as Lord's and the MCC, the Surrey county club and its ground at the Oval, Oxford and Cambridge Universities, the Army and the Navy. There is even a lengthy chapter on the connection of the British royal family with cricket – not, it might be thought, a particularly strong one, and scarcely a topic to merit such prominent treatment. There is no mention of domestic English cricket outside these narrow limits. An indication, however, that English hegemony is not forever assured in this world relationship is provided in the chapter on Australia, where the author asks 'Why is Australian cricket so good?'; he offers a series of points that might be taken as a prescription for English administrators in their own domestic game, to guard against being overtaken by the Australians. But the overriding spirit is one of solidarity; no matter what the outcome of cricket matches between the different parts of the Empire might be the universal ethic that the game bestows is sovereign. Lord Hawke, a former Yorkshire captain and a still-powerful voice in cricket lore, sums it up: 'on the cricket grounds of the Empire is fostered the spirit of never knowing when you are beaten, of playing for your side and not for yourself, and of never giving up a game as lost' (p. 1).

To explain why cricket was effectively implanted in these places requires the consideration of a number of interrelated preconditions.

1. the existence of an already well-developed game in the country of origin, with skilled practitioners able to transmit their know-how and a group of 'agents' (who might, or might not, be commercial entrepreneurs) willing to promote the game elsewhere.
2. cricket is a relatively sophisticated game requiring an understanding of its rules, and the spatial, financial and technical resources to provide the necessary equipment and playing conditions (large field with appropriate 'wicket' or 'pitch').
3. an infrastructure of voluntary association in which to establish the *club* basis of the game.
4. as a *team* game cricket requires social proximity, most likely found in an urban context.
5. a common language and a basic level of education are necessary for the cultural conditions in which a game may flourish, and not be seen as alien to local traditions of sports and pastimes.

All of these conditions were met in cricket's case in countries of the Empire. However, they were not met universally; in other words, they occurred in certain parts of the countries and among certain groups of people. In India for example, cricket was far more likely to take hold in the courts of princes, with their strong associations with the British in the system of indirect rule, or among urban-based educated intellectuals (what are sometimes referred to as the 'western-educated elite', that is, indigenous people trained in the professions or working in government service, teaching, or even manual trades based in, for example, the railways. See below, Case Study Discussions 26–28). It was thus a game for those who had been, to a greater or lesser extent, 'westernized'. Conversely, cricket was not taken up by the peasantry who lived in what Gandhi once described as India's '800,000 villages'. This pattern of dissemination applied in much the same way in all the countries where cricket became established as a 'national' game with strong grass roots. In colonies where the indigenous population far outweighed the colonizers in numbers, dissemination was circumscribed by features of social and racial exclusiveness. This was the case in the Caribbean, for example. The Trinidadian radical C. L. R. James noted with some acerbity the marked status and race distinctions that characterized cricket organization in his home country; as he put it, referring to two of the high-status cricket clubs in Trinidad, 'I would have been more easily elected to the MCC than to either.'[3] But despite this (James suggested it was *because* of this) cricket nonetheless attained a popularity in the West Indies that ultimately enabled these differences to be transcended. As elsewhere, in spite of often severe political antagonisms, especially from the 1930s onwards, the cultural bonds of language and urban environment permitted the game to become a pastime shared by more than just a small section of society.

In other contexts, however, these preconditions did not always produce the same outcome. The chief exception is North America (Canada and the United States), where cricket was implanted by English expatriates in the mid-nineteenth century but failed to take root, being overtaken by the end of the nineteenth century as the national summer game by baseball. Several different explanations have been put forward to explain this failure. Some, relating to factors such as climate and supposed American 'taste', are rather impressionistic and do not stand up to serious scrutiny; but those emphasizing resources (including the means of *promoting* new sports) deserve greater attention. In an important article Jason Kaufman and Orlando Patterson have provided a thoughtful and wide-ranging approach to this question.

Case Study Discussion 24

Jason Kaufman and Orlando Patterson, 'Cross-National Cultural Diffusion: The Global Spread of Cricket', *American Sociological Review*, 70 (February, 2005), pp. 82–110.

With much justification the authors systematically dismantle many of the explanations that have been put forward, not only about the failure of cricket in North America but also about the general responses to dissemination advanced by sociologists and political scientists. In essence what Kaufman and Patterson achieve is a switch of emphasis away from the process of *transmission* towards that of *adoption*, and they do this by focusing upon Canadian and US social relations, specifically the relationships between elites and others. Though cricket did secure a position in some sectors of North American life – notably Philadelphia and a select few New England colleges, together with some high-status educational establishments in Canada – what characterizes its development there is cricket's failure to expand from them; rather, the game was preserved there and eventually atrophied. It was the unwillingness of the elites who had espoused the game to *share* it with other social groups that partly explains cricket's inability to expand. Alongside this social inaction was the very dynamic promotion of baseball, presented by entrepreneurs such as A. G. Spalding as a vigorous *American* sport in contrast to what was depicted as an effete British one. Thus, in North America, it was not so much the dissemination of cricket that was a problem (the game exported well enough in the middle years of the nineteenth century when it rivalled baseball) but the lack of drive to internal dissemination. Cricket in America became rather like rugby union in England, a game deliberately confined to a self-defined social elite. This situation contrasted sharply with that in British colonies, where in spite of (and perhaps even because of) quite rigid racial and status segregation, cricket prospered because it was actively promoted among the masses. In territories such as India and the West Indies colonial elites felt sufficiently secure to encourage the game as a 'civilizing' influence among indigenous peoples, while in Australia and New Zealand, with larger white settler populations forging a 'new' society, there was a strong incentive to bring the classes together in a unified social and political mission.

As the game in these places developed, a process occurred similar to that which had characterized the diffusion of industrial methods across the globe. Just as early industrializers such as Britain found themselves at a disadvantage compared with later ones (Germany, the United States, Russia, Italy) who were more easily able to adopt modern techniques of production and capital formation, so the early teachers of cricket were soon overtaken by some of their pupils. Thus, quite quickly, cricket in Australia developed a high level of organization and skill, and Australian teams became more than a match for those from England, establishing a dominance in competitions (appropriately known as 'test' matches) that lasted with only a few interruptions throughout the following century. Likewise the West Indies, India, Pakistan, Sri Lanka and South Africa have all enjoyed periods, in some cases quite lengthy ones, in which the pupils have outplayed the masters.

Notwithstanding these shifting patterns of dominance, what the case of cricket demonstrates is the capacity of the game to be exported. It would be unwise to dissociate this process from the broader context of colonialism and imperialism in which it took place. In a sense, cricket was part of a movement of cultural imperialism that had its origins in Britain in the later eighteenth century. In considering the diffusion of sport in this framework there is one very obvious exception that merits consideration. It concerns American sports. The twentieth century saw the rise of American power and influence in a number of forms, both physical (military, political, financial, economic) and intellectual (ideas, entertainments, the arts). The cinema provides possibly the foremost example of these trends, which so concerned previously dominant European countries after the Second World War that people began to speak of the 'dwarfing of Europe'. Sport, however, played a relatively small part in all this. When the American businessman and former baseball player A. G. Spalding attempted to export baseball to Europe before and after the First World War he met with relatively little success. England's well-established sporting culture – both amateur and professional – made for difficulties when attempting to introduce new sports, and on the whole those coming from America put down only shallow roots. Speedway and greyhound racing, both American in origin (though the former's introduction to Britain in the 1920s owed much to Australian entrepreneurs and riders) were the two most successful, especially in the period from the 1920s to the 1950s. Baseball also established a toehold in the North West of England where, with financial assistance from the football pools promoter John Moores, a number of professional teams were established in Lancashire and Yorkshire towns during the 1930s.[4] It was never anything more than a minor sport, however, either at the commercial or amateur levels. Basketball, a game invented in America in the 1890s, was confined in England largely to the secondary-school curriculum. In other countries, however, baseball and basketball flourished. The former became very popular in Japan and Central America, especially Cuba. Basketball was rapidly exported to the outside world, with the YMCA taking the lead in introducing it to China. 'By 1915', says Allen Guttmann, 'it was popular in every modern society, and in many not so modern ones.'[5]

Clues as to why these sports caught on are provided by the case of baseball in Japan. The country was not without its native sports of course, but baseball, the introduction of which goes back to the early 1870s, was associated with 'modernity' at a time when Japanese economy and society was undergoing a process of rapid modernization. Not surprisingly the game attracted a strong following in universities, and it was at Washeda and Keio that regular fixtures were set up before 1914. By the mid-1920s the Tokyo Six Universities League had come into being, together with an extensive network of school baseball providing a summer tournament that has retained its popularity into the present day. 'Barnstorming' tours in the interwar years by Major League professionals from the United States further boosted the game, and in spite of the Second World War a professional baseball structure was established by the late 1940s. The American occupation and general cultural imperialism further strengthened the place of Japanese baseball, which in the second half of the twentieth century achieved a remarkable degree of interaction with the American professional leagues; player exchanges helped sustain the game in both countries, and a mark of Japan's strength was seen in its winning the World Baseball Classic ('world cup') in 2006 and 2009. For the Americans it was a case of the 'pupil' defeating the 'master'; Japan roundly triumphed over them in the semi-finals, and the United States only achieved fourth slot in the final standings after Japan, South Korea and Venezuela.[6]

Case Study Discussion 25

Joseph L. Arbena, 'International Aspects of Sport in Latin America: Perceptions, Prospects, and Proposals', in E. Dunning, J. A. Maguire and R. E. Pearton, *The Sports Process: A Comparative and Developmental Approach* (Champaign, IL: Human Kinetics, 1993), pp. 151–67.

Arbena's is an important piece for the scope of its vision. He takes a panoptic view of sport development in Latin America, and what his discussion might lack in specific detail it more than makes up for in its overview of the forces that shape sport across a large and much traversed region. Arbena makes clear that the nature of sport in Latin America cannot be understood apart from the area's international (global and regional) context. This is evident, first of all, in the sports that occupy a predominant place in the region – soccer almost universally, cricket in the English-speaking

Caribbean, baseball in Cuba and the Dominican Republic, as well as motor racing, polo, tennis, golf, rugby, boxing and horse racing. Arbena contends that sports such as these had an ambivalent impact upon local society. They had the capacity, to an extent, to draw local elites into a circle of dependence that assisted the creation of a neocolonial economic relationship with American and European-based interests. Equally, however, and over time, sports became the site for asserting local pride and thereby challenging overseas dominance. The boxing match in 1923 between the Argentinian champion Luis Angel Firpo and the American world champion Jack Dempsey is cited as an instance where, in spite of a controversial defeat, Firpo was hailed as having given Argentina a position of prominence in world affairs for the first time. But when it comes to assigning to sport a role in the fostering of national identity, Arbena advises caution. There are as many examples of sporting contests arousing internal conflicts (regional, gender, ethnic, class) as there are of victories on the sports field (Firpo's challenge to Dempsey, or Brazil's World Cup successes, for example) aiding the process of national unity. The contradictory effects of sport come through in other ways too. One of the continuing problems of Latin American societies has been their relationship with the outside world, and the extent to which global economic structures have enabled them to throw off dependency status and pursue a path of 'development'. Arbena pinpoints a number of ways in which sports might have served this process; through, for example, their being part of a modern civil society of clubs, schools and commerce that worked to modify traditional Latin American society; in short, to 'Europeanize' local society. Associated with this are several 'justifications' identified by modernizers for having a strong sporting culture – that it encourages hygiene, promotes teamwork and self-discipline, reduces crime and contributes to a general sense of well-being. One of the most striking features of South American sport in the second half of the twentieth century has been its increasing integration with the sporting world of Europe and North America, a process that some claim to have aided the region's economic development. But, again, Arbena notes the two-sided nature of this relationship in relation to one of its most evident features – the international migration of players. This occurs in sports such a baseball and boxing, where many Spanish-speaking athletes have long found success in the United States; indeed, reaching the highest levels of their sport is *only* possible in the United States. The exception is Cuba since the 1959 revolution, where the supply of sportsmen to the United States has dried up as Cuba itself has sought to develop a high level of sporting activity internally. For the case of association football in South America Arbena quotes a pertinent comment by the Argentinian journalist Osvaldo Bayer: 'The central countries [i.e. those of Europe], in the same manner as they carry away the riches of the Third World, likewise carry off their best soccer players' (p. 158). The movement of players, both within the Southern Cone and between it and Europe, has a long history but in recent years the loss of South America's best player does appear to have intensified. The results are varied:

- Money for the clubs with players to sell
- Income for the families of players bought by European clubs

- Decline in the domestic quality of play, with reduced attendances
- Problems for South American national coaches in assembling teams
- Consequent decline in success in international competitions

Arbena links these effects in soccer to the research of the American academic Alan M. Klein, whose studies of baseball in the Dominican Republic show similar features; the export of talent to the US Major leagues has at one and the same time detrimental and advantageous effects on the local economy and society. A sporting relationship with a bigger economy is neither a 'good' nor a 'bad' thing. [See Alan M. Klein, *Sugarball: The American Game, The Dominican Dream*, New Haven, CT: Yale University Press, 1991.]

Case Study Discussions 26–28

Sport and Imperialism: USA, France, Germany.

Gerald R. Gems, 'Sport, Colonialism, and United States Imperialism'.

Evelyne Combeau-Mari, 'Sport in the French Colonies (1880–1962): A Case Study'.

Gertrud Pfister, 'Colonialism and the Enactment of German Identity – *Turnen* in South West Africa'.

in *Journal of Sport History,* 33, 1 (Spring 2006): Forum – *Globalization as Imperialism?*.

One of the principal agencies for the spread of sport – and of many other influences – during the nineteenth and twentieth centuries has been the system of formal and informal control exercised over extensive areas of the world by countries in the 'developed' world, and known loosely by the term 'imperialism'. Sometimes this has involved the imposition of new forms of politics and culture in territories under American or European political control ('colonies' – occasionally referred to as 'mandates'); an example of such a territory was India, ruled by the British until its independence in 1947, though subjected internally to different degrees of British control – some 'direct', others 'indirect'. In other cases imperialism extended to countries that were nominally independent in political terms, though effectively colonies in respect of their economic development; examples would be Argentina, where a strong British mercantile presence existed in the earlier twentieth century, or China, which experienced economic influence from a number of western states and businesses until the Communist Party assumed power there in 1949. Few countries outside a small group of 'great powers' were free of such control and influence. A notable exception was Japan, which modernized in the late nineteenth and twentieth century in spite of (or, more accurately, because of) being free of colonial tutelage.

The three contributions to the *Journal of Sport History* forum on globalization as imperialism give us detailed examples of the similarities and differences in the process of 'sportification' in varied colonial contexts. Each should be seen in relation to a similar process that occurred in the largest of the imperial/colonial ventures, that of Britain. Historical work on this subject, which has not been extensively covered, has largely focused on British examples. In general, historians of the British Empire have emphasized the low-key nature of British colonialism. Though not without its proponents of a 'civilizing mission' British colonialism sought to stimulate trade and protect trade routes rather than promote a mass cultural transformation of native life in the colonies. So long as native peoples remained subservient to British forms of political control, the rulers of the Empire in London were content. This was particularly so after the experience of the rebellion of 1857 against British rule in India, somewhat misleadingly known as the Indian Mutiny. The threat it posed to imperial power resulted in Britain backing off attempts to change Indian society thereafter. Inevitably, however, some degree of change occurred, not only in India but also in other colonies as well. One important consequence of this change was the creation of the indigenous group often described by sociologists as the 'westernized, educated elite'. This was quite a diverse group of people who, in one way or another, had been subjected to western ways of thought and action as part of their having a role in the system of colonialism; as, for example, teachers, clerks, mechanics, legal professionals and journalists. Their education thus elevated them beyond the levels experienced by other indigenous, and usually rural-based, inhabitants, but because they were still native people (i.e. not white) they were unable to progress beyond a fixed stage in the colonial hierarchy. They were therefore in a 'no man's land' – estranged from native society, but rejected because of their colour as full members of white society. It was therefore a dissatisfied, alienated and potentially volatile group, responsible for much of the anti-colonial protest that had developed in almost all colonial territories by the second quarter of the twentieth century. Its place in both politics and sport is considerable.

Gems and **Combeau-Mari** provide a comprehensive survey of the place of sport in the American and French empires. Both were extensive territorially. The French was a diverse accretion of land totalling some 40 million peoples in 11 million square kilometres at its fullest extent in the interwar years. Its greatest concentration was in North and West Africa, and Indo-China. The American empire was less concentrated, though equally far-flung; Hawai'i, the Hispanic Caribbean and Central America, the Philippines and other smaller parts of the Far East all felt the effects of American colonial influence. In spite of the immense variety in language, geography and local traditions, as well as different forms of rule, French and American colonialism display certain common approaches.

- A variety of 'agencies' promoting sport within the colonial framework (e.g. religious, educational, military bodies; official governmental initiatives were not necessarily in the forefront of this activity)
- The idea of sport as a form of social control, though at the same time a fear on the part of colonial authorities that sports clubs might become a focus of political opposition

- A concern to suppress indigenous sports and pastimes, either because they seemed inimical to trade or because they offended religious sensibilities and notions of 'decency' (the YMCA, as the leading Protestant missionary body in the American empire, was especially active in the latter)
- The popularity of particular sports: baseball in the American sphere of influence, association football in the French
- The ability of indigenous groups both to adapt western sports to their own styles (e.g. *beisbol romantico* in Dominica) and to resurrect native sports (e.g. canoeing and surfing in Hawai'i)
- The pride experienced when native people defeated Americans or French at their western games (e.g. rugby in Madagascar or baseball in the Caribbean)
- One noteworthy difference (possibly) is the attempt by French Catholic agencies to promote sport for women in the colonies – a feature apparently lacking in the American empire (or at least not commented upon by Gems)

There was in both cases an evident intention, perhaps more publicly acknowledged in the French empire than in the American, to use sport as part of a process of cultural assimilation – to create 'black Frenchmen' as it was often claimed. The conclusions of both historians are sceptical, however, of the effect of this mission. Sport probably did as much to undermine colonial relationships as it did to cement them.

Pfister's study offers a different perspective on this problem. She focuses only on one territory (nowadays Namibia) and on one sport – *turnen*, which might loosely be translated as 'gymnastics' but which in fact encompasses a range of gym and athletics activities that differ in many ways from conventional 'sport'. Another feature of Pfister's contribution is the strong political context she constructs for understanding German colonialism. Its relationship to the recent establishment of the German state (1871) is an important factor. The perceived need to achieve international influence, and create a sense of national coherence in a country where rapid industrialization in the late nineteenth century was creating severe economic, social and political tensions, gave the colonial project a predominant place in German life. With the notable (and extensive) exception of the Social Democrats most political groups in Germany gave colonialism wholehearted support.

   In contrast to many of the American and French initiatives investigated by Gems and Combeau-Mari, which sought at least in part to use sport as a means of integrating indigenous people into colonial structures, *turnen* in South West Africa aimed at the opposite: the exclusion of native peoples through the creation of a unified Germanic white society. This part of Africa, largely left alone as unpromising territory by other European countries, was colonized by Germany in the 1880s. There resulted a harsh form of rule which intensified during and after native rebellions in the early years of the twentieth century. One distinguishing feature of the colony was the presence there of a small but vigorous immigrant settler community which sought, as similar groups elsewhere have done, to re-create its idea of 'home' in the foreign land. It was to this group that *turnen* appealed, and who transformed it into an exclusive network of ludic and cultural associations. *Turnen*, the origins of which are to be found in liberal, anti-French, patriotic movements of early nineteenth-century Prussia, had become a symbol of conservative patriotism in the years after 1871. The national *turnen* organization (*Deutsche Turnerschaft –* DT) gave unconditional support to the German regime and thus in the colonies *turnen* was a natural expression for the *enactment* (as Pfister puts it) of the idea of Germany and of white superiority. *Turnen* clubs excluded not only non-Germans and non-whites, but were also essentially male organizations; women did not participate in the athletic events, though were admitted to club membership and played an important part in the many rituals and festivals that were a crucial aspect of *turnen* social life. As a minority in a new territory, thousands of miles from their homeland and embattled by a hostile environment and resentful native population, German settlers in South West Africa took solace from the meanings inscribed in the culture of *turnen*: it was, as Pfister calls it, a 'cradle of ethnicity'.

Player movement and labour markets

The international labour market in sports players had one of its earliest manifestation in cricket. Players from the West Indies were among the first to benefit from it in a significant way in the 1930s, as opportunities were opened up for them in England. League cricket clubs in the North of England, principally those of the Lancashire League, were quick to seize on this traffic in talent, the way forward having been pioneered by Nelson when it engaged Learie Constantine in 1929. From then until the1970s, when the gradual enlargement of the international test cricket calendar created new opportunities for top-level cricketers, some of the world's leading players could be seen performing their art in the textile towns of Lancashire and the manufacturing districts of the Black Country to the west of Birmingham. The locus of international player movement in cricket subsequently shifted to the English county championship. After the Second World War there was always a significant representation of overseas players in the counties, but this intensified from the 1970s with the appearance of leading test players who had previously remained within their own countries. Mike Proctor, Barry Richards, Clive Lloyd, Kapil Dev and Muttiah Muralitharan were all to be seen, at one time or another in the later twentieth century, on the county grounds of England. Some regarded their presence as a threat to the development of the English game, since the presence of such stars was thought to be preventing opportunities for younger home-grown players; but, of course, many welcomed the celebrities simply for the lustre and excitement they brought to the game.

One of the most interesting examples of this process has occurred in the early twenty-first century in India. South Asia had by this time become one of the world's leading cricket regions, not only for the prowess of its test teams but also for the immensity of cricket's following there. It became, therefore, the obvious focal point for any new commercial ventures in the game. The appearance in 2008 of two rival professional cricket leagues – the

Indian Premier League and the Indian Cricket League – both based in India but drawing upon an international coterie of players, has raised several issues about the nature of cricket.

Firstly, the leagues represent one of those sudden incursions into the established order of the game, previously manifested in its most dramatic form by Kerry Packer's World Series Cricket initiative of 1976. Packer, an Australian media magnate, virtually revolutionized the game by introducing new ideas about the form it should take and the remuneration of its leading players. His initiative changed forever the old approach of the national governing bodies, whose power over players was altered and whose awareness of the money-making possibilities in cricket were suddenly awakened. The creation in 2007 of the Indian Cricket League by the media businessman Subhash Chandra was in some respects a repeat of the issue that had prompted Packer's original move. Like Packer, Chandra had made unsuccessful bids for television coverage of major international cricket competitions; having been rebuffed three times by the ICC, he decided to set up his own competition, and in 2008 the ICL began its first season in India. But many of the international players who had signed contracts with the ICL found themselves banned by the official national bodies, signalling their intention to regard anyone who supported Chandra's 'rebel' organization as an outlaw.

Secondly, one of Packer's greatest innovations was the 'day-night' match, bringing cricket to a television audience when they were at home to watch it, rather than when they were out at work. Adapting the game to the requirements of television was felt to benefit both parties – cricket itself and the television authorities – and both the Indian leagues, the ICL and the official Indian Premier League, have taken this further, realizing that the short form of the game suits television scheduling much better than lengthy test matches. Matches are presented amidst much razzmatazz, with Bollywood stars well to the fore in the noisy and colourful parades staged to celebrate the opening of a new series of matches. It may well be that test cricket's traditional pre-eminence will be displaced by Twenty/20. (See Case Study Discussion 29).

Thirdly, the Indian leagues point up the question of the financing, marketing and form of cricket. The system of franchising teams and hiring players, adopted by the IPL, is wholly new to the game. India is the largest test-playing country and its cricket culture is probably more deeply embedded than anywhere else. The country is also now regarded as an emerging industrial and commercial economy with a consumer society to be exploited. In this respect its development parallels that of China. The latter, never a serious part of the British sphere of cultural influence and therefore, outside Hong Kong, having no cricket, is nonetheless being spoken of as a potential area for cricket development; a 'sleeping giant' of the cricket world that might be awakened for the future.

Fourthly, the recent league principle goes to the heart of the issue of cricket's commercial potential. For much of its history, and in a great deal of the cultural representations that have accompanied it, the game has been seen as an aesthetic that resisted commercialism as being a largely baleful influence in society. Compared with association football (which also saw limitations imposed on its business development) cricket was at most a semi-commercial game during much of its development. Economic and social changes after the Second World War prompted some rethinking of finances and methods (the introduction of the Gillette Cup in 1963 was an important breakthrough) but it was the Packer 'revolution' that spurred the big changes, notably in the game's relations with television and sponsors, and in the remuneration of players.

Fifthly, the leagues have already prompted responses from the test-playing nations; there will an English Premier League was proposed for 2010,[7] and there are proposals for a southern-hemisphere competition (Australia, NZ and South Africa). The Indian leagues themselves have adopted a football-style identity, based territorially on urban districts. All these moves will affect the bases upon which the game has previously functioned.

The new leagues therefore have implications for a radical transformation of world cricket, greater than those posed by Packer 30 years ago, and are likely to usher an era in which, as the Stanford tournament in the Caribbean in 2008 showed, anything goes so long as it involves television and money. Cricket has come a long way since its amateur days of the early-twentieth century, and much of that journey has been travelled in the relatively recent past. A game which once kept commercialism at arm's length has now wholeheartedly embraced it, and not always (some would say) for the better.

Case Study Discussion 29

The Indian Cricket Leagues

Gideon Haigh, 'Who Needs First-Class Cricket?', *Cricinfo*, 26 May 2009

http://cricinfo.com/magazine/content/story/406005.html?wrappertype=print [2 September 2009].

The Indian Premier League (IPL) currently has eight teams, the Indian Cricket League nine. The IPL, organized by the businessman Lalit Modi, has official approval from India's governing body of cricket, while the ICL is a 'rebel' organization, set up in opposition to the world governing body (ICC). Thus the former is able to recruit current international stars, while the ICL, because of the sanctions applied by national governing bodies, has had problems recruiting such players and has mainly relied upon former stars whose playing careers are coming to an end.

Gideon Haigh is a distinguished Australian journalist who writes mainly (but by no means exclusively) on cricket. He is the author of several cricket books with a historical dimension (biographies, for example, of Australian players Warwick Armstrong and Jack Iverson) and a critical commentator on the contemporary cricket scene. He has been especially critical of the ECB's selling of exclusive rights for live television coverage of cricket to BSkyB, believing that the game should be made accessible on a free-to-air basis to its mass audience, as it is in Australia. Haigh has also expressed some doubts on the impact of Twenty/20. In this short article, prompted by the decision of three recently retired Australian players (Hayden, Gilchrist and Warne) to commit themselves to the IPL, he reflects on its possible consequences for the established 'first-class' game. He sees the IPL as providing a tempting opportunity to leading players such as Hayden, Gilchrist and Warne, all reaching an age where the demands of the longer forms of cricket are beginning to have their physical effects on them, to step down from this level and make big money in the far less demanding circuit of the short game. [*This fact was clearly shown when, subsequent to this article, the English test cricketer Andrew Flintoff, whose later career had been blighted by injuries of various kinds, announced in August–September 2009 his decision to retire from the test and county game and go 'freelance' in the hope of concentrating his energies on the short game.*] In spite of their relatively advanced years these players' performances in the 2009 IPL season showed that they can, as Haigh says, 'still ooze juice in the Twenty20.' It prompts Haigh to ask: might the selectors of test teams in future take players straight from T20 without needing a player to prove his form in the first-class game? The response given to Haigh by Cricket Australia suggested that this might indeed be the case. Haigh cites one example of a player who has already 'jumped the queue' for Australian selection on the basis of IPL performances. Were this to be repeated it would not only be the older players for whom IPL became a major employment attraction. The potential threat to the game, argues Haigh, would be even greater in the West Indies, where test players are disgruntled at the levels of remuneration offered them by comparison with their counterparts in other countries. [*In the summer of 2009, before the test series against Bangladesh, West Indies' leading players went on strike and the selectors had to resort to picking a new team, largely made up of cricketers brought up in the islands' universities.*] The West Indies captain, Chris Gayle, publicly expressed his boredom with test cricket in 2009, preferring the shorter, more exciting and more rewarding future that beckoned him in the form of the IPL.

The sport in which these features had one of their earliest manifestations, and in which they have now reached their most developed point, is association football. Compared with the attempts to export other sports football's dissemination seems to have been remarkably un-problematical, with none of the obstacles to expansion encountered by cricket or baseball. Both Europe and South America had been colonized by football by the 1920s, with the game well established in Asia and Africa (though with a less developed level of elite performance) by the time of the Second World War. Mason's study of the dissemination of football in South America brings out very clearly the early 'missionary' activities of British businessmen, workers and service personnel in all this, though we should probably not see their endeavours as a conscious attempt to disseminate; British people played football wherever and whenever they could, and local people followed their example. It was as simple as that. Undoubtedly one of the advantages possessed by those spreading the game was football's simplicity: it is easily comprehended and needs only a minimum of resources to get a game started. Thus what began as an elite pastime quickly became a popular one; and one, moreover, inflected with a particular South American style, until, that is, the demands of international competitions brought about a more pragmatic approach: 'perhaps this is an aspect of that globalisation ... about which sociologists excitedly chatter.'[8]

Since the development of football as we know it today the game has always had the capacity to be a world game. There has long been a transnational movement of players, beginning with the 'Scotch professors' who went south to ply their skills in England in the 1880s. This was followed by significant migrations of players between various parts of Europe, then from South America to Europe, and in recent times from Africa to Europe (often *via* France, a supply route from which Arsenal FC has profited greatly in recent years). Thus many professional footballers became used to a career of changes, involving different kinds of contacts with new places. Lanfranchi and Taylor have identified three types of migrants – *itinerants* (short-term placements, no more than a year or two, often far less), *mercenaries* (remaining 'abroad' but with several different clubs in different countries) and *settlers* (staying in one country, often with the same club, for most of their playing career). All three types can be seen in the present-day Premier League with its rich pool of talent from all over the world. The multinational nature of the Premier League is a modern, mature example of a process that has been in existence for a long time, and which has undoubtedly brought success to clubs and players, and to an extent to supporters themselves. It has not, however, been without its problems.

Case Study Discussion 30

Lennart Skoglund

Niels Kayser Nielsen, '"Nacka" Skoglund: A Swedish Soccer Player as a Welfare-Nationalistic Myth', in J. Bale, M. K. Christensen and G. Pfister, *Writing Lives in Sport: Biographies, Life-Histories and Methods* (Aarhus: University of Aarhus Press, 2004), pp. 179–89.

Lennart Skoglund (known as 'Nacka' from the working-class district of Stockholm where he grew up) was one of several Swedish players who moved to clubs in southern Europe following the successes of Sweden's national team during and immediately after the Second World War. (By the time Sweden hosted the World Cup in 1958 many of the country's best players were resident in other countries, and the Swedish football authorities were forced to rescind a previous ban on selecting 'foreign-based' players in order to assemble the national team.) Skoglund (b. 1929) was one of Sweden's stars in the 1950 World Cup in Brazil, where he was spotted and signed by Inter Milan. In Italy he enjoyed a highly successful career with Inter as a fast and clever left winger popular with the crowds, scoring 57 goals in 246 appearances. He later turned out for Sampdoria and Palermo, eventually returning to Sweden in 1964 to play for Hammarby, the Stockholm club where he had started some fifteen years before. He famously scored direct from a corner kick in his first match with Hammarby after his return. Skoglund was a popular hero whose success coincided with a period of economic and social prosperity in Sweden itself. He came to be regarded as a particular symbol of the country and its social-democratic welfare model of society, to which Swedish prosperity and well-being in the quarter century following the Second World War was ascribed.

In contrast to the stories told about 'Nacka', which portrayed him as a handsome, gifted and carefree individual who was devoid of pretence and always behaved naturally, Nielsen emphasizes another side to his life: as a burnt-out sportsman who took to drink and died an alcoholic at the age of 45 in misery and poverty. This is the downside of his fame, an experience later repeated in many ways in the case of the Irish football star George Best. Nielsen discerns three layers of myth surrounding Skoglund: the happy-go-lucky symbol of Swedish success; the victim of stardom whose life, like that of James Dean and Marilyn Monroe, became a 'common good' (p. 185); and the product of a Nordic tradition that demanded both conformity and 'being yourself'. All Swedes, says Nielsen, have to contend with some of these pressures, but sportsmen who are also heroes have particular difficulties in coping with them. Skoglund's fate was not determined by his becoming an international star, but it did not help. Nielsen's piece thus offers an unusual and important analysis of how one person's life can be affected by a sport played in an environment where particular national and international expectations are placed on him.

Skoglund was, in Lanfranchi and Taylor's term, a 'settler'. His time in Italy was successful, which partly explains why he stayed there for almost 15 years. His later decline came as a result of being unable to adapt to Swedish society and its expectations. It created tensions that the man could not cope with. Skoglund's experiences therefore represent the highs and lows of player movement. It could be a traumatic experience for everyone. For some the lows came quickly, forcing an early return back whence the player had come. Denis Law, Jimmy Greaves and Joe Baker, British footballers who had spells in the Italian league in the early 1960s, all returned home quickly, unable to deal with aspects of foreign life, which might include food, language, playing styles, management and the press. More recently problems have arisen for youngsters from Africa who have been enlisted by European clubs. Some have made the grade but most have not, and the consequences of the uprooting and cultural changes involved in the pursuit of the elusive dream can be disastrous. The film *Le Ballon d'Or* (dir. Cheik Doukoure, Guinea, 1993), while not a pessimistic portrayal of African-European football relations, hints at some of the problems involved.

Others have experienced the highs of migration. Alfredo di Stefano left Argentina after the players' strike of the late 1940s and, by way of Colombia, settled happily in Spain, played outstandingly for Real Madrid for several sea-sons in the 1950s and 1960s, and lived on a farm near the city for many years after his retirement. The very different Gary Lineker was more of a mercenary, with spells in Spain and Japan but nonetheless adapted well to Spain during his short period in Barcelona in the late 1980s. The Welsh footballer John Charles, considered by some to be one of the finest foreign players to appear in Italy, enjoyed a very successful career as a player with Juventus (Turin) and AS Roma from 1957 to 1963, but like Skoglund and many other migrants attempted a late-career return to his own country that brought only financial and domestic disappointments.

International sport organizations

Of course, football is not the only sport to witness such internationalization, and sport itself is not the only sector of business in which cross-currents of global dimensions are evident. Sport, in fact, is merely part of broader polit-ical and economic developments that saw the consolidation of nation states and national markets within a world economy by the end of the nineteenth century. George Orwell, who had a low opinion of sport, blamed the rise of nationalism for making it into 'mimic warfare ... war minus the shooting.'[9] Sport organization itself mirrored these changes, though not always with the aim of stimulating the violent competitiveness that Orwell claimed to find in sport. In Britain, by the early years of the twentieth century, all the major sports were organized under the direction of national governing bodies (the Amateur Athletics Association, Football Association, Marylebone Cricket Club, Rugby Football Union, Jockey Club and so on), and in turn these bod-ies were starting to coalesce into organizations with international authority. The forerunner of today's International Cricket Council (with its headquarters in the non-cricketing country of Dubai) was the Imperial Cricket Conference, formed by England, Australia and South Africa in 1909. In its early years it was, as its name suggested, more a forum for discussion than a body exercising real power. Association football, rugby union and athletics had created simi-lar bodies by this time, and tennis was soon to join them. One of the most interesting examples of the trend towards internationalism came shortly after the Great War, when the organized workers' movements of Europe created a sporting network in the hope of promoting 'peace through sport' (to quote one of their slogans). A series of workers' Olympiads were held in various countries during the 1920s and 1930s, some (the Prague Olympics of 1934, for example) attracting greater numbers of competitors and spectators than the rival de Coubertin version of olympism. Ultimately, however, the coming to power of fascist parties in Germany and Italy, together with the growing tensions between the social-democratic and communist wings of the workers' movement, weakened the Workers' Olympics and the event held in Antwerp in 1937 was the last.

If we take examples of international organization in two sports – association football and athletics – we can trace in some detail the development not only of the increasing interest in working together across national boundaries, but also of an intensifying business involvement that has left a deep impression on contemporary sport.

FIFA. The Federation Internationale de Football Association was established in Paris in 1904. The idea had originated in France, where there had been difficulties in establishing a unified national federation to oversee football. Belgium and the Netherlands were also part of this early alliance of forces. It was felt that an international body would be able to regulate the increasing trend towards international matches and also standardize the rules of the game. A further objective was to gain recognition for the game on the continent from Britain, to which European footballers looked as the 'masters' of the game for guidance and moral support. Ironically, until the later 1940s, the British associations gave only lukewarm support to FIFA, and were members only intermittently. Nonetheless FIFA did valuable work in regulating the international aspects of football, establishing for example standards of refereeing and ensuring that some kind of fairness was observed in the international transfer of players. But as with the ICC we must not, in the light of its later influence, overestimate the early role of FIFA. Until it moved to a larger office in Zurich in 1932 the organization was relatively small: the secretary was assisted by only one person, and income was confined to the subscription fees of affiliated member countries (30 or so in the early 1930s) and a proportion of the receipts of international fixtures (excluding those involving British teams). To a degree the body was still a European one, though during the interwar years it assumed a more global authority, largely because of the participation of South American countries. FIFA also acquired responsibility for organizing the football tournament at the Olympic Games and in 1930, after previous failed attempts, inaugurated its own World Cup competition. The initial event was a modest affair held in Montevideo but FIFA persisted and the World Cup grew into a grander form with the successful competitions of 1934 and 1938 that revealed the strength of football in countries such as Italy (the winners in both), France, Austria, Hungary and Czechoslovakia. By today's standards, though, it still was limited in scope. Neither England nor Scotland (arguably among the strongest football nations) competed until 1950, when England (though not Scotland) participated for the first time in Brazil, and the finals brought together only 16 countries, always from Europe and South America. It was, however, the proceeds from the World Cup that allowed FIFA to build up its finances and to begin to exploit the changed conditions of sport in the later twentieth century. Television and sponsorship were the two mechanisms that allowed ambitious presidents to transform FIFA into a truly global organization.

First under Stanley Rous, a former secretary of the English FA, and then more vigorously under the direction of the Brazilian Joao Havelange from

1974 and the Swiss lawyer Joseph (Sepp) Blatter (1998–), FIFA's links with the commercial world blossomed. An agreement between FIFA and Coca-Cola in 1976 enabled the latter to use the FIFA logo in its advertising and thus penetrate new markets for its product; in return FIFA earned money from Coca-Cola that provided it with the resources to launch schemes aimed at stimulating youth football in the less-developed regions of the world. A similar agreement with the German sports goods manufacturer Adidas followed, and later a lucrative structure of partners, sponsors and supporters brought in some of the world's leading brands (Hyundai/Kia, Sony, Emirates airlines, and Visa, as well as Coca-Cola and Adidas). Stricter deals with television companies increased income from this source.[10] One outcome of FIFA's greater resources was the redistribution of funds to members in the developing world, where opportunities for generating income through television deals and sponsorship are limited. The Blatter presidency, which began in 1998 and continued with his re-election in 2002, might, in spite of criticisms of his strategy from European quarters, be seen as combining the commercial exploitation of sport with an ethical distribution of resources for the good of the game. Blatter himself often speaks of having created a world family in football, and on the whole it is difficult to deny the validity of his claim when seen in a long-term historical perspective.[11]

IOC. From its small beginnings FIFA has become a powerful force in modern sport. The International Olympic Committee has followed a similar path, achieving perhaps even greater success, at least in terms of its main global event, the Olympic Games. Given the international climate in sport at the end of the nineteenth century it is no coincidence that the revival of olympism in the form of the Olympic Games held at Athens in 1896 came at more or less the same time as the formation of FIFA. In the mind of the Frenchman Pierre de Coubertin, who took a leading part in the establishment of the IOC, there was an explicit desire not only to bring athletes together but also to do so as a way of fostering peace in the world. It was a pious hope in the latter respect, but as far as creating an international forum of athletics was concerned his idea was successful. After the Olympic Games of 1908, the first commercially successful example of the event, it has gone from strength to strength, though it took the women some time to catch up with the men. Like many early football administrators, the members of the IOC were inclined towards a conservative view of their sport, tending to support amateurism and to be resistant to the involvement of female athletes on a big scale. Not until the late 1920s were women admitted to a limited range of track and field events, and it was not until much later that the amateur principle was relaxed. The presidency of the American Avery Brundage (1952–72) was marked by a particularly sectarian interpretation of the Olympic spirit: pro-western, amateur, anti-communist, male, and in the case of South Africa possibly racist.

Just as 1966 might be seen as the turning point in the history of the football World Cup, so 1984 in Los Angeles can be regarded as the first 'modern'

Olympic Games: the first time the now-familiar trinity of sport-television-advertising came into view in a big way. The financial problems of the 1976 summer Games in Montreal, which had left the host city with major debts and in spite of the many sponsors involved brought relatively little income into the Olympic coffers, prompted the IOC to restructure its financing. The chief consequence of this was the TOP (The Olympic Partner) programme, a scheme in which, in return for their financial sponsorship, a limited number of world brands receive exclusive global marketing rights and other privileges for their product in the context of the Olympic movement and Games. For the Beijing event of 2008 the TOPs were 12 in number – Coca-Cola, GE, Kodak, McDonald's, Omega, Atos Origin, Johnson and Johnson, Lenovo, Manulife, Samsung, Visa and Panasonic. Their many privileges include 'ambush' marketing protection, which means among other things that paying spectators at the Games are prevented from taking with them into the stadium anything that bears the advertising logo of non-TOP companies. As may be judged from this apparent power to restrict an individual's personal liberty TOP status is a much-coveted right, and the IOC proudly notes that the programme 'enjoys one of the highest sponsorship renewal rates of any sports property.'[12] Sponsors contribute somewhere in the region of 40 per cent of total IOC revenues, which is a slightly lower proportion than broadcasting rights, which provide just over half of all income (approximately US$ 1760 millions at Beijing in 2008). The Olympics is all very big business indeed, and for cities with outsize egos the capturing of the prize to stage the event is an opportunity not to be missed. Residents of Hackney, Stratford and neighbouring areas of east London are currently appreciating the advantages and disadvantages of their city's being the chosen one, and no doubt wondering what the 'legacy' is going to be.

For business success brings conflicts; between fractions of the powerful controlling agencies like FIFA and the IOC, and between the decision-makers and the ordinary supporters like you and me. Not all is harmony at the highest levels. Both FIFA and the IOC have their critics, who accuse the organizations of being unrepresentative and dictatorial in their actions. Havelange and Blatter have both been the subject of censure, a number of the latter's policies having elicited disapproval in various quarters, some even within FIFA itself. The collapse of FIFA's marketing partner International Sport and Leisure (ISL) in 2001 unleashed a torrent of criticism and speculation, and allegations of bribery are still being investigated in the Swiss courts. These divisions have been complicated by a serious rift – part institutional, part personal – between FIFA and one of its major constituent associations, UEFA, over the ISL case and the choice of venue for the World Cup. Further confusing the picture has been the rise to prominence in football politics of a group of leading European clubs, calling themselves the G14, who lobbied hard with both UEFA and FIFA to promote their own self interests by seeking to maximize income from European competitions. Through the influence of the new UEFA President Michel Platini, who considered the group elitist, the G14 agreed to disband in 2008 and was replaced by a less restricted European Club Association. The effect of this high-level political and business dealing on the ordinary spectator and supporter is difficult to judge. One might imagine that affairs such as the scandal over the handling of the IOC's bidding process for the 2002 winter Olympics in Salt Lake City, which led to the eventual resignation of some IOC members, the smears occasioned by FIFA's business dealings, and the way in which preparations for the 2012 Olympic Games in London are being conducted, with escalating costs and local people's interests seemingly swept aside in the rush to 'regeneration', tend to breed a cynicism among the public about the business-driven strategies of international sport.

Football, again, provides perhaps the clearest example of this (although cricket is presently coming close through its obsession with Twenty/20). The creation in 1992 of the Premier League in England broke with the long-standing practice that *all* the fully professional clubs came together in the Football League. All had never been equal in fame or wealth, but they were all part of one body. The Premier League changed this. It was an elite organization of richer clubs who imagined that by freeing themselves from the restraint (as they saw it) of the poorer ones they would be able to develop their business potential. In a short space of time some of this elite group came to see themselves as 'global brands' – capable of operating on a world stage, with big-name sponsors, international summer tours designed to boost their fan base and merchandizing, an increasingly international pool of players, huge amounts of income from television revenue, and *foreign* ownership. This last feature is seen by many fans as the most sinister development of all, and in some cases (that of Liverpool FC being an obvious one) has aroused much local opposition. For the individual fan, locally based, whose family has perhaps supported that club for maybe three or four generations, who regards the club as 'her' or 'his' club (acknowledging that this implies *moral* not legal ownership), who sees the club as an essential part of a community of people, for this fan the take over of the club by an overseas owner is tantamount to their town having been invaded by a foreign power. The clash between the local and the global is almost visceral. It can certainly shock the system. Foreign owners, often possessors of North American sporting franchises who know nothing of 'soccer', seek to supplant the local fan community with a global audience which, it is perceived, pay proportionately less to watch the local team perform on global television than does a fan in either the stadium or on television in Britain. Profits from these international transactions are not ploughed back into the grass-roots game in England or Scotland, or into providing subsidies for steeply rising ticket prices, or making available matches on a 'free-to-air' basis, but into repaying the debts incurred by the owners themselves when acquiring the club in the first place. There are several examples of local challenges to this kind of football business. One relatively effective case was the opposition of Manchester United fans to the threatened takeover by Rupert Murdoch in 1999, which succeeded (with help from the Monopolies Commission) in heading off the Murdoch bid, though the club was still acquired by the American Glazer family six years later and immediately saddled with the massive bank debt that had made Glazer ownership possible. In most cases supporters' groups are limited in what they can do to prevent this kind of incursion, and indeed often have to contend with feelings within their own ranks that new owners will bring the success a 'big club' is considered to expect and deserve.

A global playing style?

A final point to consider in a chapter that has concentrated mainly on people and institutions is the transmission of *influences* in sport through the processes we have been considering. One of the most striking examples of this is to be found in something that sport historians often overlook; namely, sport tactics and styles of play – in other words, the game itself. It was at one time common to find commentators – academic and media – speaking about *national* styles. In association football, for example, the English 'kick and rush' approach was contrasted with Scotland's more cultured passing game; teams from the communist countries of eastern Europe were often characterized as grim and methodical; South Americans were held to possess a rhythmical if over-exotic mentality. Much of this national or regional typology was, of course, based on caricatures, but some truth lay behind it, and it had to do with the forms of play that were developed in the days when there was less cross-cultural influence in the game than has appeared in recent times. The marked internationalization that occurred in the late-twentieth century created such fluidity that it became much more difficult to identify particular styles based upon particular places. It also meant that, compared with even 40 years ago, there were fewer 'unknowns' in football; that is to say, players and teams capable of taking others by surprise, much as the North Koreans did in the World Cup of 1966, largely at Italy's expense, or even as Cameroon did in 1990 (almost at England's). The game has become so thoroughly international that there are now scarcely any 'pushovers'; all teams have to be taken seriously, and even relatively weak ones now possess enough tactical acumen to combat the superior skills of their opponents and make the contest a more equal affair. Having said that, however, it remains to ask whether the example of football might be applied to other sports. As the most internationalized and professionalized sport it might be an exception. For whilst in cricket, to take another example, even though many of the same features have been apparent as in football they have not prevented Australia from exercising an almost untroubled dominance in the world game for some twenty years, with a succession of relatively easy victories over England in particular. The main difference, which might serve to explain at least part of this contrast, is in the migration patterns of professional cricketers. In the 1970s an opening up of Australian top-level cricket to overseas players began, but was then curtailed. Cricket in Australia returned to its traditional 'insular' format, although Australian cricketers themselves retained the opportunity of practising their skills in England during the northern-hemisphere summer. Thus Australia, it might be felt, obtained the best of both worlds; insulated from external penetration of their own competitions, but able to test out its own players in overseas competitions. It is said that Australia has a distinctive style of playing the game, which might be another way of saying that it has succeeded in adapting globalization in a national way. Rugby union, since its conversion to professionalism in the mid-1990s, has adapted to globalization quite readily and in its forms of play imported many of the features that characterized rugby league. The game now flows more than in the past, there are fewer set-piece stoppages, and it seems more muscular; through the influence of full-time professional coaches matches are played more according to a 'game plan', which perhaps reduces the opportunities for flashes of individual genius that were once the forte of players such as Barry John. All this is possibly the influence of southern-hemisphere rugby, the successes of which occasioned the big changes in the game that occurred in the early 1990s.

How many other sports can be examined from this perspective? Has so-called globalization changed the particular national inflections of sports and made them into games that are global not only in their organization but also in the way they are actually played? Few academic studies seem to concern themselves with these issues, preferring instead to look into the complexities of the economic, political, social and cultural aspects of sport: all are undoubtedly important, but without the game itself sport studies can become rather like *Hamlet* without the Prince of Denmark.

Conclusion

The World Cup and the summer Olympic Games are the two leading 'mega' sporting events in the world, and say a lot about sport and globalization. The term might have been bandied around overmuch by academics, to the extent that it can mean many different things, but it does convey something about the pressures and influences operating at a transnational level. The effect of them has been to make us far more into 'citizens of the world' than was the English radical Tom Paine when he first coined that phrase back in the late eighteenth century. Sport is a key element in this, even though some of us might still open the newspaper on Monday morning and first cast a parochial eye to see how Accrington Stanley of the Football League or the Columbus Catfish of the South Atlantic baseball league fared on the previous Saturday.

Looking back over the past century we may discern two overriding features in the development of sport.

- One has been the tendency for sport to outgrow its original boundaries. There has been a seemingly inexorable process taking sport out of the local, into the national, and thence to the international. The example of rugby league, a game played over many years in various countries (England, France, Australia, New Zealand) but in a localized context in each, is instructive. When embraced by Rupert Murdoch's media corporation the international potential in the game, which had only ever been partially developed, suddenly matured into a global televised Super League, with all-year-round competition. It all happened quickly in the late 1990s. We must, of course, avoid over determining this process; there is still ample room for local and national activity and identities in sport, and all the global mega events depend to a great extent on them. Where would the Olympic Games be without the national rivalries that fuel the competition and the public interest?

- The other is an increasing fixation with the *international*. Sport has always had the capacity to operate at all levels, but it would be futile to deny that in the early twenty-first century the presence and intensity of international sport is greater than it has ever been. A hundred years ago international sport – and, indeed, commercial/professional sport in general – was a small apex of a vast triangle of localized sport and leisure activity, much of it cohered through clubs and societies formed around voluntary associations, political parties and churches, especially the Catholic Church which was a major force in youth and leisure activities in continental Europe. Now, it almost seems that the pyramid has been inverted, with the latter activity forming an apex at the bottom. This image is something of an illusion (not to say a tautology) sustained in part by a dereliction of duty on the part of scholars, who have neglected to examine local amateur sport and preferred too often to fix their gaze on elite sporting performance. But it does serve to draw attention to a contemporary trend that would have dismayed those observers at the turn of the nineteenth century who felt that sport was about 'doing' and not 'watching'. Much of the changed circumstance has to do with the intimate relationship that has formed between sport, business and the media. The relationship is not new, but it is one capable of generating more profit than ever before. Sport has, we might say, become thoroughly commodified as a result of it. FIFA and the IOC, organizations once strongly committed to amateurism, have led the way in fashioning new means of extracting surplus value from their par- ticular product. Imaginative marketing, including the skilful construction of attractive media spectacles, has created a seemingly bottomless pit of public fascination with sport which in turn serves to perpetuate its business potential. Some have decried this process, and called for a return to the old amateur values of sport for sport's sake. The Stanford Twenty/20 cricket experiment in the Caribbean in 2008 – an exercise befouled by quite high levels of 'tackiness', some of it compounded by England's dismal per- formance on the pitch – highlighted some of these views. And the antics of many in the English Premier (association football) League, managers as well as players, do not assuage the opinions of those who feel that, in an unequal world, there should be limits to the rewarding of sport talent (if not other kinds of talent). Is sport in danger of being over-exposed? Might its displays of naked capitalist greed turn ordinary followers against it? So far the sports most prone to these trends (and they are all sports that emerged in the late nineteenth century, and so have a history of 'better days' to carry with them) have resisted any discernable backlash. But who is to say that a spectator counter-revolution could not happen at some point in the future?

Study Questions

1. The popular culture of America has exported very readily, but its sport less so. Why is this?
2. Explain the *uneven* impact of cricket as a world sport.
3. Thinking about a contemporary sport with which you are familiar, list some of the features that illustrate a 'global' influence, and others that appear to have resisted it.
4. Account for the changes that affected both FIFA and the IOC in the second half of the twentieth century.

Further Reading

David Goldblatt, *The Ball Is Round: A Global History of Football* (London: Viking, 2006).

Roger Levermore and Adrian Budd, *Sport and International Relations: An Emerging Relationship* (London: Routledge, 2004).

Joseph Maguire, *Sport, Power and Globalisation* (London: Routledge, 2005).

John Tomlinson, *Cultural Imperialism: A Critical Introduction* (London: Continuum, 1991).

Jonathan Wilson, *Inverting the Pyramid: A History of Football Tactics* (London: Orion Books, 2009).

Conclusion

The cultural analyst John Tomlinson, seeking in the early 1990s to disentangle the complex knots of 'modernity', 'post modernity', 'cultural imperialism' and 'globalization', pointed to a crucial theme in all this: the crisis of moral legitimacy. Capitalism, he claims, is 'technologically and economically powerful, but culturally "weak"'.[1] This was meant, I think, to describe a continuing condition, not simply a transient phase; but in the early twenty-first century, whatever moral hegemony capitalism might once have had has been severely tested amid consumer debt and banking crises, occasioned (one might argue) by cynical economic and political managers. Recognition of a moral crisis assumed a key part in President Obama's 2009 inaugural address, when he spoke of the United States' being 'ready to lead once more'. To lead, that is, not simply in military or economic terms, but to bring a moral force to bear on the world. It was a sentiment that explains the immense public expectation invested in the newly elected president early in 2009. It was as if America, and perhaps even the world, wanted a vision of where it was going, and why people were doing what they were doing; as if 'globalization', as Tomlinson suggests, is a process of *unintended* consequences – producing effects with no particular overall aim or meaning. Its effects seem greater than the capacity of political organizations to deal with them. Thus environmental problems, probably the greatest of the many problems facing the world in the twenty-first century, appear to many to be almost beyond solution.

One aspect of these impersonal processes is a diminution of identifiable sources of power and influence. We speak of the dissemination of sport in the later nineteenth century from precise centres such as Great Britain. But a hundred years later sport cannot be said to have such an easily recognized centre. At the same time it exercises a cultural power greater than it ever before possessed. In a world of uncertainty and, for many, despair, sport is perhaps the greatest culture of consolation; if not the greatest, then at least

142

a very important one (which is why I find it astonishing that sharp analysts like Tomlinson can write about these big issues without mentioning sport.) It might be one of the few ways in which we can imagine and 'live' a globalized community. The balance that the organization of sport provides between local, national and international layers which in turn intersect with various kinds of identities offers, perhaps, a way of making sense of a world that in so many other ways evades our rational understanding.

Sport is a powerful ideological force. I have written elsewhere that it has an ability to work on those who participate in it and consume it. Sport is something from which we derive *meaning*. In its manifold activities are inscribed features as diverse as gender, nationalism, hero-worship, bodily exercise and commercialism, constituting structured habits of thought and behaviour which contribute to our ways of seeing ourselves and others, to a making sense of our social relationships, and to the piecing together of some notion of what we call 'society' and 'the world'.[2] The sportswriter Simon Barnes, with whom I began this excursion, makes sport even more important than that. Apart from its being 65 million years old (part of our 'mammalian inheritance', says Barnes) sport is a constant source of fascination for us that touches on every aspect of our lives; it tests us, shows up all our strengths and weaknesses. So says Barnes. If I had to choose between sport as ideology and sport as something hard wired into us, I would go for the former. Sport is important, but not *that* important. In the end we can take it or leave it, we don't *have* to do it, and plenty of people don't. Their lives are none the worse for that. For the historian the task, it seems to me, is not to understand sport as some essential part of our psyche, but to hack through the thicket of meaning and counter-meaning inscribe in the cultural domain of sport, and to see it as an arena of discourse, contestation and negotiation: where some of the forces that shape our lives are mediated and, sometimes, resisted. It is what sport is *saying* to us, and how we respond to it, that is what really matters.

For those of you who have read through this book – perhaps the whole of it, or maybe just parts – the question might rise: what can an understanding of history add to what has already been learnt from sociology, business studies, psychology, law, cultural studies and all the other disciplines that constitute 'sport studies' these days? The answer to this question is not an easy one: perhaps it is best left to the reader to decide whether, on the evidence of *this* book, there is any value in a historical perspective. One thing that does distinguish history from all the other subjects in sport studies is that, by and large, they are concerned with the present; and not only with the present, but in many cases with *practical* problems in the present. How to organize a sporting event, understand the ethics of sporting performance, how to communicate a message about a problem in sport (drugs, fair play, injuries, crowd problems for example), raise money for local sport bodies, treat sporting injuries, sell sports goods, and so on. To an extent sport studies, as taught in contemporary colleges and universities, have as one of their chief purposes to equip people for work in the worldwide sport industry.

Historians would not claim to be doing this, except insofar as the skills they seek to develop in their students by doing history (skills, for example, of analysis, judgement, organization, working to deadlines, teamwork) are in themselves valuable in the workplace. But few would pretend that employers in sport businesses (with the exception of the museum and heritage sector) will be very attracted by a job candidate's detailed knowledge of, say, the Antwerp Olympics of 1920 or Don Bradman's role as an icon of Australian manhood in the 1930s. It's gone, it's past, it's of no value to the present. But wait. Some might argue that history has its uses: by learning about mistakes made in the past we can avoid making similar mistakes in the present. After all, does not history repeat itself? There are, to be sure, similarities between historical events across time, but I am far from convinced by the argument that we can learn valuable lessons from them. What strikes me about those who have sought to apply the (so-called) 'lessons' of history is the amount of trouble they have got themselves into as a result. To take one famous, and non-sport, example: Anthony Eden, British prime minister in 1956, was sure that his adversary Colonel Nasser of Egypt was another Hitler, and that when Nasser ordered the seizure of the Suez Canal he should be resisted; Britain should not make the same mistake as its government did in the 1930s when Hitler's aggression was appeased. This was the lesson of history. But it was the wrong lesson; the Suez crisis was a humiliating setback for the British government, and Eden had many years of life remaining in which to ponder the mistakes into which his application of history had plunged him. It is, unfortunately, far from clear that he realized the error of his ways, just as recent events in Iraq have not persuaded certain American and British politicians that they embarked on a misguided course of action in 2003. There will always be those who will make use of historical situations to justify a particular policy, and only a critical understanding of historical interpretation can safeguard us against such abuse. It is as well, perhaps, to remember Marx's famous dictum that history repeats itself – first as tragedy, then as farce.[3]

It is not in these kinds of directly practical ways that we should seek to justify the study of history. 'The past', Martin Polley has reminded us, 'features prominently in the present.'[4] One need think only of the vast array of historical material readily available in high street bookshops, DVD stores and in the television schedules. The range of material on offer is, to be sure, highly selective and limited in scope but it is there for one very obvious reason: because it sells. People like history. This fascination with the past is ubiquitous, but the implications of what people consume often go unnoticed; history happens, as it were, 'behind our backs'. How many of us are even fully aware that some of our favourite television programmes – on house hunting, or antiques, or even crime fiction – deal in subtle ways with history? In sport a similar fascination is evident – in the brief historical allusions that often appear in the opening titles of television sports programmes, or at a more mundane level in the reminiscences of sports fans about famous players and events of times gone by. It is subtly but inescapably inscribed in our memories. The problem with this kind of history is that it is prone to reproducing very particular visions of the past, perhaps in so doing distorting events and people and memories, and resulting in the production of myths which become no truer for their constantly being repeated. It is not simply a matter of factual inaccuracies creeping in; rather more it is a case of what is being chosen to remember. Certain sports over others, for example, or elite (and male) performance, or events associated with one's own country to the exclusion of other places. One instance of the perceptions that have grown out of this kind of historical selectivity is our understanding of the 'Olympics'. Most people now equate it with the four-yearly sequence of athletic events initiated by the Frenchman Pierre de Coubertin in the late-nineteenth century, and which began with the Athens games of 1896. Few seem to be aware that, in the interwar years, an equally powerful olympic movement existed, sponsored not by the International Olympic Committee but by the network of European workers' and socialist parties. After some twenty years of energetic activity the workers' olympics died out after the Second World War, and seemed to lose its place in the historical record. A conscious exercise in historical reconstruction is now needed to bring this alternative tradition, which involved a very different understanding of 'sport' and 'competition', to mind. It has passed out of the popular memory. If a sense of history is to be part of our contemporary experience of sport, then, it seems only fair that we should make the effort to understand what history is and how it has come to assume the form it has.

Martin Polley has very helpfully indicated three types of popular historical awareness present in modern sport discourse. They are as follows:

- The past as the *source* of sport
- Mythologies of the past
- Commemoration and celebration of the past

Each can be made the subject of academic enquiry, but their existence is an organic part of the general enthusiasm for sport. Polley has provided a wealth of examples on each of these categories to show that sport not only generates strong historical associations, and that people are sometimes unaware of them, or of what they mean; but, more than this, that the very existence of sport is historically determined. We cannot fully 'know' sport without recognizing its history. As Polley rightly observes, no sport began life this morning; all have antecedents. And as Markovits and Hellerman have pointed out in their book on soccer in the United States, sport organizations frequently invoke the history of their teams and players as a way of establishing the idea that they have been a long-standing and *natural* part of the sport landscape. History, in other words, conveys a *moral legitimacy*.[5]

None of us would like to think that the sports we are so passionate about today will be forgotten in a hundred years time. Were this to happen, and a large part of our contemporary life ceased to be 'history', it would tend to demean our very existence. Future historians should be aware of our present, and give our interests due accord. If, then, we are worthy subjects of history, so also are our parents, grandparents and all their antecedents.

Notes

1 Sport Matters

1. Simon Barnes, *The Meaning of Sport* (London: Short Books, 2006), p. 9.
2. Jonathan Freedland makes a similar point. 'The joy of sport is that, no matter how exciting the moment of victory, no matter how glum the defeat, we all know that ultimately it does not matter. England might well lose the fifth test [of 2009] and with it the Ashes. We will be disappointed. But nobody will get hurt.' (*Guardian*, 12 August 2009, p. 25).
3. http://deloittetouche.com; http://prospects.ac.uk
4. This phrase was first coined by Tony Mason in an unpublished paper in the 1980s, and has been used many times since by writers on sport history.
5. It is cultural in the sense of culture as a way of life, rather than as a form of elite appreciation. See Peter Burke, *What Is Cultural History?* (Cambridge: Polity, 2004).
6. Places like Sussex, Essex, York and Lancaster. Not to be confused with the later 'new universities' of the early 1990s, by which time the original new universities had become 'old' universities.
7. Re-printed in Eric Hobsbawm, *On History* (London: Abacus, 1998 edn), ch. 6; and M. W. Flinn and T. C. Smout, *Essays in Social History* (Oxford: Clarendon Press, 1974), pp. 1–22 (this edition includes an opening paragraph omitted from the later Hobsbawm edition).
8. Quoted in R. Williams and N. Garnham, 'Pierre Bourdieu and the Sociology of Culture: An Introduction', *Media, Culture and Society*, 2 (1980), pp. 212–3.
9. Peter Burke, *What Is Cultural History?* (Cambridge: Polity Press, 2004), pp. 51–62.
10. See Tony Collins, *Rugby's Great Split: Class, Culture, and the Origins of Rugby League Football* (London: Frank Cass, 1998). A good example is also provided in relation to cricket in Wray Vamplew, 'Empiricist Versus Sociological History: Some Comments on the "Civilizing Process"', *Sport in History* 27, 2 (June 2007), pp. 161–171. See also the debates in *Sport in History* 25, 2, pp. 289–306 and 26, 1, pp. 110–23.
11. Eric Dunning, 'The Social Roots of Football Hooliganism: A Reply to the Critics of the "Leicester School"', in R. Giulanotti, N. Bonney and M. Hepworth eds, *Football, Violence and Social Identity* (London: Routledge, 1994), p. 154.
12. See Neil Carter, *The Football Manager: A History* (London: Routledge, 2006), ch. 7. One of the first systematic attempts to apply psychology in sport was when the successful Brazilian football team employed a team psychologist (Dr Joao Carvalhaes) in the 1958 World Cup. However, the team manager Feola simply ignored many of his findings, which included a report that Pele did not possess the sense of responsibility needed for a team game, and that Garrincha was unsuited to

high-pressure matches. Both proved to be outstanding players in the competition, and for many years afterwards. (Jonathan Wilson, *Inverting the Pyramid: A History of Football Tactics*, London: Orion Books, 2009), p. 124.

13. Topics such as addiction to drink and gambling have been covered and mental illness in the recent life history of the cricketer Marcus Trescothick (*Coming Back to Me: The Autobiography of Marcus Trescothick*, London: HarperSport, 2008).

14. David Lavallee, John Kremer, Aidan P. Morgan and Mark Williams, *Sport Psychology: Contemporary Themes* (Basingstoke: Palgrave Macmillan, 2004), p. 7.

15. Lavallee et al., *Sport Psychology*, p. 7.

16. Murray Phillips, 'A Critical Appraisal of Narrative in Sport History: Reading the Surf Lifesaving Debate', *Journal of Sport History*, 29, 1 (2002), pp. 25–40.

17. Synthia Sydnor, 'A History of Synchronised Swimming', *Journal of Sport History*, 25, 2 (1998), pp. 252–67.

2   The Transition to Modern Sport

1. Bernard Malamud, *The Natural* (New York: Farrar, Straus and Giroux, 2004 ed.). Originally published 1952.

2. George Blake, *The Shipbuilders* (Edinburgh: B&W Publishing, 1993 ed.). Originally published 1935.

3. Allen Guttmann, *From Ritual to Record: The Nature of Modern Sports* (New York: Columbia University Press, 1978), p. 3.

4. Alan Tomlinson ed., *The Sport Studies Reader* (London: Routledge, 2007), p. 10.

5. Peter Radford, *The Celebrated Captain Barclay: Sport, Money and Fame in Regency Britain* (London: Headline, 2001).

6. The book (see above f.n.3) was re-printed in the original edition in 2004.

7. Guttmann, *Ritual to Record*, p. 49.

8. Depicted in the painting *Young Spartans Exercising* by Edgar Degas, *c.* 1860 (National Gallery, London).

9. The 'old' Wembley stadium is a reminder of it.

10. Robert Malcolmson, *Popular Recreations in English Society 1700–1850* (Cambridge: Cambridge University Press, 1973).

11. The best account in English is Richard Holt, *Sport and the British: A Modern History* (Oxford: Clarendon Press, 1989).

12. Guttmann, *Ritual to Record*, chs 3 and 6.

13. Nick Hornby, *Fever Pitch* (London: Victor Gollancz, 1992).

14. Juventus did not proceed with this plan; nor, to my knowledge, has any major football club. 'Gate' receipts are still an important income stream. The fact, however, that the scheme was at least considered is indicative of whence the *most* important income stream now flows.

15. Jeffrey Hill, *Sport, Leisure and Culture in Twentieth-Century Britain* (Basingstoke: Palgrave, 2002), p. 144.

16. Richard Holt and Tony Mason, *Sport in Britain 1945–2000* (Oxford: Blackwell, 2000), p. 38.

3   Sport and Identity

1. Eugen Weber, *Peasants into Frenchmen. The Modernisation of Rural France 1870–1917* (Palo Alto, CA: Stanford University Press, 1976).

2. See Christopher S. Thompson, *The Tour de France: A Cultural History* (Berkeley: University of California Press, 2006).
3. Linda Colley, *Britons: Forging the Nation, 1707–1837* (London: Pimlico, 1994) p. 162.
4. D. Smith and G. Williams, *Fields of Praise*, esp. chs 5–7. See also Gareth Williams, *1905 and All That: Essays on Rugby Football, Sport and Welsh Society* (Llandysul: Gomer Press, 1991); 'From Grand Slam to Great Slump: Economy, Society and Rugby Football in Wales during the Depression', *Welsh History Review*, 11 (1993), pp. 339–57. See also Martin Johnes, *A History of Sport in Wales* (Cardiff: University of Wales Press, 2005); 'A Prince, a King, and a Referendum: Rugby, Politics, and Nationhood in Wales, 1969–1979', *Journal of British Studies*, 47:1 (2008), pp. 129–48.
5. D. Smith, 'Focal Heroes: A Welsh Fighting Class', in R. Holt ed., *Sport and the Working Class in Modern Britain* (Manchester: Manchester University Press, 1990), p. 199.
6. Gareth Williams, 'The Road to Wigan Pier Revisited: The Migration of Welsh Rugby Talent since 1918', in J. Bale and J. Maguire eds, *The Global Sports Arena: Athletic Talent Migration in an Interdependent World* (London: Frank Cass, 1994), pp. 25–8.
7. It was no doubt this passage that drew from the reviewer in the *Times Literary Supplement* on the book's publication the comment: 'Mr Jenkins's real gift is for describing football matches.' ('Small Town Life', 18 June 1954, p. 389) – a clear case of being damned with faint praise.
8. Michael Cronin, 'Defenders of the Nation? The Gaelic Athletic Association and Irish National Identity', *Irish Political Studies*, 11 (1996), pp. 1–19; 'Sport and a Sense of Irishness', *Irish Studies Review*, 9 (1994), pp. 13–18; 'Which Nation, Which Flag?: Boxing and National Identities in Ireland', *International Review for the Sociology of Sport*, 32, 2 (1997), pp. 131–46; Richard Holt, *Sport and the British*, pp. 239–42. See also M. Cronin and D. Mayall, *Sporting Nationalisms: Identity, Ethnicity, Immigration and Assimilation* (London: Frank Cass, 1998).
9. Michael Cronin, 'Enshrined in Blood: The Naming of Gaelic Athletic Association Grounds and Clubs', *Sports Historian*, 18, 1 (1998), p. 93.
10. See Jack Williams, *Cricket and England: A Cultural and Social History of the Inter-War Years* (London: Frank Cass, 1999) esp. chs 1 and 6.
11. Ross McKibbin, *Classes and Cultures: England 1918–1951* (Oxford: Oxford University Press, 1998), pp. 84–98.
12. McKibbin, *Classes and Cultures*, p. 96.
13. See Philip Williamson, *Stanley Baldwin: Conservative Leadership and National Values* (Cambridge: Cambridge University Press, 1999).
14. *Daily Mail*, 26 November 1953.
15. *Daily Mirror*, 26 November 1953.
16. McKibbin, *Classes and Cultures*, p. 361.
17. Richard Holt, *Stanmore Golf Club 1893–1993: A Social History* (London: Stanmore Golf Club, 1993); John Bromhead, *Droitwich Golf Club 1897–1997* (Droitwich: Grant Books, 1996).
18. McKibbin, *Classes and Cultures*, p. 380.
19. John Lowerson, *Sport and the English Middle Classes, 1870–1914* (Manchester: Manchester University Press), p. 98.
20. See Daniel Burdsey, *British Asians and Football: Culture, Identity, Exclusion* (Abingdon: Routledge, 2008 edn).

21. It might be noted that the US army was not racially integrated until the Korean War, 1950–1953.
22. Kathryn Jay, *More Than Just a Game: Sports in American Life since 1945* (New York: Columbia University Press, 2004), pp. 32–3.

4 Sport and Gender

1. Tony Mason, *Sport in Britain* (London: Faber and Faber, 1988), p. 7.
2. Richard Holt and Tony Mason, *Sport in Britain 1945–2000* (Oxford: Blackwell, 2000), p. 11.
3. Figures from Katherine Hanson, Vivian Guilfoy and Sarita Pillai, *More Than Title IX: How Equity in Education Has Shaped the Nation* (Lanham, MD: Rowman and Littlefold Publishers Inc., 2009), ch. 5.
4. Michael A. Messner, *Taking the Field: Schools, Sports, Sex, and Title IX* (Minneapolis: University of Minnesota Press, 2002), pp. 68–76.
5. Catriona M. Parratt, 'Little Means or Time: Working-Class Women and Leisure in Late-Victorian and Edwardian England', *International Journal of the History of Sport*, 15, 2 (1998), pp. 22–53.
6. N. Dennis, F. Henriques and C. Slaughter, *Coal Is Our Life: An Analysis of a Yorkshire Mining Community* (London: Eyre and Spottiswoode, 1956), p. 163.
7. Jeffrey Hill, *Nelson: Politics, Economy, Community* (Edinburgh: Keele University Press, 1997).
8. *Sport in History* ed. Mike Huggins, 28, 3 (September 2008).
9. E. Green, S. Hebron and D. Woodward, *Women's Leisure: What Leisure?* (Basingstoke: Macmillan, 1990), p. 5 and ch. 1.
10. Angela McRobbie, '*Jackie*: An Ideology of Adolescent Femininity', in B. Waites, T. Bennett and G. Martin eds, *Popular Culture: Past and Present* (London: Croom Helm/Open University Press, 1982), pp. 263–83.
11. See Angela McRobbie, *Feminism and Youth Culture: From 'Jacke' to 'Just Seventeen'* (Basingstoke: Macmillan, 1991), chs 5 and 6; Janice Winship, *Inside Women's Magazines* (London: Pandora, 1987) esp. ch. 4. Not all magazines and comics aimed at young girls were quite so gendered. *Girl*, the female companion title to the *Eagle*, a popular boys' paper of the 1950s and 1960s, portrayed its female characters in a far more 'liberated' form, playing games, having adventures, and in no sense simply waiting to find a boyfriend with a view to eventual marriage. (See Joyce Kay, 'A Window of Opportunity? Women's Sport in the Postwar Era', unpublished paper, British Society of Sport History, annual conference, Stirling University, Scotland, 17–18 July 2009.)
12. Sheila Scraton, ' "Boys Muscle In Where Angels Fear To Tread" – Girls' Sub-Cultures and Physical Activities', in C. Critcher, P. Bramham and A. Tomlinson eds, *Sociology of Leisure: A Reader* (London: E. & F.N. Spon, 1995), pp. 117–29.
13. Ellen Ross, 'Survival Networks: Women's Neighbourhood Sharing in London before World War 1', *History Worksop: A Journal of Socialist and Feminist Historians*, 15 (1983), pp. 4–27.
14. Carol Dyhouse, *Girls Growing Up in Late Victorian and Edwardian England* (London: Routledge and Kegan Paul, 1981), pp. 111–14.
15. See Catriona M. Parratt, ' "The Making of the Healthy and the Happy Home": Recreation, Education, and the Production of Working-Class Womanhood at

the Rowntree Cocoa Works, York, c.1898–1914', in J. Hill and J. Williams eds, *Sport and Identity in the North of England* (Keele: Keele University Press, 1996), pp. 53–83.

16. Claire Langhamer, *Women's Leisure in England 1920–60* (Manchester: Manchester University Press, 2000), pp. 76–83.
17. An important contribution on this theme is G. Jarvie ed., *Sport, Racism and Ethnicity* (London: Falmer Press, 1991).
18. Hasina Zaman, 'Islam, Well-being and Physical Activity: Perceptions of Muslim Young Women', in G. Clarke and B. Humberstone eds, *Researching Women and Sport* (Basingstoke: Macmillan, 1997) pp. 50–67. On this subject see also Richard Bailey, *Muslim Women and Sport* (London: Routledge, forthcoming 2010).
19. Zaman, 'Islam, Well-being and Physical Activity', p. 61.

5 Mediating Sport

1. Women's cricket was reported in some sections of the national press, though sometimes rather condescendingly. See Jack Williams, *Cricket and England: A Cultural and Social History of the Inter-War Years* (London: Frank Cass, 1998), pp. 98–106.
2. Willy Meisl, *Soccer Revolution* (London: Phoenix Sports Books, 1955), p. 12.
3. Central Council of Physical Recreation, *Sport and the Community* (The Wolfenden Report) (London: CCPR, 1960), pp. 80–1.
4. Tony Mason, *Sport in Britain* (London: Faber and Faber, 1988), p. 49.
5. Asa Briggs, *The History of Broadcasting in the United Kingdom – vol. 1 The Birth of Broadcasting* (London: Oxford University Press, 1961), pp. 164–83; P. Scannell and D. Cardiff, *A Social History of British Broadcasting: vol 1 1922–1939, Serving the Nation* (Oxford: Basil Blackwell, 1991) ch. 1.
6. Mike Huggins 'BBC Radio and Sport 1922–39', *Contemporary British History*, 21, 4 (Dec. 2007), pp. 491–515.
7. Garry Whannel, *Fields in Vision: Television Sport and Cultural Transformation* (London: Routledge, 1992), p. 29; ch. 2 provides a good summary of the development of sports coverage at the BBC from the 1920s to the 1950s.
8. BBC Written Archives, Reading. File SA 1953–54, T 14/93/15, 1 December 1953. It was a commentator brought up in the 'Lobby' school – Kenneth Wolstenholme – who delivered probably the most memorable wisecrack of all, at the close of the 1966 football World Cup Final: 'there are people coming on to the pitch – they think it's all over. [Hurst scores]. It is now'.
9. Briggs, *The History of Broadcasting*, IV, p. 854.
10. See the study of listening habits conducted in a working-class neighbourhood of Bristol in the later 1930s: H. Jennings and W. Gill, *Broadcasting in Everyday Life: A Survey of the Social Effects of the Coming of Broadcasting* (London: BBC, n.d.), pp. 37–9.
11. P. Scannell and D. Cardiff, 'Serving the Nation: Public Service Broadcasting before the War', in B. Waites, T. Bennett and G. Martin eds, *Popular Culture: Past and Present* (London: Croom Helm/Open University Press, 1982), pp. 161–88. Briggs, *History of Broadcasting*, I, pp. 327–47.
12. Briggs, *History of Broadcasting*, IV, p. 854.
13. Briggs, *History of Broadcasting in the United Kingdom*, II, p. 315.

14. See Geoffrey Moorhouse, *At The George: And Other Essays of Rugby League* (London: Sceptre, 1990), pp. 44–5.
15. Benjamin Rader, *In Its Own Image: How Television Has Transformed Sports* (London: Collier Macmillan, 1984).
16. A. and J. Clarke, '"Highlights and Action Replays" – Ideology, Sport and the Media', in Jennifer Hargreaves ed., *Sport, Culture and Ideology* (London: Routledge and Kegan Paul, 1982), pp. 62–87.
17. Michael Oriard, *Dreaming of Heroes: American Sports Fiction 1868–1980* (Chicago: Nelson Hall, 1982), p. 30.
18. M. Cadogan and P. Craig, *'You're a Brick Angela!': A New Look for Girls' Fiction 1839–1975* (London: Victor Gollancz, 1976) esp. ch. xiii.
19. See Daniel A. Nathan, *Saying It's So: A Cultural History of the Black Sox Scandal* (Urbana: University of Illinois Press, 2003).
20. Allen Guttman, *From Ritual to Record: The Nature of Modern Sports* (New York: Columbia University Press, 1978), p. 101.
21. It is due to reopen in November 2009.
22. Since this book went into production the museum has moved from Preston and will become part of the Urbis centre in Manchester.
23. For a very good analysis of a sport museum, in the context of sport tourism, see: Daryl Adair, 'Where the Games Never Cease: The Olympic Museum in Lausanne, Switzerland', in Brent W. Ritchie and Daryl Adair eds, *Sport Tourism: Interrelationships, Impacts and Issues* (Clevedon: Channel View Publications, 2004), pp. 46–76. Adair suggests why visitors to the Olympic Museum might come away with a slightly cynical attitude about it.
24. Gary Imlach, *My Father and Other Working-Class Football Heroes* (London: Yellow Jersey Press, 2006), pp. 114–15.

6   Sport in a Globalized World

1. Pierre Lanfranchi and Matthew Taylor, *Moving with the Ball: The Migration of Professional Footballers* (Oxford: Berg, 2001), pp. 7–10.
2. England, India, Pakistan, Sri Lanka, Bangladesh, West Indies, South Africa, Australia. New Zealand and Zimbabwe.
3. C. L. R. James, *Beyond a Boundary* (London: Stanley Paul, 1969 ed.), p. 56.
4. See Mike Huggins and Jack Williams, *Sport and the English 1918–1939* (Abingdon: Routledge, 2006), pp. 64–73, 113–14.
5. Allen Guttmann, *From Ritual to Record: The Nature of Modern Sports* (New York: Columbia University Press, 1978, p. 41).
6. Many American attitudes towards the World Baseball Classic are not dissimilar to those of England in relation to the early football World Cup – a feeling of superior detachment from the tournament. On baseball in Japan see Jonathan Fraser Light, *The Cultural Encyclopedia of Baseball* (Jefferson, NC: McFarland and Company, 2nd ed. 2005), pp. 496–503.
7. Because of financial problems and opposition to the original scheme the plan was modified and the name dropped.
8. Tony Mason, *Passion of the People? Football in South America* (London: Verso, 1995), p. 157.
9. *Penguin Essays of George Orwell* (Harmondsworth: Penguin Books, 1984), pp. 328–9.
10. www. Fifa.com/about fifa/marketingtv/partners/fifapartners.html

11. Pierre Lanfranchi, Christiane Eisenberg, Tony Mason and Alfred Wahl, *100 Years of Football: the FIFA Centennial Book* (London: Weidenfeld and Nicholson, 2004).
12. www.olympic.org/uk/organisation/facts/programme/sponsors_uk.asp

Conclusion

1. John Tomlinson, *Cultural Imperialism: A Critical Introduction* (London: Continuum, 1991), p. 174.
2. Jeffrey Hill, *Sport, Leisure and Culture in Twentieth-Century Britain* (Basingstoke: Palgrave, 2002), p. 2.
3. Made in the opening paragraph of his essay 'The Eighteenth Brumaire of Louis Bonaparte' (1852); Margaret Macmillan covers some of these issues in *Dangerous Games: The Uses and Abuses of History* (London: Profile Books, 2009).
4. Martin Polley, *Sports History: A Practical Guide* (Basingstoke: Palgrave Macmillan, 2007), p. 15.
5. Andrei S. Markovits and Steven L. Hellerman, *Offside: Soccer and American Exceptionalism* (Princeton: Princeton University Press, 2001), pp. 20–22.

Select Bibliography

Bale, J., *Sport and Place: A Geography of Sport in England, Scotland and Wales*. London: C. Hurst & Company, 1982.
——, *Running Cultures: Racing in Time and Space*. London: Routledge, 2004.
——, *Anti-Sport Sentiments in Literature: Batting for the Opposition*. Abingdon: Routledge, 2008.
Bale, J., Christensen, M. and Pfister, G., *Writing Lives in Sport: Biographies, Life Histories and Methods*. Aarhus: Aarhus University Press, 2004.
Barnes, S., *The Meaning of Sport*. London: Short Books, 2006.
Bateman, A. and Bale, J., *Sporting Sounds: Relationships between Sport and Music*. Abingdon: Routledge, 2009.
Beckles, H. and Stoddart, B., eds *Liberation Cricket: West Indies Cricket Culture*. Manchester: Manchester University Press, 1995.
Birley, D., *Land of Sport and Glory: Sport and British Society 1889–1910*. Manchester: Manchester University Press, 1995.
Blake, A., *The Body Language: The Meaning of Modern Sport*. London: Lawrence & Wishart, 1996.
Brailsford, D., *British Sport: A Social History*. Cambridge: Lutterworth Press, 1997.
Briggs, A., *The History of Broadcasting in the UK*.
——, Vol. I *The Birth of Broadcasting*. London: Oxford University Press, 1961.
——, Vol. II *The Golden Age of Wireless*. London: Oxford University Press, 1965.
——, Vol. IV *Sound and Vision*. Oxford: Oxford University Press, 1979.
——, Vol. V *Competition, 1955–1974*. Oxford: Oxford University Press, 1995.
Booth, D., *The Field: Truth and Fiction in Sport History*. Abingdon: Routledge, 2005.
Burke, P., *What Is Cultural History?*. Cambridge: Polity Press, 2004.
Carrington, B. and McDonald, I., *'Race', Sport and British Society*. London: Routledge, 2000.
Carter, N., *The Football Manager: A History*. Abingdon: Routledge, 2006.
Central Committee of Physical Recreation. *Sport and the Community* (the Wolfenden Report). London: CCPR, 1960.
Clark, P., *British Clubs and Societies, 1580–1800: The Origins of an Associational World*. Oxford: Oxford University Press, 2000.
Collins, T., *Rugby's Great Split: Class, Culture and the Origins of Rugby League Football*. London: Frank Cass, 1998.
Cox, R., Jarvie, G. and Vamplew, W., *Encyclopedia of British Sport*. Oxford: ABC-Clio, 2000.
Dennis, N., Henriques, F. and Slaughter, C., *Coal Is Our Life: An Analysis of a Yorkshire Mining Community*. London: Eyre and Spottiswoode, 1956.
Dunning, E. and Rojek, C., *Sport and Leisure in the Civilizing Process*. Basingstoke: Palgrave, 1992.

Giulianotti, R., ed. *Sport and Modern Social Theorists*. Basingstoke: Palgrave Macmillan, 2004.

Goldblatt, D., *The Ball Is Round: A Global History of Football*. London: Viking, 2006.

Griffin, E., *England's Revelry: A History of Popular Sports and Pastimes, 1660-1830*. Oxford: Oxford University Press, 2005.

Guttmann, A., *From Ritual to Record: The Nature of Modern Sports*. New York: Columbia University Press, 1978.

——, *Sports: The First Five Millennia*. Amherst/Boston: University of Massachusetts Press, 2004.

Hargreaves, Jennifer, ed. *Sport, Culture and Ideology*. London: Routledge and Kegan Paul, 1982.

Hargreaves, Jennifer, *Sporting Females: Critical Issues in the History and Sociology of Women's Sports*. London: Routledge, 1994.

Hargreaves, John, *Sport, Power and Culture: A Social and Historical Analysis of Popular Sports in Britain*. Cambridge: Polity Press, 1987.

Hill, J., *Nelson: Politics, Economy, Community*. Edinburgh: Keele University Press, 1997.

——, *Sport, Leisure and Culture in Twentieth-Century Britain*. Basingstoke: Palgrave, 2002.

——, *Sport and the Literary Imagination*. Oxford: Peter Lang, 2006.

Hill, J. and Williams, J., eds *Sport and Identity in the North of England*. Keele: Keele University Press, 1996.

Holt, R., *Sport and the British*. Oxford: Oxford University Press, 1990 edn.

——, *Stanmore Golf Club, 1893–1993: A Social History*. Stanmore: Stanmore Golf Club, 1993.

——, ed. *Sport and the Working Class in Modern Britain*. Manchester: Manchester University Press, 1990.

Holt, R. and Mason, T., *Sport in Britain, 1945–2000*. Oxford: Blackwell, 2000.

Hornby, N., *Fever Pitch*. London: Gollancz, 1992.

Houlihan, B., *Sport and Society: A Student Introduction*. London: Sage, 2003.

Huggins, M. and Williams, J., *Sport and the English 1918-1939*. Abingdon: Routledge, 2006.

Inglis, S., *The Football Grounds of Britain*. London: CollinsWillow, 1996 edn.

James, C. L. R., *Beyond a Boundary*. London: Stanley Paul, 1969 edn.

Jarvie, G., ed. *Sport, Racism and Ethnicity*. London: Falmer Press, 1991.

——, *Sport, Culture and Society: An Introduction*. Abingdon: Routledge, 2006.

Jay, K., *More Than Just a Game: Sports in American Life since 1945*. New York: Columbia University Press, 2004.

Johnes, M., *History of Sport in Wales* (Cardiff: University of Wales Press, 2005).

——, *Soccer and Society in South Wales, 1900-1939: That Other Game* (Cardiff: University of Wales Press, 2002).

Jones, S., *Sport, Politics and the Working Class: Organised Labour and Sport in Inter-War Britain*. Manchester: Manchester University Press, 1992 edn.

Kimmel, M. and Messner, M., *Men's Lives*. London: Allyn and Bacon, 2001.

Korr, C. and Close, M., *More Than Just a Game: Football v Apartheid*. Collins, 2008.

Lanfranchi, P. and Taylor, M., *Moving with the Ball: The Migration of Professional Footballers*. Oxford: Berg, 2001.

Langhamer, C., *Women's Leisure in England, 1920–60*. Manchester: Manchester University Press, 2000.

Lavalee, D., Kremer, J., Morgan, A. and Williams, M., *Sport Psychology: Contemporary Themes*. Basingstoke: Palgrave Macmillan, 2004.

Levermore, R. and Budd, A., *Sport and International Relations: An Emerging Relationship*. London: Routledge, 2004.

Lowerson, J., *Sport and the English Middle Classes, 1870–1914*. Manchester: Manchester University Press, 1993.

Maguire, J., *Sport, Power and Globalisation*. London: Routledge, 2005.

Mangan, J. A., *The Games Ethic and Imperialism: Aspects of the Diffusion of an Ideal*. Harmondsworth: Viking, 1986.

Markovits, A. and Hellerman, S., *Offside: Soccer and American Exceptionalism*. Princeton, NJ: Princeton University Press, 2001.

Mason, T., *Association Football and English Society, 1863–1915*. Brighton: Harvester Press, 1981 edn.

——, *Passion of the People: Football in South America*. London: Verso, 1995.

——, ed. *Sport in Britain: A Social History*. Cambridge: Cambridge University Press, 1989.

McKibbin, R., *Classes and Cultures, 1918–1951*. Oxford: Oxford University Press, 1998.

Moore, K., *Museums and Popular Culture*. London: Cassell, 1997.

Oriard, M., *Reading Football: How the Popular Press Created an American Spectacle*. Chapel Hill: University of North Carolina Press, 1993.

Pegg, M., *Broadcasting and Society, 1918–1939*. London: Croom Helm, 1983.

Polley, M., *Moving the Goalposts: A History of Sport and Society Since 1945*. London: Routledge, 1998.

——, *Sports History: A Practical Guide*. Basingstoke: Palgrave Macmillan, 2007.

Pope, S., ed. *The New American Sport History: Recent Approaches and Perspectives*. Urbana, IL: University of Illinois Press, 1997.

Rader, B., *In Its Own Image: How Television Has Transformed Sports*. London: Collier Macmillan, 1984.

Rae, S., *W. G. Grace: A Life*. London: Faber & Faber, 1998.

Remnick, D., *King of the World. Muhammad Ali and the Rise of an American Hero*. New York: Random House, 1998.

Ritchie, B. and Adair, D., *Sport Tourism: Interrelationships, Impacts and Issues*. Clevedon: Channel View, 2004.

Russell, D., *Football and the English: A Social History of Association Football in England, 1863–1995*. London: Carnegie Publishing, 1997.

Scannell, P. and Cardiff, D., *A Social History of British Broadcasting, Vol. I 1922–39: Serving the Nation*. Oxford: Basil Blackwell, 1991.

Scraton, S. and Flintoff, A., *Gender and Sport: A Reader*. Abingdon: Routledge, 2002.

Smith, D. and Williams, G., *Fields of Praise: The Official History of the Welsh Rugby Union, 1881–1981*. Cardiff: The University of Wales Press, 1980.

Stacey, M., *Tradition and Change: A Study of Banbury*. Oxford: Oxford University Press, 1960.

Steen, R., *Sports Journalism: A Multimedia Primer*. Abingdon: Routledge, 2008.

Stoddart, B., 'Cricket and Colonialism in the English-Speaking Caribbean to 1914: Towards a Cultural Analysis', in Mangan, J. A., ed. *Pleasure, Profit, Proselytism: British Culture and Sport at Home and Abroad, 1780–1914*. London: Frank Cass, 1988, pp. 231–57.

Storey, D., *This Sporting Life*. Harmondsworth: Penguin Books, 1962 edn.

Struna, N., *People of Prowess: Sport, Leisure and Labor in Early Anglo-America*. Urbana, IL: University of Illinois Press, 1996.

Taylor, M., *The Association Game: A History of British Football*. Harlow: Pearson Education, 2008.

Tomlinson, A., ed. *The Sport Studies Reader*. Abingdon: Routledge, 2007.

Tomlinson, J., *Cultural Imperialism: A Critical Introduction*. London: Continuum, 1991.

Tygiel, J., *Past Time: Baseball As History*. Oxford: Oxford University Press, 2000.

Vamplew, W., *Pay Up and Play the Game: Professional Sport in Britain, 1875–1914*. Cambridge: Cambridge University Press,1988.

Whannel, G., *Fields in Vision: Television, Sport and Cultural Transformation*. London: Routledge, 1992.

——, *Media Sport Stars: Masculinities and Moralities*. London: Routledge, 2002.

——, *Television, Sport and Cultural Transformation*. London: Routledge, 1992.

Williams, Jack, *Cricket and England: A Cultural and Social History of the Interwar Years*. London: Frank Cass, 1999.

——, *Cricket and Race*. Oxford: Berg, 2001.

Williams, Jean, *A Beautiful Game: International Perspectives on Women's Football*. Oxford, Berg, 2007.

——, *A Game for Rough Girls: The History of Women's Football in Britain*. London: Routledge, 2003.

Wilson, J., *Inverting the Pyramid: A History of Football Tactics*. London: Orion Books, 2009.

Young, K. and Wamsley, K., *Global Olympics: Historical and Sociological Studies of the Modern Games*. Oxford: Elsevier, 2005.

Index